PRAISE FOR NOW'S THE TIME

MUSICIANS

I have found working with Doug Goodkin to be an absolutely delightful and enlightening experience. His approach is an extremely comprehensive method of teaching the essentials of jazz harmony, ear training and rhythm.

—STEFON HARRIS, JAZZ VIBRAPHONIST AND COMPOSER

I have thoroughly enjoyed my guest teaching in Doug Goodkin's jazz course. I'm always impressed with how teachers with little jazz background can get swingin' after just a few days. The book is also terrific and impressive. Great work!

—EDDIE MARSHALL, ACCLAIMED JAZZ DRUMMER, JAZZ RECORDER VIRTUOSO AND COMPOSER

Doug is a highly skilled and gifted educator who communicates a wealth of information, insight and connectivity. His jazz education work is solidly researched and pedagogically sound, but more important, his ideas and methods quickly enable young students to access the joy of playing this remarkable music. An accomplished writer, Doug articulates his information so clearly in this groundbreaking book—*Now's the Time* is a must-have for teachers pursuing jazz studies with younger students.

—KEITH TERRY, PERCUSSIONIST, BODY MUSICIAN, EDUCATOR

Doug Goodkin is one of the most creative music instructors I've ever met. He has developed ways to get students and teachers alike to fearlessly embrace their own creativity. He makes it easy for the beginner to make music quickly and therefore remain involved in the creative process. This book captures that process as work.

—LINDA TILLERY, VOCALIST, PERCUSSIONIST, PRODUCER

Doug Goodkin's understanding and approach to teaching, learning, and performing jazz, and indeed music in general, underscores the principle of holistic education. In *Now's the Time: Teaching Jazz to All Ages*, Goodkin's use of the Orff approach invokes the basic historical, philosophical, cultural, theoretical, aesthetic, and methodological dynamics that underpin the jazz genre. Each and every music lesson epitomizes the qualities that make Doug Goodkin one of the best in music education.

—STEPHEN GBOLONYO, GHANAIAN MUSICIAN, PHD CANDIDATE IN ETHNOMUSICOLOGY

Oh, man, that's marvelous!

—MILT JACKSON, LEGENDARY JAZZ VIBRAPHONIST AND COMPOSER
(AFTER HEARING DOUG'S 5TH GRADE STUDENTS PLAY)

NOTED MUSIC EDUCATORS

Doug Goodkin has written a must-have book for teachers who teach and treasure Blues and Jazz. A consummate musician, teacher and clinician, his passion for this music and love of teaching has yielded a masterful book to guide teachers and students alike into our rich musical heritage. The spiraling sequential learning from the known to the unknown is poetry in communication!

—ROBERT ABRAMSON, INTERNATIONALLY RECOGNIZED DALCROZE TEACHER AND AUTHOR

Doug Goodkin brings years of experience and expertise as a teacher and musician fluent in both Orff Schulwerk and jazz to the task of encouraging you to deepen your own knowledge of—and appreciation for—America's music. Your musical life—and that of your students— will be greatly enriched by exploring *Now's the Time*. It is a splendid achievement.

—JANE FRAZEE, INTERNATIONALLY RECOGNIZED ORFF SCHULWERK TEACHER AND AUTHOR

General music teachers take note. *Now's The Time: Teaching Jazz To All Ages* is a compelling text for including jazz in every child's education and offers a sequential approach for teaching it to all ages by combining theory and practice. What makes it unique is that it integrates the Orff approach to music education with effective jazz education.

—JOHN KUZMICH; IAJE MAGAZINE

INTERNATIONAL MUSIC TEACHERS

My 6th graders made their headmaster and their other teachers cry with big tears as they performed *Blue Moon*. From the moment the violinist started to play the first note through the vocalist singing like an angel and the boys joining in, they stood there crying so hard that the kids didn't know how to react!! These were boys who often have to visit the headmaster when they get in trouble—now they made him cry for a different reason! WE LOVE THIS BOOK and we're going to go through piece after piece!!

-NANNA HLIF INGVADOTTIR; ICELANDIC MUSIC TEACHER,
PRESIDENT OF THE ICELANDIC ORFF ASSOCIATION

Now's the Time has the possibility of serving as a base for a long- term profound revolution in the musical educational system here in Spain and in the rest of Europe. It already has made a profound difference on teachers in my school who work with children or teach jazz to young adults. Doug's approach to the music is at the same time practical, intelligent, musical and fun. Using his ideas we can get the people to play music without going through the traditional traumas often associated with "music" class here in Europe. Highly recommended.

—ANDY PHILLIPS, TEACHER, JAZZ MUSICIAN, COORDINATOR
CREATIVE MUSIC SCHOOL, MADRID SPAIN,
MEMBER EMMEN EUROPEAN MODERN
MUSIC EDUCATIONAL NETWORK (BRUSSELS)

Many teachers tend to use materials without digesting the history behind it. The song sounds good, the play seems to be enjoyable and not every teacher takes care to investigate what is lying behind these materials. This book tries not only to encourage us to under-stand the roots of all musical material we are using, but it contains very useful hints according to teaching models. Although its primary purpose is to teach jazz, these ideas are essential in teaching any kind of music. Because there are no books like this in Turkish, we have translated parts of *Now's the Time* in our Orff Magazine to awaken the attention of the Turkish teachers.

—FATOS AUERNIG, EXECUTIVE DIRECTOR OF TURKISH ORFF SCHULWERK ASSOCIATION

The theoretical concepts are broken down into simple and easy to manage parts, yet the overall approach is an integrated, holistic and problem-solving way that honors the individual and invites play and discovery.

—Dr. Christina Grant, jazz educator, Toronto, Canada

ORFF MUSIC TEACHERS

I have been using the materials in *Now's the Time* extensively for the past two months and have found great life in them. Doug has taken this sublime art form and distilled it down to its elements that are such wonderful seeds. This work is so valuable because it SPECIFICALLY speaks to the music that lives in the bones of American children. It SPEAKS to my students. My 5th graders come running in the door and ask, "Are we gonna *Lindy Hop* today? Are we? Are we?" And we jump and jive until the room is unbearably hot and sweaty. This is good stuff!

—Dave Thaxton, Orff teacher, Reno, Nevada

Doug has taken part of the history of American roots music and interwoven the Orff Schulwerk in a way never known before! He has captured the essence of how and why Jazz and Blues were born, connecting it to the roots of how we learn music. This music is a part of all of us, especially children, and this book provides the tools for developing the skills to improvise. In the tradition of the Schulwerk, vamping the bass ostinati and developing "riff's" open a doorway that allow children to experience first hand the thrill, freedom and beauty that is Jazz & Blues and the roots of our music. For music educators that are not comfortable with the limitless complexities of jazz, Doug unveils the integral elements and hands "it" right to you!

—Michael Wray; Primary/Middle School Teacher, Jazz Musician

Now's the Time has been an invaluable resource in both my academic classroom and music teaching. It is an exceptionally clear, logical and inspirational guide to bringing children into the world of jazz. The lessons have totally changed how I teach music and history.

—Nancy Kaye, veteran classroom teacher

I so appreciate the integration of dance, drama, poetry, philosophy, history and performance—I've been searching for an approach to jazz education like this for years! It really seems like a more authentic approach to learning the music. Jazz players in the past didn't usually learn in a classroom, they learned from church from home life, from hangin' with the elders—Doug's approach seems to mirror that old way.

—Ryan Murtfeldt; jazz musician and music teacher

Drawing from a lifetime of work with children and adults, Doug has captured splendidly in this book the universal qualities of this remarkable art form, jazz. Having witnessed his work with diverse populations—Brazilian and Spanish children, Turkish and Taiwanese teens, professional musicians and music teachers, hospital patients and school parents—I've seen the magical effect that playing jazz produces. This can only happen with a teacher who knows how to release the natural musical impulses we all share in common—in Doug's hands, we are all jazz musicians.

—Sofía López-Ibor, Internationally recognized Orff teacher, author, San Francisco School colleague and president of the Spanish Orff Association.

ALSO BY DOUG GOODKIN

Name Games: *Activities for Rhythmic Development.* (Alfred Publishing/Warner Bros.)

A Rhyme in Time Rhythm: Speech Activities & Improvisation for the Classroom
(Alfred Publishing/Warner Bros.)

Sound Ideas: Activities for the Percussion Circle (Alfred Publishing/Warner Bros.)

Play, Sing and Dance: An Introduction to Orff Schulwerk (Schott)

The ABC's of Education: A Primer for Schools to Come (Pentatonic Press)

Do It First! Guidelines for Effective Teaching (Pentatonic Press—forthcoming)

Intermediate Jazz Arrangements for Orff Ensemble (Pentatonic Press—forthcoming)

NOW'S THE TIME

TEACHING **JAZZ** TO ALL AGES

BY DOUG GOODKIN

PENTATONIC
PRESS

For futher information, point your browser to www.douggoodkin.com

ISBN Number 0–9773712–1–2

Cover design by Sue Sandlin Design.
Photos by Doug Goodkin, Sofia Lopez-Ibor, Jeanne Makanna, Ira Schrank, and Drew Story.

Editor: Peter Greenwood
Copy Editor: John Tyler Evans
Book design, typesetting, and music engraving: Bill Holab Music

CONTENTS

PREFACE TO THE
SECOND EDITION

There are few pleasures more satisfying for an author than writing a preface to a second edition of one's book. It means that the book has sold well and one is confident that there are other readers still waiting for it. But mere sales don't tell the whole story. What is most gratifying is the testimony from those who have used the book—it works. The directions seem understandable, the scores playable, the comments valuable—and most importantly, children who I will never meet are going home at the end of the school day a bit happier from having played a good piece of jazz.

This new edition gave me the chance to add a few more details of process teaching, a couple of new homework assignments from the kids, some new resources now available and a new arrangement or two. Because of the length of the book, I resisted including any of the 60+ new jazz pieces I've done with my students in the past few years, saving that for another book down the line. However, I have made available a double CD of my students at The San Francisco School playing the arrangements in the book. This both helps bring the music off of the page and gives a reality check for how it sounds with real kids playing. (The CD available separately—see my website or check with your vendor).

The need for quality jazz education for all children of all ages remains as strong now as it was when this book was conceived. It is my hope that this book continues to contribute to that need and brings culture, pleasure and beauty to children worldwide.

—DOUG GOODKIN (12/2006)

INTRODUCTION

This book arrives as a labor of two loves—Orff Schulwerk and jazz. The first, a dynamic approach to music education, has framed the center of my life these past 28 years of teaching music to children. The second has been my passion for even longer as I've listened to, practiced and performed jazz. Here I bring these two worlds together and the result has been surprising—it turns out that they have a lot to say to each other. Few music teachers using the Orff approach include jazz in their curriculum and few jazz teachers know anything about Orff Schulwerk—I hope that this book will help change that.

Working with children has been a lifetime's delight. Their perpetually moving bodies, observant senses and inquiring minds keep me fresh and alert and remind me of the pleasures of the beginner's mind. I go home at the end of the day remembering the three year old who looked me in the eye and breathlessly exclaimed, "I love to dance!" I think about the third grader who ran to tell me he figured out on the piano the song we sang. I read the eighth grader's report about Bessie Smith and feel that my day has been well spent. I have the satisfaction of introducing them to some lifelong pleasures. They, in turn, teach me what it's like to listen to Duke Ellington with fresh ears free from preconceptions and remind me how it feels to take your first blues solo.

And jazz. How poor my life would have been if I never heard Louis and Ella "call the whole thing off" or heard Billie "laughing at life." How could I have survived without Count Basie's infectious joy, Miles's muted tones, Dizzy's exuberant proclamations or Coltrane's swirling passion? How I would have missed all those hours alone at the piano when the music rolled off my fingers and the blues sang out. When I needed it, jazz was always there—a companion for a joyful moment, a medicine for an aching soul, a tonic for the thirsting spirit.

And so this labor of two loves, combining the freshness of children improvising their way through each day with the maturity of a jazz spirit that's been around the block a few times. All the material and ideas presented here come from almost three decades of experimentation with children from three to thirteen years old at The San Francisco School. I began investigating the possibilities of jazz for young children around 1980 and out of our collective experimentation, a few choice pieces, ideas and processes began to crystallize. In 1988, I taught my first week-long class on Jazz and Orff Schulwerk to music teachers and found that the work I had already done with the children arranged itself effortlessly into a coherent order. It occurred to me that something approaching a jazz curriculum could be possible without killing the spirit of inquiry that had begun the whole process. That same year I initiated a full year jazz curriculum for my eighth graders. Some fifteen years of that curriculum, combined with working and re-working the jazz course for teachers, helped separate out the inspired activities from the merely effective. By 1993, I had written the first draft of this book—it would be another ten years of thinking and re-thinking before I finally arrived at this work.

There is not a single activity, thought or process in these pages that has not lived many lives in many classes with people from three to seventy three years old in places as diverse as the U.S., Australia, Taiwan, Russia and Spain. Where it succeeds, I have all these fellow students to thank. Where it fails, I can only blame my own inability to capture in print what comes forth so joyously in the class.

How to Use This Book

This book is not a jazz curriculum, though it presents a logical sequence that could be used as such. It is not a jazz theory book, though it gives enough information to help the reader learn to play basic jazz on any instrument. It is not a jazz history book, though it sketches out some important moments in that history. It is not an Orff Schulwerk book, though many fundamental principles of that approach are illuminated. It is not a songbook, though there is a wealth of arrangements ready to play as written.

There are many books here—one, purely practical, outlines specific class plans for the practicing teacher. Another gives some crucial cultural background and aesthetic criteria that helps to frame the subject. Yet another follows the thread of music theory as it applies to jazz style. Tips on teaching and general pedagogical principles are peppered throughout these pages. Cultural criticism and sociological concerns leak in here and there, and my personal love affair with jazz is given voice at different points. The tone shifts between preaching, poetry and prosaic postulates.

To assist the reader, I have generally put historical background near the beginning of chapters and my subjective thoughts at the end, with the practical "how-to" information and theory in the middle. However, even here, a particular exercise may turn our attention to the next piece in the puzzle and we will reach for it as we need it. The linear threads of history, theory and educational practice are there, but are spread across the chapters.

An ambitious teacher eager to launch an entire jazz curriculum will find enough in these pages to do so. Yet teachers do not adopt other's curriculum lock, stock and barrel; nor should they. We look to ideas and material as models and then adopt and adapt them to fit our own situations, experience, ways of thinking and ways of doing. Though I have taken the time to suggest a certain order to events and present a logical sequence, it is likely that most readers will skim through the book and take whatever serves their needs or attracts their interest in the moment. To assist in that process of choosing, there is a summary of the practical material at the end of the book.

Who Can Use This Book

There are no prerequisites for the teacher-training course I teach in jazz and Orff Schulwerk. The class is often a mix of jazz musicians with little teaching experience and no Orff background, Orff teachers with little jazz experience, classroom teachers with little musical background, and every combination of the above. I have found the jazz musicians and band teachers intensely involved in learning how to cook their knowledge down to child-size portions and Orff teachers fully awake in the sections illuminating jazz aesthetics and theory. The mix of background and knowledge adds to the class—everyone has some time when they feel stretched and some time when they find their knowledge affirmed.

This book is for anyone with a sincere interest in learning more about jazz. Jazz musicians who teach will want to follow the process of presenting the material. Orff teachers will pay closer attention to the theory. Band teachers might consider putting the instruments down and playing some of the games. Theory teachers might be inspired to bring xylophones into the classroom. Piano students can learn an approach to reading jazz tunes, and jazz aficionados might find new ways to listen to the music they already love.

The arrangements set forth here are scored for Orff instruments, but can generally be adapted to all sorts of ensemble situations, from bands to orchestras to keyboard labs to choir. As will be made clear later, the Orff instruments are a compromise and a dilution of the genuine band sound of jazz, but are an important avenue in light of their accessibility to young children and their relatively effortless technique. But by all means, adapt my adaptation to fit your particular needs.

Re-learning Music

Having taught my summer teacher-training course for fifteen years now, I've had the pleasure of seeing some results as teachers share their successes. Adults never trained in jazz can indeed learn enough to get their students started. Here is what one teacher wrote in her course evaluation:

> "I took this class to fill a gap in my musical and teaching experience. Stepping into the world of jazz constituted a risk for me—it meant facing a fear. Improvisation is scary stuff to the uninitiated. Yet it is knowledge that dissipates fear—now it all makes a great deal of sense."

Five years later, she wrote to me again:

> "The jazz ensemble has become one of the most popular electives in my junior high and certainly my favorite class to teach. I basically knew nothing about jazz before I took your workshop. Thanks so much for starting me down this wonderful path."

Her testimony is ample evidence that it is never to late to learn jazz. And my own story bears this out. My musical life began with traditional piano and organ lessons that taught me the valuable lessons of Bach and reading music. But when at 18 years old, I realized that I couldn't a) Sing in tune b) Dance c) Improvise rhythmically d) Improvise melodically e) Read a simple lead sheet with chords, I knew that something was radically missing from my musical education. My adult remedial education mostly came from two sources—training and experience in Orff Schulwerk and independent study in jazz piano.

If jazz is new to you, by all means dive in, no matter what age you are. My most recent jazz course included a 70-year-old dancer, a 65-year-old college philosophy professor and a 60-year-old Scottish storyteller, none of whom had ever played a note of jazz in their lives. By the end of the week, they were soloing on the xylophones, singing the blues and playing the drum set. And having a great time doing it!

ACKNOWLEDGEMENTS

Any book that has come into the light of print has been urged along by countless unseen helping hands, and this is no exception. I am particularly indebted to all those who believed in this project in the face of so many rejections from publishers who couldn't imagine how to fit it into their catalogs. First conceived in 1988, this book has had an elephantine pregnancy, with many stillborn versions sitting for years in a closet gathering dust. When it was clear that no one else was going to bring it to life, my decision to self-publish it came from the children and adults in my jazz classes who responded so joyfully to the material. It was with them in mind that I tried to summarize and capture in print our experiments over the past twenty years.

First thanks are due to my mentor Avon Gillespie, who at once brought me into the world of Orff Schulwerk and introduced me to the work of Bessie Jones. Thanks to Jane Frazee for the invitation to teach my first jazz class for adults at Hamline University in 1988 and for the conviction to run the class with an enrollment of only six students. Thanks to "the first six," who endured my beginning efforts to formalize the approach—

you know who you are. Thanks to John Harper, who first shared my vision that this work was worthy of publication.

In the world of jazz, I am indebted to Art Lande for his always inspiring playing and his equally inspired teaching. I am grateful to Keith Terry for his approach to body percussion that opened up both my own rhythmic potential and that of my students. Thanks to Milt Jackson for his visit to my school and to Stefon Harris for his continuing visits and his work with the children. Thanks to all the wonderful guest teachers in the jazz course—Linda Tillery, Keith Terry, Joni Haastrup, Lester Cobb, Herb Gibson, Michael Smolens, Rebecca Mauleon, Mary Fettig, and more. Thanks to the musicians whose children I taught at The San Francisco School who gave so much to the music program—Bobby McFerrin, Eddie Marshall and Bill Douglass, among others.

In the world of teaching, I thank Susan Kennedy for sharing the jazz course with me and bringing movement to the forefront, James Harding for sharing the 8th grade teaching at The San Francisco School, Melissa Martinez for her enthusiastic generosity, and again, all my 8th grade classes at The San Francisco School and all my Orff colleagues who have attended my jazz workshops. Thanks also to the company Peripole-Bergerault for their chromatic instruments that allowed this work to unfold.

For assistance on the manuscript, immeasurable thanks are due to Sofia Lopez-Ibor for her numerous suggestions for improvement and her help in gathering photos, to Susan Kennedy for her help on the Jazz Movement chapter, to Jeanne Makanna, Ira Schrank, Sofia Lopez-Ibor, and Drew Story for taking many of the photos, to Sue Sandlin for her fabulous cover design, and to Bill Holab for all his work on the typesetting and music engraving.

The lion's share of thanks goes to Peter Greenwood, my editor, who has stayed with me through the thick and thin of the past twelve years. He improved my writing exponentially and continued to take me to task even when I thought I had it right. Where the manuscript sings, I have him to thank.

A final thanks to my daughter Talia for the years of our piano-saxophone duets, to my daughter Kerala for her insights on writing, to my wife Karen for keeping the home fires burning, to my mother Florence Goodkin for clipping out articles on jazz musicians in the newspaper, to my father Jim Goodkin for playing jazz standards on the organ, to my childhood friend Bill "Lump" Blackshear for walking me across to the other side of the tracks, and to all the jazz musicians who taught me the true meaning of "triumph in the face of adversity" by bringing beauty into this world.

Talia Goodkin playing Alto Saxophone.

The author with Bill Blackshear at his record store.

Three Orff-trained musicians join the band.

CHAPTER 1: JAZZ GOES TO SCHOOL

*"I ain't been to Frisco, I ain't been to school,
I ain't been to college, but I ain't no fool."*

—Verse from African-American
clapping play *Head and Shoulders*

Imagine walking through a school and hearing the beat of a tambourine echo in the hallway. You peek through an open door and see an exuberant group of three year olds waving their arms while they sing, "Shoo, turkey, shoo, shoo!" In the next classroom, the five year olds are having a circle time. "Funga Alafia" sings out the teacher and they all respond in unison, "A shay, a shay!" Here is a school where children sing their way through the day.

Down the hall, a third grade student stands in front of the music class and recites "I said, a boom chick a boom" and her classmates echo it back. Then they go to the xylophones and make up melodies to the text. Here is a school where all children not only play music, but create it as well.

The third graders leave and the fifth graders come in to the sound of Dizzy Gillespie's trumpet. They start walking in line, bouncing to the beat, snapping their fingers and following the leader. Soon they partner up, try out their own motions and begin to choreograph a dance. Here is a school where children take off their shoes and dance.

Across the way in the Middle School music room, eighth graders are listening to both Thelonious Monk and Art Tatum play *Tea for Two*. They hear some stories about these two pianists and share their insights on their different uses of space and silence. Here is a school where children think about music and learn about its theory and history.

This imaginary walk through a school is what you might experience should you visit The San Francisco School, where I teach. This is neither a special arts school nor a special "jazz" school. It is simply a place where music is one of many ways for children to express what they feel, what they think and what they imagine. They don't "study"

7

music as a subject with rules, but learn to speak music as a language. Like all languages, music begins with the simple need to communicate and is built from the trial-and-error of daily conversation. Music class is a formal time to practice speaking while also learning essential diction, structure and grammar.

Because many schools don't recognize children's need to speak the languages of sounds, gestures and images just as fluently as those of words and numbers, this school takes on the aura of a special place, and the Orff approach to teaching music becomes a special practice. But these ideas are timeless and found in all cultures—music is simply part of being human and no person or community of persons is quite complete without it. The children who have passed through The San Francisco School know this because they have sung, danced or played music every day of their eleven-year school life.

Any school that commits to a serious and playful music education is to be commended for serving its students. Yet in this book, I hope to take this one step farther. Though *all* music is a joy and a pleasure, *jazz* is of special importance to American children. I hope to give convincing cultural, aesthetic, political and historical reasons why this is so, but the strongest statement comes from the children themselves. Like the second grade boy who heard the jazz ensemble at an assembly and commented: *"I loved the music the jazz group played. You know, it's like it turns on the dance inside of you and it just has to come out."*

Cultural Literacy

As your students' response will testify, jazz is *our* music. And yet we don't know it as thoroughly as we should. Part of our resistance is embedded in its very history—jazz began as an outlaw, neither accepted nor welcomed in mainstream culture. Every step it made deeper into our American psyche came from its own irresistible and infectious rhythms, at once joyful, triumphant and exuberant and yet also singing of great pain, suffering and despair. One approach to the story of jazz is to trace its journey from the whorehouse to the White House.

Jazz has come a long way, but not far enough. If once it was deemed crass and low-brow, it is now distinguished and erudite—worthy of a nine-part series on PBS, $50 tickets in concert halls, and a place in virtually every university and conservatory music program. Every high school has its jazz band and most middle schools as well. It would seem that jazz is well known and well respected. And yet we don't know it as well as we should.

A child can grow up in Toledo, Ohio and never know that Art Tatum was born there. A high school student can hear the name Billie Holiday and ask, "Who's he?" A college student might see the graffiti "Bird Lives" and assume it came from the Ornithology Department. People in most regions of the United States can scan through their radio dial and never hear a note of jazz.

To assure a spot in mainstream culture, jazz needs schools. Schools are where we can guarantee exposure to what E. D. Hirsch Jr. calls "cultural literacy—what every American needs to know." * Schools are where we can publicly and openly acknowledge this great American achievement. Schools are where we can learn the stories of the people who created this timeless art form and thank them for their efforts.

Yet consider the nature of universities, high schools and middle schools. They are all institutions in which music is an *elective*. That means only those with the interest, tal-

---

* This is the title of a book Hirsch wrote in 1988 listing 5,000 names, phrases, dates and concepts essential to an American identity. Jazz, the music that more than any has helped define that identity in the 20th century, is conspicuous in his book by its glaring absence.

ent, and opportunity will even take music classes. Of those students, only some will go into jazz programs. Once in those programs, they still might spend all their time reading notes on jazz charts and never listen to *Ellington at Newport* in class or know what was going on in Minton's club in the mid-40's.

By contrast, elementary schools theoretically have a general music program required for *all* students. Shouldn't this be a place where we can ensure exposure to jazz as a major part of our cultural heritage? Shouldn't all children be given the chance to hear jazz, dance to jazz, learn about jazz and play jazz? If we are to change with the times and add computer education, drug education, and diversity education to the traditional curriculum, shouldn't we include jazz education as well? This book answers with an exuberant "yes!"

Our walk through The San Francisco School gave a taste of what a preschool through middle school jazz curriculum might look like at a glance. The rest of this book will fill in the details. But before delving into the "what" of a jazz curriculum, let's look at some of the generating ideas that form the basis of the activities to follow.

The author with Art Tatum's sister, Arlene, in front of their house in Toledo, Ohio.

Building the Foundation

This book ends where others begin. The territory it marks off is the largely uncharted landscape of developing a *foundation* for jazz. There are countless books describing the next step—the scales and chord progressions, the specific instrumental techniques, the band arrangements and orchestrations—but few (if any) concerned with giving the beginner a chance to get inside of the music from the very start. How can we introduce jazz to children? How can we open this world to them in a way that meets their needs, capacities, interests and learning styles? Does there exist a pedagogically sound and proven approach that can equally handle the inspired, spontaneous act of creation and the sequenced presentation of increasingly complex theory? Is there a process that can simultaneously get down with the body and spiral up to higher thinking skills, a way of working that is playful and a way of playing that is serious work?

Such an approach to music education already exists. It was not designed to teach any specific style of music, yet its approach to learning and its method of building musical skills and understanding is remarkably compatible with the demands and sensibilities of jazz. Very few people trained in this approach use it to teach jazz and perhaps fewer jazz band teachers are aware of its potential. It is known as Orff Schulwerk.*

Eighth grade Orff ensemble at The San Francisco School.

---

* For a more thorough look at this dynamic approach to music education, see my book *Play, Sing and Dance: An Introduction to Orff Schulwerk*: Schott 2002

Orff Schulwerk and Jazz—A Natural Integration

Our tour through the school gave us a bit of the flavor of the Orff approach. Kids, along with their teacher, were singing, dancing, playing games, playing with music and playing music. They were patting their bodies, exploring their voices, creating motions and gestures. They were playing xylophones and drums and recorders and a potpourri of percussion instruments. They were marching in lines, dancing in circles, swinging with partners. Sometimes the kids were the leaders, with everyone else (again, including the teacher!) copying *their* motions, their vocal inflections, their rhythmic patterns. There was laughter and giggles and quiet reflection and boisterous enthusiasm, loud crashing cymbals and the delicate tinkle of glockenspiels. There were moments where the children stood out, improvising their own melodies on the xylophone and moments when they blended in, joined as one voice in the chorus. Above all, the children were not competing against each other for first chair in the orchestra—they were weaving anew each day the cloth of community.

Herein lie the first connections between Orff process and jazz. The roots of jazz lie in the music and dance of the slaves, where the people danced barefoot in rings, clapped, slapped the body, sang and moved, played tambourines and any available percussion instruments. They lived communally, worked communally, suffered communally, exulted communally—and made music communally. Cut off from their tradition, they improvised their way into the newly emerging forms, passing it down through the ears, bodies and memories of each generation. They were alert to every musical idea that crossed their path, filtering it through an African genius that inevitably made it into something new. Out of their deep need for music making and shared experience came an original expression that was destined to become one of the greatest influences on world musical culture.

The African slaves brought over an entirely different relationship to music making (and thus, music *teaching*) that informed every African-American form that grew from it. Though there are noteworthy differences, the underlying bond between the African-American practices and Orff sensibility is clear. Taking off our shoes, forming a circle and playing around with musical ideas through our bodies and voices will bring us closer to the heart of jazz than copying the jazz scales and chords from the board. How strange that the musical innovations of transplanted African cultures meet the experimentations of a few key people in Europe and discover they have much to share!

Cornerstone Principles

When giving an Orff workshop, I invariably begin in silence and lead the group through many activities before the first word is spoken. We discover that understanding begins from doing. After we play, sing and dance, we sit down and reflect on what we have done. I tell the participants, "You are anthropologists in this strange country of Orff Schulwerk and your passport has just expired. You must go home and describe the nature of this community. What would you say?" Out pour the adjectives—"fun, involving, playful, friendly, risky, energetic, rhythmic, spontaneous, sequenced." Having experienced something together directly in their bodies, these words carry so much more meaning to the participants than if I had begun a lecture describing Orff Schulwerk as "an approach to music education that is fun, involving, playful, etc."

The transition from active workshop to fixed print is a difficult one—how to give you, the reader, a similar experience? As you try out the material presented here, its success will depend partly on your understanding of the thinking behind it, a thinking embodied in a workshop setting, but abstract when presented in print. Why teach all the parts to everyone? Why switch instruments? Why should the students move as well as play? Why is improvising important? Why should we talk about the meanings of songs? Though the answers are stitched into the activities, a few words in advance about the key ideas of teaching jazz in this style are in order.

What follows are the basic cornerstone principles that inform both the choice of material and the process in which it is taught. Some of these principles come from Orff pedagogy, some from jazz practice, and some from plain common sense. Though many jazz programs may include elements of each, it is the commitment to them all that makes this approach to teaching jazz—or indeed, any musical style—unique.

1. The Whole of Jazz Must Be Taught to the Whole Class Using the Whole Range of Our Intelligences.

We can learn more about flowers in the field than in the laboratory. The laboratory may make it easier to distinguish pistil from stamen, but the field reveals the community of plants the flower lives amongst, the insects it attracts, the cycles it lives through. If we are to keep jazz alive as it crosses the threshold into schools, we must keep it connected to its history, its culture, its aesthetic, the whole of its being. We will have our share of laboratory moments, but most of the learning will take place out in the fresh air.

Why the whole class? Both Orff practice and West African culture proceed from the assumption that *everyone is innately musical*. Naturally, everyone is not equally talented or interested at the same level, but that should never be an excuse to neglect a significant part of our humanity. All children can make and create music and we will give them both the opportunity and the confidence.

We will teach all the parts to everyone before choosing our parts and also make sure that children switch parts in each new piece. This gives them an opportunity to experience the whole of the music by being inside its different components—the bass, the drums, the melody, the chords.

Finally, we will draw on the full range of our intelligences—learning by doing, by feeling, by thinking—in a wide range of mediums—voice, body percussion, movement, dance, instruments. When we have played, sung, danced, listened to and analyzed each piece of music, we get the whole picture.

2. A Study of Jazz Is a Study of Culture.

> *"whatever you have to say, leave*
> *the roots on, let them*
> *dangle*
>
> *And the dirt*
> *Just to make clear*
> *where they come from"*
> —CHARLES OLSON [1]

The insistence on keeping the notes tied to their cultural origins is not simply a humanitarian gesture, worthy as that is—it is a musical consideration as well. I have found that *all* music sings clearer and truer when we understand where it comes from. Much music education treats notes as disembodied patterns of sound, but all music is born from a specific time, place and group (or groups) of people. Knowing something of life in the Georgia Sea Islands, New Orleans funeral customs or the Harlem Renaissance will give us new insight into the music that grew out of each. By connecting the practices and principles of a culture with the practices and principles of the music, children learn that *all* music is a form of cultural expression.

Connecting music to culture means coming to grips with both the dark and light side of cultural expression. Much music made for and taught to children has been commercialized, homogenized and processed, the roots pruned and dirt washed away. The twists and turns that give character to culture are straightened out and the children are left with music without a soul. As appropriate, we will keep those dangling roots and gritty dirt alongside the blossom of the flower.

3. A Study of Jazz Is a Study of History.

> *"To listen to jazz without any knowledge of its history is to miss much of its charm."*
>
> —DUKE ELLINGTON

Intimately tied to jazz culture is jazz history. "No him, no me," said Dizzy Gillespie of Louis Armstrong, and the excitement of history is for the children to be able to hear how Louis begat Roy (Eldridge) who begat Diz. One author lamented that many high school jazz players *"did not know the names of such jazz greats as Count Basie, Miles Davis, John Coltrane, Bill Evans…* [2] To teach jazz minus its history is akin to teaching literature without ever reading Dickens, Dickinson or Dostoyevsky. Not only is the rich vein of tradition left untapped, but the *pleasure* of the story is also missed.

Eighth grader Will Gaines agrees. He wrote: *"I definitely think that knowing the history of the music you're listening to and of the artist playing it gives it much more depth. To hear the African drummer charged with magnetic energy and then to hear Louis Armstrong blowing his trumpet with that same fire is just magical."*

Recordings, videos and biographies of the musicians will keep our learning tied to the actual development of the music. In front of all our words *describing* the music and its growth will be the music itself, a glorious sounded history vibrating from a struck cymbal and pouring forth from the bell of the trumpet.

4. A Study of Jazz Is a Study of the Repertoire.

A first step in learning jazz is hearing jazz. Whether immersed in it as background music, moving to it in music class or engaged in a formal listening lesson, we need to hear jazz—especially the key pieces in the repertoire played by master musicians. Listening helps us hear what we're aiming for. The more we listen, the better we speak. The more we speak, the harder we listen.

We can learn something of jazz by listening alone, but until it passes through our hands, we only have a partial understanding. The premise of this book is that we learn about jazz by playing jazz. When we try *The C Jam Blues* and then listen to Duke playing it, we listen with different ears. And after we listen to Duke, we return to playing with new ears. Eighth grader Kira Carlin affirms the importance of both playing and listening: *"When I first listened to the music, I just heard the plain music. But after playing it, I saw the layers that come together to form the piece. Then when I went back and listened again to the music, I heard the complexity of the layers and that brought the music alive for me."*

Playing jazz means playing the repertoire—the real pieces played by real jazz musicians. So much of what we offer children in schools is "jazz-y"—taking a poem or a song from a completely different context and swinging the rhythm while snapping our fingers—but very little is jazz itself. Playing authentic jazz pieces connects the child's beginning first steps with the master musician's lifelong journey.

5. A Study of Jazz Is a Study of Theory.

When we play, the hand understands. When we listen, the ear grasps the essentials. Yet both together are still not enough—we need the head to contribute its area of understanding—theory. Once the foundation is poured, music theory frames our understanding. When we can articulate the general patterns involved, name them, apply them and re-apply them in the next piece, we gain greater control over the material. We can learn a great deal of music by rote and feel our way through a portion of the repertoire, but when we truly understand the thinking behind the playing, we have the tools to continue teaching ourselves. Our goal as teachers to lead the students towards a greater independence and theoretical understanding is one of the central pillars of that independence, freeing us from shouldering the beam.

When novices begin to study jazz, they are shocked—and often scared off—by the vast storehouse of theoretical information necessary. What appears to the outsider as an effortless spontaneous expression is built from a meticulous and often tedious theoretical study. Our job at this beginning stage is to give just enough information to clarify what makes jazz sound like jazz, but not too much to overwhelm and to keep the hand and head in constant conversation, sometimes one leading, sometimes the other.

6. A Study of Jazz Is a Study of Ourselves.

If we are to implement a national movement towards jazz in every child's education, how can we avoid reducing the sublime idiosyncrasies of each region, district, school, teacher and child to a homogenized monolithic standard? Orff Schulwerk sidesteps this dilemma by calling itself an approach rather than a method. The models it offers resist slavish imitation and invite creative participation. Each teacher may begin by imitating others' lesson plans, but only as a step to finding his or her own authentic and unique teaching style. Jazz likewise insists that imitation of existing models is not an end in itself, but a means to discovering your own voice.

Though it takes a lifetime to discover who you are and what you have to say, the first signs come early. Jazz traditionally has a long waiting period to begin improvisation, dependent on sufficient instrumental technique and a grasp of complex forms, but Orff Schulwerk starts the process much earlier. From the early years on, children learn to make any musical idea—a rhythm, a text, a scale, a dance—their own through improvisation. Who they are in that moment—their experience, their character, their level of technique and understanding—all go into the improvisation and make it distinct.

Some high school players in a jazz band may read well and play with good technique and yet have trouble improvising. How ironic that an Orff student improvising movement or experimenting with vocal sounds may be closer to the heart of jazz than a saxophone player reading the chart to *Take the A Train*! If jazz becomes just a particular combination of notes played in a certain style, we will have missed its greatest gift—a relentless search to fully express the depth of our feeling.

Eighth grader Matthew Watson puts it this way: *"What makes jazz amazing is that most of it was written or performed by people with lives full of hardship. It is what makes what they play come from the heart. Jazz has a deep feeling to it because the musicians are playing about their own lives."*

Lead Sheet Activities

These principles are the themes that form the background of all to follow. The beginning activities give the practical details of how such lessons are taught. As the lessons progress, it is assumed that the teacher has gained facility in the approach and doesn't need the details of the process spelled out.

Here we follow the same route as the evolving jazz player, who first may need to play from sheet music with all the notes written out and then progress to the lead sheet with only a melody and chord symbols. At this level, each player decides his or her own voicing, tempo and interpretation. The tune is not a rigid composition, but a flexible song that inspires further improvisation and exploration.

That is the spirit of this material—fixed improvisations that generate further improvisations. Not only must each teacher bring the full force of his or her background, knowledge and creativity to each activity, but equally must consider how to bring the children's ideas into the mix. Setting anything into print always runs the danger of fixing that which is fluid—it is the teachers' and students' job to make it come off the page.

With these in mind, we are ready to answer the fundamental question at the start of any enterprise—how do we begin?

Endnotes

1. Olsen, Charles: *These Days*: Poem included in the collection *The Rag and Bone Shop of the Heart* edited by Robert Bly, James Hillman & Michael Meade: HarperCollins

2. CMEA Newsletter Feb./March '93

Bibliography

Play, Sing & Dance: An Introduction to Orff Schulwerk: Doug Goodkin: Schott

Name Games: Doug Goodkin: Alfred

A Rhyme in Time: Doug Goodkin; Alfred

Sound Ideas: Activities for Percussion Circle: Doug Goodkin: Alfred

The ABC's of Education: A Primer for Schools to Come: Doug Goodkin: Pentatonic Press

The Schulwerk: Carl Orff (V. III of *Documentation)*: Schott

Orff-Schulwerk Music for Children: Volumes I–V (Margaret Murray Edition): Carl Orff and Gunild Keetman: Schott

Music for Children: Orff Schulwerk-American Edition: Volumes 1,2,3: Edited by Hermann Regner: Schott

Discography

The San Francisco School Orff Ensemble Collection: Volumes 1 to 21: www.sfschool.org

Orff-Schulwerk: Music for Children (3 CD's): Schott

The author considers a new approach to teaching jazz.

CHAPTER 2: GAMES

"Let's go Zudio, Zudio, Zudio, let's go Zudio all night long."
—AFRICAN-AMERICAN SONG

We begin with the child's natural mode of learning: games. In this case, *African-American* games. Clapping plays, singing games and ring plays are the living textbooks that teach us historical information, stylistic considerations, social values, physical attitudes and postures, musical concepts and forms. *How* they teach us—from the hand through the heart to the head—is as important as *what* they teach us. When we start to play, get the toes tappin', the knees knockin', the hips happenin' and the hands clappin'; the heart opens wide, the voice rings out and we pass over the threshold of mere *information* into the house of *transformation.*

A generation ago, these games could be found in city playgrounds, suburban backyards and country fields, played by children of all ages without any adult supervision. Today, the child's world is markedly different. Free play has been largely supplanted by adult-organized activities, and oral tradition replaced by media. In some places, the music classroom is the wildlife refuge that preserves the endangered species of children's games.

If this must be, we must understand something of the nature of the species. What is its place in the ecology of the school curriculum? What does it offer us generally and what can each specific game teach us?

Though the games are complete in themselves, our concern here is quite specific—to trace how the acorn of African-American folk music grows to the tree of jazz. Though the details change, the essential qualities of jazz are already present in seed form in these games in a kind of cultural genetic code. We will reveal the DNA blueprint by playing the games and then naming the names—key musical concepts that clarify our understanding. In keeping with the tradition, we will keep these abstract concepts held close to the chest of their mother songs. We will learn how to play the music by first playing the games.

Bessie Jones and the Georgia Sea Island Singers

Without written manuscripts or recordings to preserve the music of the slaves, how can we come to know the roots that eventually grew to jazz? One solution is to search for an unbroken oral tradition, and there is no better place to begin than the Georgia Sea Islands. Three factors helped the inhabitants of these islands preserve their culture:

1. Island cultures in general tend towards more stable traditions because of their isolation.

2. The mosquito-ridden islands were breeding grounds for malaria, a disease the English plantation owners were more susceptible to than the African slaves. As a result, the owners didn't generally live on the islands, leaving the slaves freer to maintain their own culture. To this day, there still is an Africanized form of English known as Gullah spoken on the islands.

3. When a young woman called Bessie Jones came to St. Simon's Island in 1933, there already existed a group formed by Lydia Parrish called the Coastal Georgia Spiritual Singers Society, dedicated to preserving the musical heritage of slavery times. Bessie joined the group and eventually took over the leadership of what became The Georgia Sea Island Singers.

In 1972, Bessie Jones collaborated with Bess Lomax Hawes to set down this oral tradition in the book *Step it Down* and later made a recording of the same title (see the Bibliography and Discography). These remain the quintessential sources of this tradition, infused with the love, wisdom, and spirituality of Ms. Jones. Now others have carried on this research, most notably Linda Tillery and the Cultural Heritage Choir, Bernice Johnson Reagon and Sweet Honey on the Rock, and Doug and Frankie Quimby, the two remaining members of The Georgia Sea Island Singers.*

1972 was also the year in which Avon Gillespie, an African-American Orff teacher, opened the door for me to the world of Orff Schulwerk. Avon briefly studied with Bessie Jones and was one of the first Orff teachers to integrate this material with the Orff approach. The games presented here are the versions I learned from Avon.

---

* The Quimbys still travel around sharing this material at schools, conferences and music festivals. To contact them, write: quimbys@gacoast.com

Bessie Jones's house on St. Simon's Island.

Guidelines for Games in the Classroom

As we shift these games from the playground to the classroom and open them up to people outside the culture, we create radical changes. We take something from the child's world and pass it through adult hands before returning it to children. We take a learning experience based on the African model of music—a functional part of daily life learned informally through immersion in a musical community—and place it within the classical European model of music—an academic subject learned formally through a special discipline of drill, exercise and understanding of the rules. This transplanting requires care and attention if we are to keep the roots intact.

The following are some suggestions to ease the transition.

1. Invite everybody to play.

The community as the center of musical activity is a theme that resurfaces throughout the African-American musical experience. Though most are called children's games, adults and grandparents at community gatherings would often join in the fun. The games are for *everybody*—as the teacher, you should get into the circle and play with the children.

2. Teach the songs by rote.

These games come from an oral tradition worlds removed from formal musical training. Since many are call and response, the response can be quickly taught aurally, with the teacher singing the verses or improvising the couplets. Other longer songs can simply be sung by the teacher while playing the game. The repetition built into the game allows the children to absorb the words and start singing along.

3. Play the games with musical integrity.

To teach these games effectively, we must understand the style that sets African-American music apart from other forms. We will be outlining some of the specifics of that style as we learn the games. The problem with people from outside the black culture singing these songs is the unconscious (or conscious) tendency to "clean them up"—change the vocal timbre, even out the syncopations, ignore the ornaments, revise the language (Georgia Sea Island singer Doug Quimby remarks: *"You don't say 'Juba this and Juba that,' say 'Juba dis and Juba dat, Juba killed a yella,' not yellow, but a yella, y-e-l-l-a. If we change it, it wouldn't be our oral tradition."*) [1] Scraping the dirt off the roots (and I'm using dirt in the wholesome, earthy sense here) changes the character of the game.

Likewise, be aware of the complete physical involvement called for in singing and clapping. Bessie Jones taught, *"Use your feet. You hardly can clap without using your feet, not and stay on time. That clap didn't go so good for me because you've got to get it all over!"* [2] Motion ignites e-motion in the African-American aesthetic and is an essential part of "how to do."

4. Play the games often.

These games demand a high level of rhythmic precision, movement coordination and social cooperation, goals not easily achieved in one or two playings. They may appear simple, but require constant repetition to be played *well*. There is always one more thing that can be improved—the singing, the clapping, the shape of the circle, the quality of the movement, the group spirit.

5. Play the games with a playful spirit.

Bess Lomax Hawes (co-author of *Step It Down*) describes the experience of white students first learning these games, and reveals yet another cultural gap:

> "Ms. Jones would urge everyone on their feet to play; the students, meanwhile, with pencils and notebooks ready, waited to be told *what* to play and *how* to play it. As I watched first the Islanders play, and then the students, it seemed that the game was the same (we had learned the "rules"), but the play was not (our emotional commitment and consequent emotional gratification was different). As the Islanders, most of them grandparents, several in their sixties, danced their way through countless repetitions of "Little Johnny Brown" with fresh joy and humor each time, it seemed to me that I could never recall having played any game with that much involvement, that much gaiety, even as a child." [3]

Stephen Nachmanovitch, in his excellent book *Free Play*, makes a useful distinction between play and game. He says:

> "'Play 'is different from 'game.' Play is the free spirit of exploration, doing and being for its own pure joy. Game is an activity defined by a set of rules, like baseball, sonnet, symphony, diplomacy. Play is an attitude, a spirit, a way of doing things, whereas game is a defined activity with rules and a playing field and participants." [4]

Game is replacing play in the lives of many American children and as children borrow adult models of organized sports, a piece of their childhood is lost. Watching children in Ghana playing games, I was struck by their lighthearted energy. Even in games that had "winners and losers," winning seemed incidental to the overall feeling of playing together. The games were punctuated by constant smiles and much laughter. Teaching one of these games to my 4th grade students revealed that kids brought up in a culture of winning created a different kind of atmosphere. Within two minutes, there were accusations of "You cheated!," "I did not!," rooting for friends, laughing at losers, hurt feelings, etc. The contrast was enlightening and depressing. If our children can learn to play these games in the spirit of enjoyment and community (and my students have improved over time), we will have given them a lifelong gift.

6. Keep to the original purpose of the games.

Avon Gillespie once told me of a workshop he gave at a music education conference. Coincidentally, he and a colleague had chosen the same game to present to the teachers. In his class, the participants were barefoot, singing and dancing with a rousing spirit, while his colleague next door was teaching the song from notation on the board, analyzing the scale and discussing the song's place in the conceptual curriculum. The contrast spoke volumes. We teachers are notoriously nervous about making sure our students have "learned something." We bring the games into the classrooms only to reduce them to a means of achieving pre-programmed learning objectives. We play the games to prove a point, but miss the essence—the playing *is* the point.

This is not to say there is no place for reflection. Indeed, we will see how an analysis of these games leads us to an understanding of jazz. But the first step is to play them as they're meant to be played and learn their primary lessons—communication, celebration, and jubilation! With that in mind, take off your shoes, grab a partner and let's play!

Head and Shoulders (as learned from Avon Gillespie)

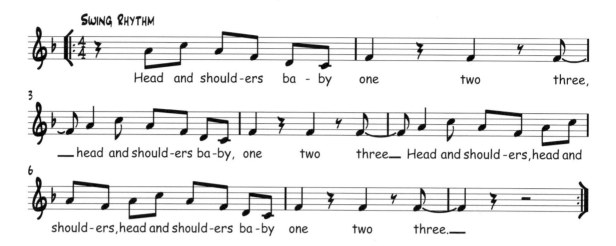

Head and should-ers ba - by one   two   three,

— head and should-ers ba-by, one   two   three— Head and should-ers, head and

should-ers, head and should-ers ba-by one   two   three.—

2. Knee and ankle baby, 1- 2- 3
3. Bounce the ball, baby, 1- 2- 3
4. Milk the cow, baby, 1- 2- 3

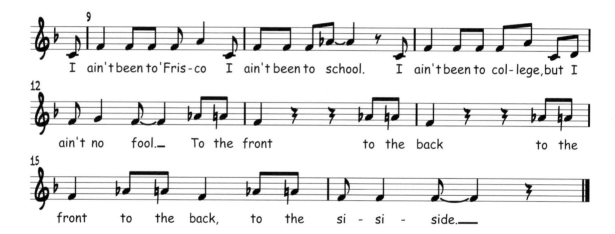

I ain't been to 'Fris-co   I ain't been to school.   I ain't been to col-lege, but I

ain't no   fool.— To the front   to the back   to the

front   to   the back,   to   the   si - si - side.—

Children from St. Simons Island.

1. Head and Shoulders

Focus: Offbeat, Syncopation, Swing

Activity

- I enjoy teaching all the motions silently before singing the song. When the group is ready, all sing the song with the motions.

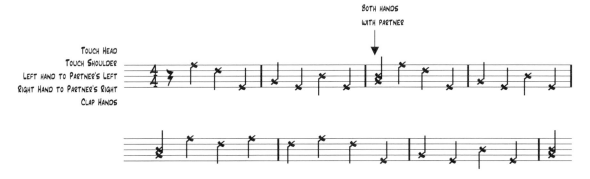

- In a circle, create partners as follows: One person turns to partner on right, next two face each other, next two, each pair waiting for those before them to turn. (I call this the "domino method.") If there is an uneven number, the teacher can join in. Repeat the whole song with a partner, touching partner's hands on cross right, cross left and both. In the second part of the song, bounce and snap on beats 2 and 4, clap twice after words "front" and "back," moving as the words dictate.

- At the end of the song, all turn around and repeat with a new partner.

- Turn and change partners after each verse.

Variations

- Partners create two new verses (each one contributes one verse) based on things they do each day. They must follow the form and create an accompanying motion:

Brush your teeth, baby, one two three, Brush your teeth, baby, one two three, Brush your teeth, Brush your teeth, Brush your teeth, baby, one two three.

Ride your skateboard, baby, one two three (2x)
Ride your skateboard, Ride your skateboard, Ride your skateboard, baby, one two three

- All perform at the same time.
- Half perform, the other half watches. Switch. Notice if any were the same.

Comments

The silent teaching technique mentioned here is a wonderful way to start any class. It captures the attention of the students, wakes up the brain and lets the students know that something is different here than the standard lecture/listen model. The game itself is also a great opener—the motions warm up the body, the partner play stirs up the community spirit and the invitation to make up new lyrics exercises the imagination. In one activity, the students experience the full scope of the Orff approach—moving, singing, clapping, and creating through joyful play.

An Orff class is like a piece of music in which every detail must be thought out in advance. What formation serves the activity? How will I teach this song? How will they choose a partner? How can I develop the material? Some helpful class process hints are folded into the directions that are worth bringing to attention.

The Circle: The circle is the basic form for these games and many other activities in the Orff classroom as well. It allows for complete visibility, places the teacher as one of many points on the circle playing *with* the children, helps focus the energy and allows for some effortless variations. Simply standing in a circle with children already speaks volumes about the class—no desks in rows, no looking at the back of other student's heads, no elevated teacher and those at the head of the class and those at the foot. As Bess Lomax Hawes so eloquently describes it:

> The notion of a ring has always had a quality of magic; during play it is, literally, a
> "charmed circle." It includes and excludes at the same time. It surrounds and enfolds
> while it walls off and repels. Inside a ring, within its bounds, you are safe from what it
> "outside;" you are in a special world in which you may be either king or prisoner. The
> ring is without gap or weakness—perhaps strength is its underlying symbolic quality." [5]

Choosing Partners: One of my missions in my professional teacher-training life is to get the "domino method" of choosing partners instituted as a common practice! I've attended countless workshops where momentary chaos reigns as the teacher tells the people in the circle to "turn to a partner." I turn to the person on my left just as she turns to the person on her left—and the flow of the activity is broken as we look up helplessly trying to figure it out. The domino technique begins by two people turning, then the next two, then the next two and so on around the circle in a wavelike motion, each waiting to turn until the people before them do. Shaking hands as you turn makes this even more concrete.

Changing Partners: For the children, this structure avoids the hurt feelings of "choose a partner." For those ready to complain," I don't like my partner," the circle provides another wonderful effortless possibility—simply by turning around, everyone automatically has a new partner. Changing partners gives the children the repetition they need to practice with the variety of interest—each partner is a whole new experience!

Often children who can't succeed with one partner can with another. A fun variation in this game is to change partners in the middle of a verse, i.e. sing the first phrase with one partner, then turn and sing the second phrase with another partner.

Style: In children's culture, the older children would impart the full body rhythmic bounce. Model that quality in your presentation and call attention to the children who have it. The repetition of practice alone is insufficient if the children don't know what they're aiming for—the bounce, strong singing, relaxed and gentle hand pats with the partner, eye contact and joyful energy.

New Lyrics: As with so many of the activities presented in this book, the invitation to make up something new keeps the creative urge well oiled. It also keeps the song contemporary. The given text came from a particular time and place that is markedly different from many people's experience these days—very few of my students, children or adults, have ever milked a cow! Not only is it an interesting musical challenge to create a new text that fits the phrase length ("Eat, baby" is too short, "Eat a double-scoop vanilla chocolate fudge ice cream cone, baby" is too long), but it is also a fascinating cultural study. In my adult workshops, hygiene and driving tend to be the most popular themes. If you get a group of kids with verses like "play Nintendo," "change the channel," "hit the mall," you'll have your work cut out for you. Good luck!

Overview of Jazz Rhythm

The rhythmic elements characteristic of African-American folk music that later appear in jazz are all present in this clapping play. When children sing these songs, clap and move these games, they internalize these essential characteristics. Let's look at some of these qualities as they appear in this song.

Offbeat: In most African-American music, the strong beats (in European terminology) are felt internally and the weak beats are accented. In 2/4 time, the *offbeat* is accented (1 <u>and</u> 2 <u>and</u>), in 4/4 time, beats 2 and 4, the *backbeat*, are stressed (1 <u>2</u> 3 <u>4</u>). (To keep it simple for the kids, I use the term *offbeat* for both experiences).*

Historically, the offbeat emphasis was a natural polyrhythmic response to European folk material in 2/4 and 4/4—the complex African drumming tradition couldn't breathe in those metrical boxes. African sensibility shifted the European emphasis of beats 1 and 3 to a *complementary* texture—accents on beats 2 and 4.

Head and Shoulders, like virtually all African-American clapping plays, has claps on beats 2 and 4. They complement the text by filling in the intervals between the words "One, two, three." Playing these games gets the sound in the ear and the feeling in the

---

*Some modern black pop music augments this feeling over two measures-1 *2 3* 4 / 1 *2 3* 4. From the 2/4 Ragtime and Dixieland to the 4/4 Swing and Be-bop to the 8/4 Funk and Rap, there is a progression of increased augmentation that leaves space for different styles of dancing and rhythmic improvisation. Though the offbeat changes from 1 *and* to 1 *2* to 12 *3*, the *feeling* remains intact. Parenthetically, there also seems to be an increase in *volume* of the offbeat, from the subtle hi-hat to the ear-expanding syntho-sound!

body. Clapping plays are more effective than the abstract counting of beats because they establish the rhythm in relation to a *text*. This is of utmost importance; rhythm is never abstract and isolated in the African sensibility—even drum pieces are called songs.

Syncopation: The Harvard Dictionary of Music defines syncopation as "a momentary contradiction of the prevailing meter or pulse" while Elson's Pocket Music Dictionary describes it as "a temporary displacement of the natural accent in music…with attacks falling *between* the beats." To give the children the feeling of this in their bodies, I have them walk to a beat and suddenly slip on an imaginary banana peel—the steady beat is interrupted through the release of weight, a sense of falling. This quality of momentary imbalance translates musically as well, creating rhythmic movement and dramatic tension.

Compare "1 2 3"

with "1 2 *3* "

Syncopation in combination with the offbeat emphasis accounts for the rhythmic energy that catches the listener's attention. To emphasize the difference, compare these three different interpretations of the last phrase from our song:

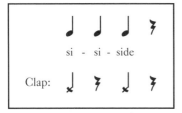

The claps reinforce the strong beats and the texts falls squarely on the beat.

The text remains square, but the claps emphasize the "weak" beat and fill in the rest on the fourth.

The text and clap never meet, creating complementary rhythms and a sense of movement.

Swing Rhythm: *"It don't mean a thing if it ain't got that swing..."*

Playing in swing rhythm, like snapping on 2 and 4, is one of the gates that separates the jazzer from the non-jazzer. Singing these game songs is your admission ticket! Because swing rhythm is difficult to capture in notation, many speak of it as an elusive quality that defies explanation. That may make the musicians who "have it" feel good, but teachers are paid to *reveal* mystery, not perpetuate mystification. If we come in through the right door, we can all join the party.

Simply put, *the swingin' is in the singin'*. This not only supports our choice of starting our study with these songs and games, but leads us to a principle developed in Chapter 5—

if we begin with songs that have a natural swing feel, *our subsequent improvisations are likely to swing.** Many a frustrated band teacher might rejoice to discover this simple truth— put down the instruments for a while, get into the dancing ring, return to the bandstand and listen to what happens. Voila!

Can we come up with a dictionary definition of swing? Even the Harvard Dictionary backs off—*"an intangible rhythmic momentum in jazz... swing defies analysis..."* Duke Ellington gives it a try: *"An extra lift above and beyond the basic beat."* [5] One route towards definition is through what it is *not*—8th notes performed evenly. In swing, the first note in the pair of 8th notes is slightly longer—most call it a triplet feel:

♩ ♪ ♩ ♪ ♩ ♪ This notation comes close to the feeling, but an oral tradi-

Head and should-ers ba - by

tion from one continent cannot be easily represented in a literate tradition from another. The notational compromise in jazz is to assume an aural understanding and notate tunes in normal eighth notes with the simple direction "Swing rhythm." Our job here is to provide that aural foundation by *listening* and *imitating*—which of course, is how children naturally learn anyway.

One useful distinction between a swing triplet feel and a kind of swing you might find in an Irish reel or hornpipe is that in the latter, the quarter note is given a slight accent ♩ ♪ whereas in jazz, the eighth note has a subtle emphasis ♩ ♪. This makes perfect sense given the Western European tendency to accent the beat and the West African tendency to emphasize the offbeats.

The above analysis is for the teachers. Children, prepared by nature to be perfect mimics, only need to hear genuine swing models to get the right feeling.

Pedagogical Pointers

The three rhythmic qualities introduced in *Head and Shoulders*—offbeat, syncopation and swing— are present in much of the music that led to jazz and in most of jazz itself. Each alone is not the exclusive property of jazz—polka music uses offbeats, Stravinsky and Balinese gamelan music abound with syncopation and some Baroque music has a kind of rhythmic swing. Rather, it is the unique *combination* of these three qualities that defines the jazz rhythmic style and sets it apart from any other.

Should we explain these concepts to the children? Two things will guide us here— our own understanding of developmental levels, pacing and age-appropriate information and the reaction of the children themselves. There are few things so gratifying as helping children learn things they're eager to know and few things so disturbing as killing their curiosity by telling them too much at the wrong time. These games are complete in themselves—"the playing is the point"—while simultaneously helping children hear and feel the musical elements that they later will come to name and understand conceptually.

"Later" for me means the upper elementary years. When organizing a class or group of classes around specific concepts, the general rule is to concentrate on one concept at

---

* One of the most tragically amusing stories about swing rhythm is reported in a book titled *Jazz: A Century of Change*. Unwilling to accept that such a marvelous musical feeling could have originated in black culture, Dr. Smith Ely Jellife, a noted neurologist, gave a talk to the New York Society for Clinical Psychiatry in 1928 in which he claimed, *"I propose the idea that Irving Berlin may have been born with a talent for irregular rhythms of jazz by the possibility of his mother's having had an irregular heart."* [6] The idea was that her heartbeat "swung" and had a prenatal influence on her son!

a time. For example, a 5th grade class plays the game one time and afterwards identifies and defines the *offbeat*. In another class, *syncopation* is the focus and the students try the examples given to compare and contrast accents on the beat and accents between the beats. In the next class, *swing* is at the center and the students try singing in both straight and swing rhythm. This one game can be played over six or seven classes with a shifting conceptual focus. Meanwhile, there might be a new *skill* goal in each class—smoother bounce, better singing, choreography, etc.

In the games that follow, these key rhythmic qualities will appear again and again with much variation—offbeats at different tempos, new combinations of syncopations, swing rhythm in body percussion as well as voice, each gradually moving from the body to the instrument. Let's see how these elements come together in our next game— *Soup, Soup.*

Playing *Head and Shoulders.*

Soup, Soup (as learned from Avon Gillespie)

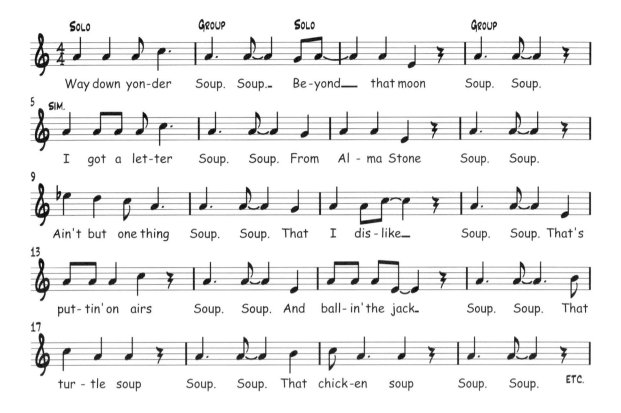

Way down yon-der / Soup. Soup. / Be-yond that moon / Soup. Soup.

I got a let-ter / Soup. Soup. From / Al - ma Stone / Soup. Soup.

Ain't but one thing / Soup. Soup. That / I dis - like / Soup. Soup. That's

put-tin' on airs / Soup. Soup. And / ball-in' the jack / Soup. Soup. That

tur - tle soup / Soup. Soup. That / chick-en soup / Soup. Soup. ETC.

Ballin' the Jack in *Soup, Soup.*

2. Soup Soup

Focus: Syncopation, Vocal timbre, Call and Response

Activity

• One person walks around the inside of the circle singing the verse while all sing the response. Those singing the response clap on the offbeat and find a comfortable step in place.

• On the words "ain't but one thing," the player stops, faces a player in the circle and shakes a finger. On "puttin' on airs," both mime the action, nose up in the air, flipping the hair with one hand while turning around. On "ballin' the jack," both do the "ballin' the jack" motion—knees together, rotating in a circle, hands on knees. (One challenging variation is to clasp hands together and "stir the soup," rotating arms in the opposite direction of the knees.) Encourage everyone to find their own style—small, large, fast or slow. Partners "ball the jack" while the leader sings out different types of soup.

• When the leader begins the song again, the two players switch places and the new person walks around the center of the ring.

Variations

• As above, but in a cumulative fashion. After two people finish "ballin' the jack," *both* players walk inside the circle and choose two more. Each of the two new people steps behind the person who chose them rather than both falling to the end of the line. Now there are four people who will choose four more. Continue in this fashion until all are walking. Then, all face the center of the circle and sing one more time.

• At the end of the above sequence, go around the circle with each person singing in turn a different kind of soup. Continue the offbeat clap and the "Soup, Soup" group response. Challenge the students to get all the way around the circle without repeating a soup choice.

  Remind the students that the premier soup in New Orleans is gumbo, made from the mixture of whatever ingredients are on hand. This is how jazz developed—from the mix of distinct and diverse cultural flavors all thrown together.

• Repeat the above in Spanish with a straight instead of a swing rhythm, as follows: Call: "Sopa de cebolla" Response: "¡So-pa!" "Sopa de tomate." "¡So-pa!" etc.

Comments

I prefer to play this game in the cumulative version and often include it in workshops on integrated curriculum as an example of geometric progression. It is a living example of the classic math problem, "Would you prefer a penny doubled every day for a month or a million dollars?" The unsuspecting student choosing the latter loses over seven million dollars! In addition to being a living demonstration of math, these cumulative games offer a powerful metaphor as well—when one person spreads an idea that catches on—

say, the importance of jazz in American music education—and each person who receives the message passes it on to someone else, the news spreads fast!

Soup, Soup reinforces the three rhythmic concepts introduced in *Head and Shoulders* and illuminates other key qualities of the African-American aesthetic as well—particularly the call and response form. (We will return to an instrumental version in Chapter 5.)

The song also helps expand the culinary vocabulary of the student, introducing such delights as gazpacho, miso, and vissychoise. For a culminating experience, host a soup potluck with the parents and play the game.

Key Qualities In *Soup, Soup*

Syncopation: One of the prominent qualities of this song is the syncopated rhythm expressed in the response "Soup, Soup." ♩ ♪♩ This is a prototypical jazz rhythm. Here are just a few examples:

Charleston:

C-Jam Blues:

Stompin' at the Savoy:

Moanin':

So What:

Whenever students miss the syncopation in tunes like the above, I remind them to think "Soup, soup" and they correct themselves instantly!

Polyrhythmic Clapping Patterns

Many of the older style African-American folk songs are accompanied by polyrhythmic clapping—two or more patterns clapped simultaneously that interlock to create a larger rhythmic pattern.* The most common of these is the powerful 3+3+2 pattern, an archetypal rhythm found not only throughout the African diaspora, but in musical cultures as distant as the Middle East and Bali. Notice the "Soup, soup" rhythm within the pattern.

Divide the group in half, with one group accompanying the song with the above clap and the other with offbeat. Separate the timbre by playing the first pattern with cupped hands to create a bass clap and the offbeats with one hand cupped to create a higher timbre.

Notice the combined effect of the two:

The double offbeat clap is another variation, often clapped on the fourth beat, but sometimes on the second and sometimes on both.

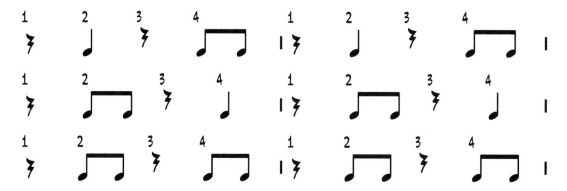

It is permissible for one group to clap lightly on the beat as part of the overall texture. The following is a polyrhythmic pattern whose combined effect produces a rhythm spoken with this mnemonic:

---

*Examples of this kind of polyrhythmic clapping can be found on the Folkways recording *Georgia Sea Island Songs*. and on the CD *Good Time, A Good Time:* Linda Tillery and The Cultural Heritage Choir, particularly the song *Old Lady From Booster* (see discography).

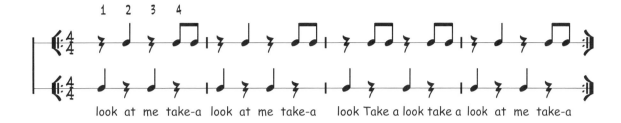

look at me take-a look at me take-a   look Take a look take a look at me take-a

Tambourine

Traditionally, this is the only instrument other than the body and voice used to accompany some of these games. Generally, tambourines with skin heads are used, held in one hand with the other hand striking the drumhead. Affirming Orff's perception that rhythm moves from the body to the instrument, the tambourine can play the composite polyrhythms in the examples above. (Indeed, I heard the above mnemonic "take a look at me" on an obscure recording of Doug Quimby explaining how to play tambourine that I've never been able to find since. If anyone knows of it, please contact me!)

But how to play it? Hearing a recording will not give the details of how to strike it. Indeed, after years of trying it my own way, I finally had the opportunity to observe some players who knew the technique and was discouraged to realize that whereas I held the tambourine in my left hand and struck it with my right, they held it in the right hand and produced the rhythm by moving the tambourine over a mostly steady left hand. If you are fortunate enough to find someone to study with, by all means do it!

MELODIC ELEMENTS

Melodic interpretation

The *Soup, Soup* version I learned is in minor pentatonic, a mode of crucial importance for learning melodic improvisation (see Chapter 5). The version printed in *Step It Down* transcribed from Bessie Jones's singing is in major pentatonic. The version on the recording *Step It Down*, also sung by Bessie Jones, adds a b7[th] to the major pentatonic base. African-American melodic interpretation is as flexible as its rhythmic expression.

All folk music undergoes some degree of melodic variation as it passes from one performer to another, but the aesthetic found in many of these game songs is unique in its melodic conception. The "melody" is a loosely organized group of tones that is re-invented spontaneously by the performer. Not only might the melody change from one singer to another, but the same singer might also change the melody from one day to the next—or even with each repetition. Thus, a printed or recorded version represents a moment frozen in time. To honor the tradition, the singer must understand the fluid nature of these melodies.

This sensibility is also present in much blues singing. Naturally, not all African-American music is organized so loosely—most of it has recognizable melodies. However, the expectation is to interpret the melody in a personal way, to re-create it by shifting the rhythms, embellishing the tones, adding or deleting notes. This is common practice in a variety of African-American musical styles—five jazz musicians playing the same tune (or one musician playing it five times) would produce five distinct versions. This is in marked contrast (remember—not better or worse) to the European classical aesthetic that demands adherence to the composer's intention and aims for a higher degree of uniformity in performance.

Vocal timbre

Vocal timbre is an essential means of expressing melody in a personal way. Once again, where the European tradition aims for more uniformity of tone and tonal production, the African-American welcomes diverse vocal qualities—witness the gruff, gravely chest voice of Louis Armstrong and the pure head tone of Ella Fitzgerald—and then listen to them sing a duet!

The emphasis on personal sound, most immediately realized through the distinct timbres of each person's voice, carried over into the instrumental aesthetics of jazz. The trumpet player Roy Eldridge said: *"When I came up, I got my own vibrato. You could tell me anywhere you heard me. Any of the cats that had any kind of name, you could tell them by the sound they got."*

The *sound* of the voice and its subsequent instrumental extensions are inseparable from the other stylistic elements that make jazz jazz. In our attempts to reach out towards a broader repertoire of diverse musics, duplicating authentic timbres has proven to be the most difficult barrier to overcome. We are most conservative in our taste in accepting the vocal timbre of a musical style. Because it hits the ear before any of the other musical elements, many wonderful musics are dismissed without a second hearing as offensive to our (narrow) standard of beautiful tone. Well-meaning children's choruses singing songs from other lands invariably reduce the notes of every song to a European aesthetic of timbre.

This seems to be more of a problem for teachers in the music classroom than for the children themselves. Because the African-American vocal aesthetic has influenced so much popular music in America, children understand the need to match timbre with style. The mix of head and chest voice, the ambiguity of pitch achieved through swoops, slides, growls, bent notes and other expressive devices, and street diction all contribute to the "soul" of the various African-American styles. Take it away and we are left with a pale rendition.*

Lyrics

We will come to see how improvisation informs virtually every level of African-American music. In addition to the constantly shifting melody, *Soup, Soup* introduces another important aesthetic—verbal improvisation. Making up different kinds of soups is a good way to develop this skill. (Wednesday is "Soup Day" at my school, so my students have a large repertoire from which to choose.)

FORM

Repetition

The cumulative power of repetition (with slight variations) is an important African aesthetic tied to the experience of dance. Dancing for long periods of time *in* time achieves a physical, communal and spiritual harmony far beyond the enjoyment of pleasing sounds. Here again, we must judge a musical style based on its own cultural criteria. The African cosmology is based on a cyclical experience of time. This is reflected in the great West African drum repertoire, in which repetitive and interlocking patterns gain power over

---

* The Leonard Bernstein recording "What Is Jazz?" gives a priceless example of this, comparing Bessie Smith's version of the *Empty Bed Blues* with an opera singer's attempt. The result is as humorous as it would be for Louis Armstrong to sing a Bach cantata in his style. If teachers can go past their culturally-induced notions of "beautiful tone/ ugly tone" to the place of "beautiful in this *style*, ugly in this style," they can get out of the way of the young children's open embracing of all sound.

time. Because of their complex interrelationship, a variety of sub-patterns and supra-patterns emerge within the cycles, often accented by the variations of the master drummer. For the uninitiated, the repetition may seem boring; for the initiate, the unheard (the musical equivalent of the *unseen* Ancestors) gradually reveals itself. The listener is actively engaged through the body—singing, clapping, dancing—and through the soul, moved by the power of the music and joined with the social and spiritual community. Though the great polyrhythmic traditions could not carry over into African-American culture after the banning of the drums, the relationship to the music through the body and soul remained intact.

By way of contrast, the European historical view and concept of time is based on a linear, forward movement dependent on the notion of progress, change and improvement. Consequently, much of its art music thrives on a linear development of musical material with constant variation and contrast. The listener's involvement is through the mind, enjoying the composer's musical thought, through the ear, charmed by the changing orchestral texture and through the heart, moved by the different emotional responses the music evokes.

Some might scoff at the simplicity of the repetitive form of *Soup, Soup*, but those who play it know that it is just right for its purpose.

Call and response

This call and response form is fundamental to much West African music, both vocal and instrumental. This sensibility remained dominant in much African-American music, as well as informing other aspects of cultural life (as in the affirmations from the congregation to the preacher). *Soup, Soup* is a good model of the basic call and response form—a varied, often improvised call from a soloist and a fixed response from a group.

There is a great deal of comfort and reassurance in knowing the correct response. When everybody in the group knows exactly how to respond, the community is affirmed. Community shares an etymological root with the word "common"—it comes alive when the group acts on common knowledge. Especially in today's multi-cultural society, with its shifting rules of language and etiquette (Does the man open the door for the woman? Is this an Indian or Native American community? Can you wear jeans to this party?), the security of knowing the response to the call is a social blessing.

I teach at least six call and response songs to the children at my school and like to surprise them by singing the first line of a song to hear how quickly they can respond. Sometimes I sing a medley and mix up the first lines to sharpen their attention. I sense their deep need for order and structure and their subsequent satisfaction in answering correctly. These songs also serve as great attention-getters in those moments that every teacher dreads—large group chaos! I love to impress visitors when 100 noisy kids come in from recess to sing. Just at the moment when I sense the visitor is skeptical of me ever bringing order to the scene, I casually whisper, "Watch this," and fire off a first line. The noise immediately congeals into a focused response, followed by another and another. When I have the children's attention and they're waiting expectantly for the next line, I stop for a moment of deep silence and then greet them with the next order of business, with 100% attention!

CULTURAL VALUES: The body and the spirit

The lyrics of *Soup, Soup* bring up one of the fundamental dividing points between European and African culture—the relationship to the body. In African religious practices, the body is the vessel of the spirit and celebrated as such through dance. In the European Christian ethic (and particularly in American Puritanism), the body is separate from spirit and its celebration through dance disdained. Where the African saw a spiritual expression of fertility, the Puritans saw the dances as lewd, disgusting and indecent. The distance between these two points of view created much confusion in the forced conversion of Africans to Christianity.

Soup, Soup is a marvelous vehicle to sidestep this cultural rift. Outwardly, it expresses disdain—*"Ain't but one thing that I dislike"*—for "balling the jack" (hip movement was considered particularly distasteful amongst the sexually repressed Puritans), but while speaking out against this impropriety, the player gets to demonstrate repeatedly the forbidden motion!

Group of Ewe dancers in the village of Dzodje, Ghana.

Johnny Brown (as learned from Avon Gillespie)

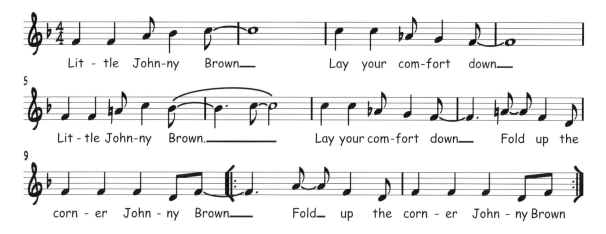

Show us the motion, Johnny Brown (2x)
We can do the motion, Johnny Brown (2x)
Take it to your friend now, Johnny Brown (2x)

3. Johnny Brown

Focus: Tempo, Movement improvisation, individual/group interplay

Activity

• Leader sings the song and demonstrates the sequence as follows:

"Little Johnny Brown, lay your comfort down"—Strut into the circle and lay out a scarf or
   handkerchief (square is best) in the middle of the circle.

"Fold up the corner, Johnny Brown" —Fold each corner precisely on the syllable "corn."

"Show us the motion, Johnny Brown"—Pick up the scarf and make a clear, repetitive motion.
   (Later, make sure that the group does not copy while singing this phrase.)

"We can do the motion, Johnny Brown"—The whole group imitates the motion.

"Take it to your friend now, Johnny Brown"—Strut over to someone else and hand over the
   scarf. That person now goes into the center and the whole song starts again.

• Continue playing until everyone has had a turn. If the group is too big, there can be
   several Johnny Browns (each with a handkerchief) going in the center at once, with
   the remaining people in the circle choosing whose motion they want to copy.

Variations

• Sing *Julie Brown* for girls or substitute each child's name as he or she goes into the
   center; *"Little Manuel Brown," "Little Jessica Brown," etc.*

• Play at a slow tempo.* A faster tempo. Begin slowly and gradually increase the tempo
   as the game progresses.

---

* The slower tempo of *Johnny Brown* allows for more subtlety in the movement. Many people often miscon-
ceive of African-derived music as always fast and lively and the dancing as wild, free and uninhibited. Author
John Miller Chernoff, offers a different perspective:

   "...I was amazed when I saw some Congolese dancing to one of their popular Rumba tunes; in spite
   of their reputation for lively dancing, it seemed that they were not even moving. One dancer raised
   his knee as if he intended to take his foot off the ground, but he never lifted it. He stayed poised to
   move. Gideon [the author's friend from Ghana] said, 'Wow! Look at him dance!' and had a beer sent
   to the man's table." [8]

Comments

Johnny Brown is a game that involves risk and is terrifying to some. The handkerchief provides some security for shy students. If a student freezes up when it's time to show the motion, follow the cue of her body and copy whatever comes up. If the student shrugs her shoulders as if to say, "I don't know what to do," or shakes her head no, copy the motion immediately. Sometimes a simple model or suggestion before the game as in, "Your movement doesn't need to be fancy. Wiggling your pinky is fine," helps the insecure student.

Though you may have to carry the singing at the beginning, remind the students to sing, clap and sway to the music. The better the singing and clapping, the more inspired the dancing in the middle. If students move *too* much while singing, remind them to save their motion until they're in the center of the circle.

Everyone's natural tendency is to immediately imitate the motion in the center. Remind them to be patient and *wait* until they sing *"We can do the motion..."*. This both allows for better observation—and thus, imitation—and sets up the exciting moment when one motion becomes many.

I once played this game at a teacher workshop where there was a one year old baby. Near the end of the game, the baby crawled into the center of the circle and sat down. We all immediately copied his posture. When he waved his arm up and down, we waved our arms up and down. He soon caught on to what was happening and laughed with glee as his every motion came back to him a hundredfold! Forget computer games—*these* are the kind of "interactive" experiences our children need!

Folding up the scarf for *Johnny Brown.*

CULTURAL VALUES: The group and the individual

Johnny Brown reveals a particular relationship between the individual and the group that I believe is much needed in contemporary culture. It is the meeting point of the two important goals I communicate to my students:

1. "Blend in—align yourself with the group energy and become part of a greater whole."

2. "Stand out—express yourself as a unique individual with something to contribute."

These two goals are useful in setting the tone for class discipline. The students must understand that they will be given the opportunity to do both—blend in *and* stand out. Part of their learning is to understand when each is appropriate. Thus, students who are acting out inappropriately can have their bid for attention channeled into an appropriate form by being invited in the center for *Johnny Brown* (four times out of five, they will refuse!). They will also understand that their ability to blend in is necessary for the success of the game. It is a great moment when the recalcitrant student discovers that it is more fun to play the game well than poorly!

Likewise, the shy students who like to hide can grow to accept the responsibility of expressing themselves in front of the group and even learn to enjoy it. If no one wants to "show us their motion," the game suffers—indeed, it loses its point.

The dancing circle is a primary form in West African communal celebration. The participants sing, clap, and move in place. Individuals go into the center when the spirit moves them to "show their motion." If the circle is unified in rhythm, movement and song, the dancers in the center are inspired to dance their best. Likewise, they in turn inspire the group with their dancing and evoke stronger music.

This aesthetic lives on in jazz. The ensemble plays together, the soloist steps out (into the circle) backed by the ensemble. The soloist calls, the group responds. The group sends forth ideas, the soloists picks them up. When the conversation feels finished, the soloist re-enters the group to make room for the next soloist. This two-way flow of energy is a beautifully balanced system in which two basic human experiences are honored, played out and enhanced—our individuality and our common humanity. Jazz is amongst the most democratic of musical forms, in many cases giving *each* player an opportunity to step forward. The roots of this practice lie in the African dancing circles, transferred to African-American ring plays in games like *Johnny Brown*.

What precisely is the individual trying to express? Our competitive mentality might imagine the task is to create the "winning" motion—the fanciest, most technically complex, our "personal best," but the African aesthetic suggests something different—dancing from the heart. Someone once told me of her experience witnessing such a dancing ring in Ghana. She watched many people go into the center and dance, but after one dancer, there was an obvious surge of appreciation from the crowd. She hadn't noticed anything particularly accomplished about the dancer—indeed, others had seemed more acrobatic, dynamic or rhythmic. Her African friend patiently explained—"In that moment, the dancer was most like herself."

This is true in jazz as well. The immature soloist will try to impress with flash, technique, complex jazz "riffs," but at the end of all their efforts may be met by Duke Ellington's comment to an aspiring pianist: *"My, you play so many notes!"* The jazz soloist, like the Ghanaian villager, is working towards the moment when the notes (or motions) speak the full radiance of her unique personality. When she is most fully herself, the whole group is inspired and celebrates.

Johnny Brown formalizes this interplay one step further with a built-in means of letting the individual know his contribution to the group. After the center player shows the motion, it is magnified by the group taking it up. This allows the children (or adults) to actively realize a primary Orff aesthetic—*everyone is both student and teacher*.

I know a teacher who told her students that the comfort (comfort is short for comforter) was like Linus's security blanket. When you're in the middle of the circle, surrounded and supported by friends, you don't need it any more, so you can lay it down. This is a beautiful statement about how the game evokes risk-taking in an atmosphere of trust.

Though the form is similar, the experience of the dancing ring in traditional West African culture is markedly different from a contemporary American version. In the African community wedded by common values and experiences, the meaning of the individual improvisation can be very specific. J.H. Nketia writes:

> "The dance can be used as a social and artistic medium of communication. It can convey thoughts or matters of personal or social importance through the choice of movements, postures, and facial expressions. Through the dance, individuals and social groups can show their reactions to attitudes of hostility or cooperation and friendship held by others towards them. They can offer respect to their superiors, or appreciation and gratitude to well-wishers and benefactors. They can react to the presence of rivals, affirm their status to servants, subjects, and others, or express their beliefs through the choice of appropriate dance vocabulary or symbolic gestures." [9]

In a classroom of children from different cultural backgrounds, the game takes on a new meaning. Instead of a shared movement vocabulary, there is the possibility of learning a wide range of movements. What we lack in depth of uniform movement style, we can make up for in breadth. This is the very process of cultural exchange that has informed the evolution of art.

Finally, the invitation to "stand out" is not an "anything goes" attitude, but is contained within the boundary of the circle. Many young people attempt to express themselves in ways devoid of responsibility (literally, ability to respond) to the group and thus damage the community and alienate themselves. The American view of the creative individual is the superstar or the alienated artist. The West African aesthetic is markedly different:

> "Like a drummer, a dancer should not try to do too much or he will lose clarity and become pretentious. A dancer's subtle refinement and good taste will enliven the music by enriching the occasion, pulling the whole scene into a movement rather than attempting to project the strength of one performer." [10]

More than any single game, *Johnny Brown* strikes me as the quintessential expression of the African-American spirit.

Old Lady From Brewster

Well, there was an old la - dy from Brew-ster   She had two hens and a

roost-er   The roost-er   died   and the old la-dy cried. Now she can't get eggs like she

used to.   Oh.   Ma.   You look so.   Oh.   Pa.   You look so.

Who's been here since   I   was gone   Two   lit-tle boys with a   red cap   on.

Hang them with a   hick' ery   stick.   Pa-pa's gon-na parch them soon.   Whap! I got a

pain in my   head   Rank - y tank-y.   Pain in my head   Rank - y tank - y.

CONTINUE, AD LIB., IN CALL/RESPONSE FORMAT WITH DIFFERENT BODY PARTS (E.G., PAIN IN MY SHOULDERS, PAIN IN MY KNEES)

Last time:

Pain   all   o-ver   Rank - y   tank - y   Pain   all   o-ver   Rank - y   tank - y.

4. Old Lady From Brewster

Focus: Limerick form; call and response

Directions

- Teach the response "Ranky tanky." All find clapping accompaniment.

- Sing the first part of the song, leaving off the rhyming words for the students to fill in:
  "There was an old lady from Brewster,
  She had two hens and a _____
  Well, the rooster died and the old lady _____
  Now she can't get eggs like she _____."

- Invite all to sing along with the first part of the song as possible while finding motions to tell the story (miming an old lady, a hen and rooster, the rooster dying, etc.)

- During the call and response, all move the body part in the lyric while continuing to clap and sing.

- For variety, all touch the body parts sung.

Comments

Like all these games, *The Old Lady From Brewster* operates on several levels at once.

One story it tells is how the slaves borrowed from Western sources to keep their need for music-making alive. With their ancestral music prohibited and, by the 1800's, buried in an obscure past, slaves by necessity had to borrow from European models. The first part of the song is a limerick, a poetic form created by English poet Edward Lear. Generally in 6/8 meter, it is a four line poem with rhymes in first, second and fourth phrases and internal rhymes in line 3. Sometimes line four repeats line one and sometimes it uses the same last word, as in this example by Lear:

> There was an Old Man with a beard,
> Who said, "It is just as I feared!—
> Two Owls and a Hen, four Larks and a Wren,
> Have all built their nests in my beard."

As in all models they adopted, this song is infused with a variety of Africanisms—the 6/8 meter changed to a 4/4 meter with offbeat clapping and a second section moving into a call and response form.

A second story it tells is about rural courting practices. Young boys would arrange to meet young girls behind the henhouse, away from the eye of the protective father. The girls would go to gather eggs and find their own excuses for why they took so long. In this song, the father gets suspicious because there are not as many eggs since the rooster died. He goes out to investigate and finds the boys, chasing them with his hickory stick and "parching" them on different parts of their body as they run away. Naturally, telling this story will need some further discussion with the children about corporal punishment.

A third story it tells is of the whippings the slaves got and their need to sing about their pain in disguised form. "I got pain all over"—the singing helps shake it off.

Pedagogically, there are a few points of interest. Isolating body parts is always a good practice for children learning to dance. The practice of leaving out rhyming words keeps the children's linguistic intelligence active. Whereas *Head and Shoulders* tells the children where to clap, now they have to find the offbeats for themselves. The two-part response—first up and then down—is an extension of the *Soup, Soup* idea.

Doug Quimby says that this is not a ring play, but played with a line singing behind a person in front acting it out. However, I prefer to play it in a circle. It's also worth noting that some variants sing "The Old Lady from Booster" while others replace *"Hang them boys on a hickory stick, Papa's gonna parch them soon,"* with *"Ranky tanky down to my shoes, Buffalo Boy's gonna buy it back."* What is that about? I'll leave it to you to figure out!

Middle Schoolers performing body percussion.

Summary of African-American Musical/Cultural Qualities Expressed in the Games

Since music and culture are inseparable, we must approach the music by first coming to terms with the cultural elements that inform every note. If we are entering the story of jazz from outside the culture, we have to learn how it's taught, how it's received, how it's felt by its creators. These games are marvelous teachers in illuminating not only essential musical qualities, but also history, culture and aesthetics as well. We've already noted many of these characteristics as expressed in these four games. Now it is time to telescope out further and examine these qualities within their social context—an American society whose dominant culture derives from Western European values.

Observing the tension between these two world-views—the West African and West European—accomplishes many things at once. It sheds light on *history*—the real life struggle of Africans trying to adapt in an alien land; on *sociology*—the continued story of the difficulty of accommodating difference; and on *psychology*—how it feels to be marginalized in a mainstream culture. But in addition to these important issues that we insist on including in the discussion of jazz, there is a crucial *musical* reason for accenting the differences between the two parent cultures. When we understand the extremes of each separate aesthetic, we will be better prepared to both teach and learn the material.

Instead of making European material "jazzy"—putting a swing beat to Bach or English nursery rhymes—and making African-American material "cleaner"—head-toned children's choirs singing arranged spirituals—we can apply the appropriate cultural understanding to pieces in either tradition. When we finally come to grips with how markedly different these two worlds are, we will be better prepared to understand how jazz is one of the bridges that can connect them.

The following list compares the European art music tradition with the African-American and West African folk tradition. Why European *art* and African-American *folk*? Aren't these apples and oranges? Though it is true that an Appalachian folk song has much in common with its African American counterpart—much repetition, improvisation, connection with dance, oral transmission and communal function, for example—at its root it lies closer to its European art music cousin. More importantly, it is the European art music tradition that has set the standard in the United States for the definition of music, how it is to be performed, how it is to be appreciated and most important for our study here, how it is to be taught. It is the standard against which jazz has had to push in its slow climb to acceptance.

Our list makes clear how much of African-derived folk culture survived in African-American *art* music—i.e., jazz. By noting how much of the right-hand column has informed jazz, we can begin to see the shifting influence of the left—from Louis Armstrong's virtuosity to Duke Ellington's compositions to Charlie Parker's long melodic lines to John Coltrane's vertical *Ascension*.

Of course, sacrificing the similarities and the exceptions to the exercise of generalizing the extremes can be dangerous, treading the thin line between archetypal qualities and stereotypical assumptions. Some may object to this as divisive and simplistic, too black and white in a real world with many shades of gray. Let us be clear—the hope in accenting difference is to move towards an inclusive understanding, an intellectual *Johnny Brown* that invites each quality to stand out and be honored and blend in and be joined. With those intentions held clearly in mind, let us look at the two distinct parents that gave birth to jazz.

EUROPEAN-AMERICAN ART MUSIC	AFRICAN-AMERICAN FOLK MUSIC
• Beat	• Offbeat
• Straight rhythm	• Swing rhythm
• Head tone in singing	• Chest tone
• Clear timbre	• Mixed timbre (growls, buzz,etc.)
• Precise articulation	• Relaxed articulation
• Long melodic lines (Gregorian chant)	• Short phrases (riffs)
• Polyphony	• Polyrhythm
• I–V	• I–IV
• Variation	• Repetition
• Composition	• Improvisation
• Interpretation	• Self-expression
• Written	• Oral
• Individual (composer, virtuoso)	• Communal
• Serious	• Playful
• Select participation	• Complete participation
• Polite detached audience	• Involved, responsive audience
• Formal study, separated from daily life	• Informal, integrated with daily life
• Dance incidental	• Dance essential
• Absolute music	• Story
• Conceptual meaning	• Emotional meaning
• Linear time conception	• Circular time conception
• Vertical (ascending)	• Horizontal (gettin' down)
• Spirit	• Soul

Games for a Healthy Childhood

"Skip-rope rhymes are fascinating because within the invisible world of the turning rope, children can relieve pain by chanting their need for romance and identity, respond to the mysteries of life, protest real or imagined injustices and even cruelties inflicted by adults and the adult worlds, compensate for loneliness, and above all, dream of a happy and self-determined future.... It is sad that so many children—and the adults they soon become—are now deprived of this rich nourishment, in which all things are recognized as a part of life." [11]

—Francelia Butler

We're now well on our way to an understanding of what makes jazz jazz. The games presented here (and the many others not included here as well) serve as a pedagogical pushing-off point for our study. They reveal an African-American aesthetic in its seed form, one whose inflections change as jazz evolves, but whose root sensibilities are constant. By attending to the text, the rhythms, the melodies, the motions, the spatial formations and the actions of children's games, we learn the essential qualities that inform the adult music of the culture. As such, this is an excellent way to enter *any* musical style, not only for children, who will naturally gravitate to a learning style that comes from their world, but for college students and adults as well.

Yet as compelling as the musical reason is for playing these games, there is an equally vital social and emotional argument to include such games in the school curriculum. The American child is in crisis, cut off from a sustaining collective morality and a sense of belonging. Statistics paint a portrait of passive children with poor muscle tone sitting in front of the TV, their imaginations stifled through pre-programmed entertainment and their feelings shut down by the relentless violence they see. They don't know about the past and have no hope for their future. Their hopelessness becomes depression expressed through drug abuse and rage expressed through crime, violence and suicide. Childhood as a time of innocence, wonder and great dreams is giving way to artificial sophistication, cynicism, and despair.

These games will not solve such overwhelming problems, but they *can* help children focus their rhythm, breath, and motion. They can help tone and coordinate the body. They can stimulate imagination, connect children with their peers and activate a healthy sense of play. They can provide a safe container for acting out fears through ritual play. They can help children make friends. They require no special equipment, need no adult supervision, demand no special time or place and cost nothing.

While school boards, parents and politicians meet to discuss strategies for revitalizing our failing educational system, I've yet to hear one suggest that the school community get together daily to play these games! Instead we spend money on remedial therapies that try to correct what children miss by not playing games. We develop artificial curricula about self-esteem, fund police systems to curb the violence of children disconnected from community, invent new drugs to calm them down or help them focus. We hook them up to computers that further atrophy the body and reduce human interaction. The "experts" look outside for smart answers to fix the problems of today's children, but the wisdom of a Bessie Jones knows that the truth is closer at hand—as simple as turning to a partner and singing out,

"Head and Shoulder Baby, One- Two- Three."

Endnotes

1. Jones, Bessie: *Put Your Hand on Your Hip and Let Your Backbone Slip* (CD liner notes): Rounder Heritage Series 1166

2. Jones, Bessie and Hawes, Bess Lomax: *Step It Down*: University of Georgia Press

3. *Ibid.*

4. Nachmanovitch, Stephen: *Free Play*: Jeremy P. Tarcher, Inc.

5. Jones, Bessie and Hawes, Bess Lomax: *Step It Down*: , p 87

6. Ellington, Duke: *Music Is My Mistress*:

7. Porter, Lewis: *Jazz—A Century of Change*: Schirmer Books

8. Chernoff, John Miller: *African Rhythm and Afircan Sensibility*: University of Chicago Press

9. Nketia, J. H. Kwabena: *The Music of Africa*; W. W. Norton & Company

10. Chernoff, John Miller: *African Rhythm and African Sensibility*

11. Butler, Francelia: *Skipping Around the World*: Ballantine Press

Bibliography

Step It Down: Games, Plays, Songs & Stories from the Afro-American Heritage: Bessie Jones and Bess Lomax Hawes: University of Georgia Press

Let's Slice the Ice: A Collection of Black Children's Ring Games and Chants: Eleanor Fulton and Pat Smith; MMB Music

Circle Round the Zero: Play Chants & Singing Games of City Children: Maureen Kenney: MMB Music

Discography

Put Your Hand on Your Hip and Let Your Backbone Slip: Bessie Jones and The Georgia Sea Island Singers: Rounder Heritage Series 1166

Good Time, A Good Time: Linda Tillery and The Cultural Heritage Choir: BLHCD746

Front Porch Music: Linda Tillery and The Cultural Heritage Choir: Earthbeat R272881

Hippity Hop: Linda Tillery and The Cultural Heritage Choir: Music for Little People R275951

Wade in the Water: African American Sacred Music Traditions: Compiled by Bernice Johnson Reagon: Smithsonian Folkways: CD SF40076

Websites

For information about The Georgia Sea Island Singers:
http://www. gacoast.com/navigator/quimbys.html

For information about Linda Tillery and The Cultural Heritage Choir:
http://www.culturalheritagechoir.com/

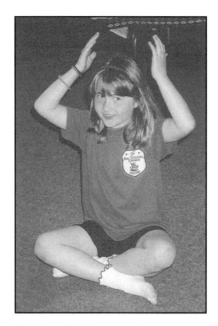

The joy of body percussion.

Kids snapping on offbeat.

CHAPTER 3:
SPEECH AND BODY PERCUSSION

"The speech exercise comes at the beginning of all musical practice, both rhythmic and melodic."

—Carl Orff

"Oop bop sh'bam, a klook a mop."

—Dizzy Gillespie

Language opens the door to the house of rhythm. If we can say it, we can play it. When we count, we're in our head and out of our body. But when we anchor rhythm to words, we're connected hand to tongue and the most astounding music emerges effortlessly.

Our earliest rhythm lessons are the nursery rhymes. Not only do we feel the bounce of the beat and the flow of the rhythm, but we also tune our ear to the singing of the words. Dylan Thomas writes:

> "The first poems I knew were nursery rhymes, and before I could read them for myself I had come to love just the words of them, the words alone… These words were, to me, as the notes of bells, the sounds of musical instruments, the noises of wind, sea and rain… I did not care what the words said, overmuch… I cared for the shapes of sound that their names made in my ears." [1]

Orff Schulwerk not only tunes us to the inherent musicality of vowels, consonants, words and phrases, but uses speech as a means to awaken and enhance our understanding of rhythms, rhythmic structures and forms. Speech play in the Orff classroom takes on a variety of shapes, as follows: [2]

- **Vocal exploration:** The rhyme becomes the vehicle to explore the expressive range of the voice, speaking a poem high, low, loud, soft, nasal, clear, smooth, choppy, etc. This is both self-sufficient and an excellent springboard into song.

- **Wordplay:** The child's inherent fascination for nonsense speech is given shape and permission to unfold. The specific timbres and articulations of vowels and consonants in nonsense syllables are validated as an integral part of musical texture.

- **Teaching rhythm:** Words become the notation for learning and remembering rhythms, making concrete that which is essentially abstract. This begins as simply as reciting and clapping the rhythm of one's name, following the natural accent pattern of the syllables. From a single name—Monk—to a group of names, a rhythmic phrase emerges:

Rhythms can come from a proverb:

Rhythmic texture can arise effortlessly by combining the two above and made more complex yet by adding another ostinato:

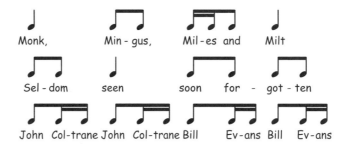

A typical sequence: Speak the phrases, then clap (pat, snap or step) the words while speaking, and finally, think the words silently while clapping or playing on an instrument.

Rhythmic accompaniment: A poem or song is accompanied by rhythm patterns that complement the text, from a simple beat to a repeated rhythm pattern (ostinato) to a shifting rhythm pattern.

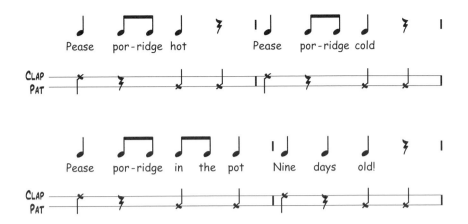

Composition: The poem serves as a springboard for group composition. This is one of the most exciting developments of the Schulwerk, the moment when all the separate strands of the music and movement work come together as a unified whole. The poem may be set rhythmically with body percussion and percussion instruments, melodically through voice, recorder, xylophone or other melodic instruments, texturally through a combination of instruments and speech qualities, kinesthetically through choreographed movement or in some combination of all of the above. The mediums can be predetermined (use only voice and body percussion) or left open. In either case, the task is to let the poem speak for its own appropriate realization. The meaning of the text, its mood, its structure, its quality of language will all affect the resulting composition.

Speech in Jazz Study

Speech is the key to teaching music "without chops." Traditional music education assumes mastery of an instrument is essential before real music can be made and understood. Orff practice suggests that we can begin with something close to us all—language— and develop an ear and feeling for the entire spectrum of musical expression—rhythm, accent, melody, dynamics, articulation, timbre, texture, form and more. When we arrive at an instrument, we will have already internalized the essentials.

In this chapter, we'll see how to turn these existing Schulwerk models towards jazz, to discover where they are already present and to imagine where they might lead us. Traditional games like *Boom Chick a Boom* and *Mama Lama* and invented activities like *Name Sounds* and *International Language* will tickle the child's fascination with vocal exploration and wordplay while putting them at the doorstep of scat. Rhymes like *Tom Greedy Gut*, *Juba* and *Hambone* will use language to teach rhythms and use rhythms to accompany language. Because the language and rhythm are so intricately connected, I've chosen to explore the medium of body percussion, found both through Orff Schulwerk and African-derived music, in this chapter.

In speech, as with movement, the development of jazz and the ideas of Carl Orff meet in their respective deep structures. One of the dangers teachers new to Orff Schulwerk run—and I speak from my own experience here—is to miss the depth and apply only the surface. The well-meaning teacher might make a chant like "Dixieland, Swing, Be-bop, Cool," or make a speech piece built on "cool" jazz phrases—"That cat sure is blowin', Daddy-o." Though some of the following exercises approach the dangerous ground of the contrived, the intention is to look at existing models of African-American speech, speech patterns, phrases, rhymes and poems that will naturally lead us to jazz rhythms, phrasing and inflection.

BOOM CHICK-A BOOM

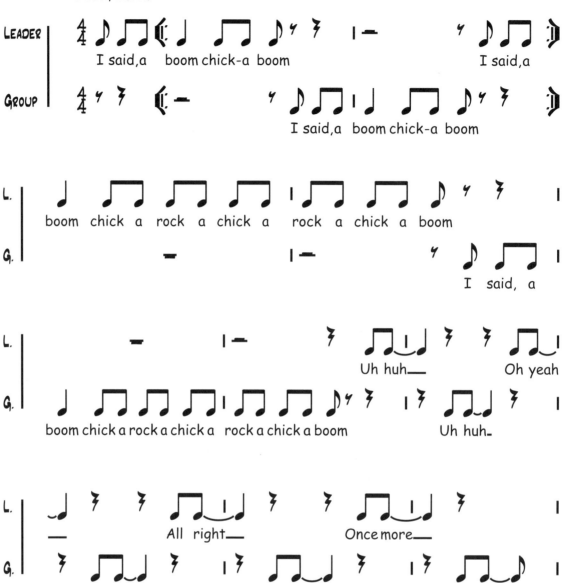

5. BOOM CHICK-A BOOM

Formation: Circle

Focus: Expressive variation

Activity

- Leader speaks each phrase; group echoes, all snapping on offbeat

- Leader repeats with a different vocal quality for each phrase (high, low, loud, soft, gruff, sweet, happy, sad, with an English accent, etc.) or varies the rhythm, accents or tempo. Group echoes.

- Half group joins leader, other half echoes. Switch.

- All do whole poem, speaking with one hand acting like a puppet, echoing with the other. (Also fun to do with actual hand puppets!)

- Play with partner, one leading, one echoing. After "once more," switch roles.

- As above, with dramatic gestures.

- As above, one moving with steps while reciting and freezing at the end of the phrase, the other copying both vocal inflection and movement.

- Each set of partners (or groups of them) perform for others.

Comments

The text is a child-size example of the jazz dictum—"say it your own way." With the same text, children explore the various expressive possibilities of speech. For children adept at foreign accents, this is a wonderful showcase for their talents.

This activity can be done as suggested or immediately lead into the next step, as outlined in the version of the same game in Chapter Five (page 124).

6. NEWSPAPER SERMON

Focus: Expressive speech/ border of speech and song

Activity

- Bring a newspaper into class and have students take turns reading out loud in a flat monotone.

- Each takes turn again with expression—attention to inflection, rhythm, tone, phrasing, volume, attack.

- Play an excerpt of a recording of an African-American preacher: Some examples:

  I Have a Dream speech by Dr. Martin Luther King (Share the Music-Gr. 5)

  I'm Going to Heaven: Rev. J.M. Gates: *History of Classic Jazz*: Riverside

  Easter Morning Sermon: John's Island, South Carolina: *It's People & Songs*: Folkways Records FS 3840

- Read the article again imitating the black oratory style. Group members must participate by affirming and echoing in call and response format, listening for the pauses at the end of the leader's phrases.

Variations

- As above, moving from speech into song.

Comments

I am indebted to my colleague James Harding for this idea. The intent here is to get a feeling for the unique African-American oratory style through a playful approach appropriate for a school setting (in contrast to reading Bible verses). The random articles in the newspaper allow the students to focus more on style than content (though in some cases, such an emotional involvement in the article may be *more* appropriate than our accustomed bland newscasters approach!). The Riverside Recording is an especially remarkable example of the fine line between speech and song as the speaker/ singer moves back and forth between the two.

Not only is this a good game for the leaders to get a feel for vocal expression and phrasing, but a fantastic exercise for those responding to listen for the gaps in the "melody." In addition to the kind of affirmations from *Boom Chick a Boom* ("Uh-huh," "oh yeah", etc.), they should also listen to the text and occasionally echo the words spoken. The total effect is that of the jazz soloist and the accompanists (mostly piano and drums) "comping" by filling in the spaces.

7. MAMA LAMA KUMA LAMA

Formation: Circle of partners
Focus: Nonsense "scat" speech

Activity

- Teach first and last phrase echo fashion, four beats at a time.

- Teach middle phrase as a call ("Oh no no no no") and response ("na beesta").

- Perform first two phrases with partner and following clap pattern:

- "Jazzwalk" while reciting third phrase and find new partner by the end of the phrase.

- Resuming clapping, one partner introduces herself to the other by scat-speaking the first sound of her name for 14 beats and then saying the name on beat 15. Other partner does the same. At the end, both say the rhyme again, leaving to find new partner and third phrase as indicated above.

- Repeat as desired.

Variations

- Ask the children if they know a similar version and compare.

- Have them share a different partner clap pattern that they know, or create a new one.

Comments

Nonsense speech is as old as language itself and found in the rhymes and songs of all cultures. This African-American version, with its swing rhythm, offbeat, syncopation, and musical text, serves as a child-sized bridge into the world of jazz scat-singing.

Turning this game towards a means of introducing group members to each other, I changed the last phrase (originally "x-a-y-z" in my version) to "Who are you?" Like virtually all of the material in this book, the aim is to stay as close to the original source material as possible while simultaneously keeping it alive and contemporary by adapting it to one's particular situation. From changing the words to *Head and Shoulders* to using *Boom Chick-a-boom* to introduce hi-hat to arranging *Soup Soup* for Orff instruments to playing *Bag's Groove* on recorder, this entire book is an exercise in swinging back and forth between past and future by keeping alert to the needs of the present. New directions that ignore the old ways and undue reverence to an established canon both fall short of the mark. As Leroi Jones so eloquently states it: *"Ornette Coleman uses Parker only as a hypothesis; his conclusions are quite separate and unique."* [3]

This rhyme can be sung as indicated, or spoken.

8. SCAT WITH NAME SOUNDS

Formation: Partners

Focus: Phrasing

Activity

- Partners carry on a conversation using the first sounds of their names.

- One partner asks an 8-beat "question" in the jazz style (swing rhythm, snaps on 2 and 4), the other gives 8-beat answer, still using the first sounds of their names (Dan uses "D," Bill uses "B," etc.).

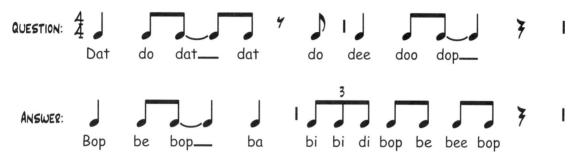

- Return to the freer conversational phrasing of step one (short questions, long answer, long questions, short answers, partially overlapped), but keep the jazz rhythmic feel.

- As above, but each student creates his or her own improvisation based on the above question/answer format.

Variations

- As above, using any vocal sounds.

- As above, adding melody.

- Over a "rhythm section" background. (Teacher playing drums, bass, guitar or piano chords minus melody or a Music Minus One tape of a blues progression.)

Comments

This exercise is an excellent jumping off point to enter a crucial area of jazz: phrasing. When various classical musicians have good-naturedly ventured into a jazz recording, occasional trouble with swing rhythm alerts the listener that something is "off," but even more telling is difficulty getting the feeling of jazz phrasing. Much European classical phrasing is quite formal, reflecting both a composer's mentality and the aristocratic milieu in which it thrived. Jazz is more conversational, reflecting an improviser's mindset and the informal social setting of the bars and nightclubs in which it lived. Here we try to create a conversational ambience within different approaches to phrasing.

The first is entirely free, unconcerned with meter, rhythm or formal phrase length, trying to capture the gestalt of real conversation in an abstract musical way. The second is tied to the offbeat and swing feel of jazz, and then restricted further to an eight-beat question/answer form. By limiting expression, we gain clarity, form and a sense of jazz style. The final challenge is to combine the freedom of conversation in the first step with the form of jazz rhythm and phrasing.

SUGGESTED RECORDINGS

It is always a good idea to connect the activities in the classroom with the world of existing music. The following recordings support and extend the discoveries the children have made in this exercise.

- **Free conversation:** *What Love*: Charles Mingus/Eric Dolphy: *Charles Mingus Presents Charles Mingus*: Candid 9005

This remarkable piece is a superb example of an instrumental "conversation" between Charles Mingus's bass and Eric Dolphy's bass clarinet. Recorded in 1960, on the cusp of the "free jazz" movement, Mingus and Dolphy abandon the beat and formal structure after eight and a half minutes of playing and let their instruments *speak*, approximating both the sound of the human voice and the nuances of real spoken conversation. To help students focus on their listening, have them imagine what the two musicians are saying.

- **Eight beat question/answer:** *Trumpet Blues*: Dizzy Gillespie/ Roy Eldridge: *Roy & Diz*: Verve 314 521 647-2

This tune from this fabulous CD (also mentioned in the Jazz Movement chapter) begins with some overlapping "conversation" between the two trumpet players, is followed by several choruses of individual solos and moves into a series of eight-beat exchanges over a blues background. Within the structure of eight beats, both players maintain a conversational tone—venturing over bar lines and responding to each other's statements.

Tenor Madness, a tune on a CD of the same title, features a similar conversation between the two great tenor sax players Sonny Rollins and John Coltrane.

- **Varied phrase lengths over beat:** *St. Thomas*: Sonny Rollins: *Saxophone Colossus*: Prestige 24050

Any good jazz solo would serve as an example of the solo conversational style of phrases of various lengths, but I enjoy using Sonny Rollins's saxophone improvisations here to demonstrate the variety of phrase lengths. For a challenging active listening exercise, have the students attempt to graph the improvisation by drawing lines parallel to the length of the phrases *while* listening!

9. GROUP IMPROVISATION

Formation: Groups of four to eight.

Focus: Vocal improvisation/texture/small group composition.

Activity

• Divide group in 3, teaching the parts above. Each person goes in the middle to sing a short solo. Group changes background with each soloist.

Variations

• In small groups of four to eight people, one student begins with a sung ostinato based on his/her name. The next person does likewise, but fitting with the first.

• When all the ostinati are set, one person can go in the middle and sing a solo using sounds from each person's name in the group.

Comments

After a workshop activity, a student once asked me, "Was that an exercise or a piece?" This activity takes the exercise of exploring sounds of names and turns it towards an improvisational *piece*. Pieces like this help strengthen the primary jazz muscle—the listening ear. Before it starts, no one can predict what it will sound like, but by listening, the music starts to grow. The soloist in the center is now carving out a musical *Johnny Brown*, expressing him or herself within the boundaries of the group ostinati.

   This kind of exploration can be supported by some big band recordings, particularly those of Count Basie, where short riffs like those above call, answer and overlap with each other.

10. SCAT IMPROVISATION

Formation: Circle

Focus: Scat improvisation/ phrasing

Activity

• Leader sings out "question"

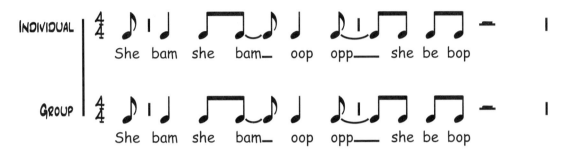

and group improvises answers all at the same time.

• As above, with individual responses around the circle.

• As above, with group calling out the "question" and also echoing each individual's response. (Ex.: Group: *Oop-Bop-Sha-Bam-a-Klook-a-Mop'*)

• Listen to recording *Oop Bop Sh'Bam* (*Birdology*: Charlie Parker: Black Label)

Variations

• Improvise scat words to the instrumental response in above recording.

First response rhythm:

Second rhythm :

Comments

This exercise begins with an existing jazz scat phrase as the springboard for the students' own inventions. The sounds and rhythm of the parent phrase may now begin to affect the subsequent improvisations. The variation narrows the field further by giving the rhythm.

From our beginnings freely exploring the sounds of our names, now we move towards some of the standard vocabulary of traditional jazz scat. The choice of consonants and vowels should reflect both the sounds and articulations of the instrumental music. In jazz, the African qualities of percussive attack are reflected in the explosive, hard consonants—*p, d, b*—the sizzle of the cymbal in *s*, the swish of the brushes on the snare drum in *sh*, the wail of the trumpet in *w*. Like all jazz improvisation, the particular choices within these loose parameters are highly individualized. Yet also characteristic of both instrumental and scat improvisation is a basic store of characteristic riffs and short phrases from which the player draws.

Brief Overview of Jazz Scat

When Louis Armstrong reportedly dropped the music and had to improvise nonsense words in his historic 1926 recording, *Heebie Jeebies*, scat singing was officially introduced to the public at large. (It was likely that this practice had long been a part of African American folk culture and that perhaps, if Louis *did* drop the music, it was only his way of recording something that might not have been approved by his producers!). It was fitting that the first great scat singer was a great instrumentalist. Many conjecture that scat arose as a means to both practice and communicate phrases away from the instrument. When black musicians first began playing Western instruments, from guitar to cornet to piano, their primary impulse was to make their instruments *sing*. The instrument became an extension of the voice. With scat, it was reversed—the voice now duplicated the sound of the instruments.

The singer and bandleader Cab Calloway popularized the scat tradition through the 30's with songs like *Jumpin' the Jive* and his famous *Minnie the Moocher*. Scat was given a new infusion in the be-bop experimentation of the 40's, with trumpeter Dizzy Gillespie at the forefront. Ella Fitzgerald, one of the all-time great scat singers, describes her initiation into the form joining in the verbal games Dizzy used to play with his friends after hours.

> "That to me was my education in learning how to really bop. We used to do 'Oop-Bop-Sha-Bam-a-Klook-a-Mop'... that's one of the things I remember he used to do. And 'She-bop-da-ool-ya... that really fascinated me. When I felt like I could sing like that, then I felt that I was in... and I followed him everywhere they went." [4]

Scat singing brought vocalists like Ella Fitzgerald into a new dimension, for not only did she have to invent nonsense syllables spontaneously in the moment, but also improvise melodically over the chord changes of the song in the same manner as instrumentalists. This was a challenge that was not up to everyone's taste or ability. Many of the great singers of the 40's, 50's and beyond—Billie Holiday, Dinah Washington, Sarah Vaughan—were not scat singers and based their reputation on interpretation of lyrics and melody.

The next boost for scat singing came in the 50's and 60's from Jon Hendricks, Dave Lambert and Annie Ross in their work as the vocal trio Lambert, Hendricks and Ross.

They also popularized an idea called "vocalese"—putting words to a variety of instrumental be-bop tunes and famous solos. Some of the vocalists of the next generation, like Betty Carter and Carmen McCrae, continued the scat tradition while others like Johnny Hartman and Nancy Wilson rarely sang it. Bobby McFerrin took it to a new level with his imitation of many instruments in the ensemble—bass, drums and horns.

Classic Scat Singing Examples

- *The Louis Armstrong Story, Volume 1*: Louis Armstrong and his Hot Five: CL 851

  Heebie Jeebies: The ground-breaking recording.

  Skid-Dat-De-Dat: Short phrases in the breaks at a slow tempo.

  Hotter than That: A remarkable solo with exquisite cross-rhythms, followed by a call and response section with guitarist Lonnie Johnson. Comparing the vocal solo with Louis' trumpet solo reveals the close relationship between the instrumental and vocal expression.

- *Ella Fitzgerald Sings the Duke Ellington Songbook*: Verve Records: MGV 4008-2

  It Don't Mean a Thing if It Ain't Got That Swing: Some scat words are built into the melody- "doo-wah-doo-wah...". Ella later sings a superb solo alternating words with scat that proves the title.

  Cottontail: Ella scat sings the instrumental melody, re-enters later with a scat solo that includes a "shave and a haircut" quote and trades phrases with sax player Ben Webster (and includes a "Jingle Bells" quote).

  Take the A-Train: This tune begins with the lyrics and goes right into Ella's scat solo. She returns after the instrumental solos alternating scat with improvisation using the words.

- *Ultimate Ella Fitzgerald: Selected by Joe Williams:* Verve 314-539 054.2

  How High the Moon-In this classic tour-de-force, Ella combines improvising new lyrics with some fiery scat (including scatting the melody to the be-bop tune *Orinthology* based on this tune, quoting "A Tisket A Tasket," and Ferde Grofe's theme from "Grand Canyon Suite." By the end, it gets paired down to Ella and drums, with some new vocal techniques thrown in!

- *Roy and Diz*: Roy Eldridge/ Dizzy Gillespie: VE 2-2524

  Pretty-Eyed Baby: Living proof that the best jazz improvisers are not just playing notes, but bringing out the song inside. The great swing and be-bop trumpeters side by side singing extended scat solos in their respective styles.

- *Dizzy Atmosphere:* Dizzy Gillespie: DRIVE: DE 2-4201

  Oop Bop Sh'Bam: Dizzy himself helps sing this scat melody and then lets his trumpet do the talking.

- *Bobby McFerrin: Spontaneous Inventions*: Blue Note

  Walkin': In duet with Wayne Shorter playing soprano sax, not only matching musical ideas, but timbres as well.

  I Hear Music: A solo version of this jazz standard with an echo section with the audience (have the kids try it!).

  Mañana Iguana: An original goodbye song alternating rhymed farewell sayings with scat singing.

"Vocalese" examples: Text put to jazz solos

The Jazz Singers: Prestige Records P-24113

Moody's Mood for Love; *Twisted*; *Tickletoe*; *Doodlin'*; *Billie's Bounce*.

RHYTHM AND SPEECH

One of the Schulwerk's distinguishing trademarks is teaching rhythm through speech. In choosing this approach, Orff was echoing a common practice in oral musical culture. Set or improvised rhythmic syllables that teach note values, rhythms and often approximate the sound of the particular percussion instrument played are found in India, Bali, Korea, Japan, the Middle East—and throughout the African diaspora.

Many of the varied West African languages are tonal—inflection of tone is fundamental to the meaning of specific words. The now well-known "talking drums" reflect this intonation in their playing. But the words offer something else in addition to intonation—the *rhythm* of the syllables, the particular accents and phrases implicit in the language. Listening to a master drummer improvise, we may imagine him creating abstract permutations of divisions of the beat and meter, but in actuality, he will be drawing from a repertoire of proverbs and phrases transferred to the drum.

If we come to understand how the songs and rhythms of a musical culture are natural extensions of the varied rhythms and pitches of its language, we gain insight into another dimension of the cultural loss of African slaves. Not only was their music banned, but their language lost as well. Now they learned to speak English, a language that gave birth to a distinctly different music—the strophic form of metered verses found in much European and American folk music. The example below [5] comparing a phrase in the Twi language of the Akan people of Ghana with its English translation shows how much music is lost even when the rhythm is almost the same:

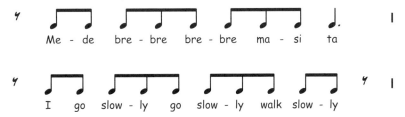

We can imagine the initial dilemma of maintaining an African rhythmic feel within the limitations of the adopted English language. The result was that language, like dance, music and religion, became transformed when picked up by the slaves and was passed down to this day. Though looked down upon by "high" culture, much of the African-American vernacular speech represents a re-vitalization of American English through accent, vocabulary, phrasing and rhythmic emphasis. Rap is an obvious example of a rhythmic use of the language markedly different from the English child ballads.

Though teaching specific rhythms through specific syllables didn't formally crystallize in African-American culture, the practice manifested in different forms. We already touched on the use of the phrase *"Take a look at me"* in polyrhythmic clapping. Tap dancing likewise developed phrases to teach tap patterns—*"Thank you for the buggy ride"* is a verbal device to remember a particular time-step. As suggested, scat may have developed partly as a pedagogical device to teach rhythmic phrases.

These next activities highlight the teaching of rhythms through speech and accompanying speech.

11. TOM GREEDY GUT

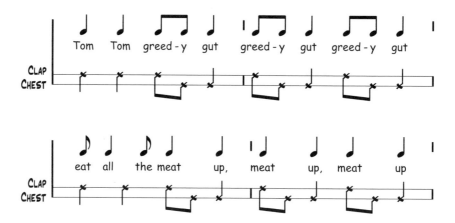

Focus: Parallel and contrasting rhythm

Activity

• Teach the first line with the body percussion motions. The dominant clapping hand slides into the chest with a flat, resonant stroke, followed by the other hand.

• Continue the body percussion motion without the text. Add the second line while continuing body percussion.

• Ask students to describe the differences between the two lines. (In the first line, the hands play the rhythm of the words. In the second, they play a contrasting rhythm.)

Variations

• Create form: (A) speak once alone, (B) speak with body percussion, (C) body percussion alone (think words), (B) speak with body percussion.

• As above in two-part canon (group 2 enters after second "Tom").

• As above in four-part canon (each group enters after first "Tom").

Comments

This delightful rhyme from *Step It Down* is listed under Baby Games, traditionally played with a baby on the lap. Here I've adapted it for older children. It is an excellent vehicle to demonstrate the contrast between playing the exact rhythm of the words (1st phrase) and a contrasting rhythmic accompaniment (2nd phrase). The suggested forms in the variations of alternating the speaking and clapping and performing in canon are classic Orff procedures that offer some challenging musical extensions.

  This game is also an excellent introduction to an extended body percussion technique that includes the deep resonance of the chest and leads us to the work of Keith Terry.

12. KEITH TERRY'S BODY PERCUSSION

Formation: Circle

Focus: New techniques in body percussion

Activity

- Clasp the hands in front of the body with one palm facing up and the other down, with students imitating. (The hand which naturally falls on top is the "active hand" and will always go first in the patterns to come.)

- Slide active hand and strike chest with a flat hand, following with the other hand. This three-stroke motion with a rest at the end will be called "three." (As in *Tom Greedy Gut.*)

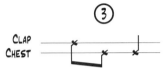

- When students are comfortable, non-verbally indicate a change and continue with the active hand followed by the other hand to the pat the thighs. This is called "five."

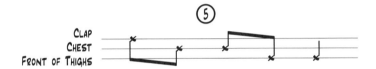

- Continue to "seven" by patting the back of the thighs.

- Continue to "nine" by taking two steps in place.

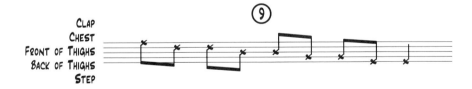

- Try a combination of patterns, as in 3, 3, 7.

- Repeat above, adding speech to match the rhythms.

To the East, to the West, to the one you love the best

- Repeat as above, but shift the accent to East as the downbeat.

To the East, to the West, to the one you love the best To the
4   1   2   3   4   1   2   3   4

- Divide the group in two, half doing one pattern, half the other. (This will create a speech/rhythm canon). Set a simple form, as in 2 times, just speak, 2 times, just do, 2 times, speak and do.

- Repeat above sequence with swing rhythm.

Keith Terry (far left) teaching Body Music in the author's jazz class.

Comments

I was delighted to discover the *Tom Greedy Gut* rhyme as it introduced a first step in a dynamic new approach to body percussion that considerably changed my teaching. Developed by percussionist Keith Terry, "body music" is the term he uses to describe the "music/dance created by the sounds the body can produce via clapping, slapping, stepping and vocalizing."[6] Combining interests and skills in trap-set drumming, rhythm dancing and comedy, Keith has created a performance art that synthesizes body percussion, movement and cross-cultural rhythmic concepts. His work is an excellent medium for rhythm training at all levels. The rhythm is experienced in the whole body through simultaneous vocalization, movement, gesture and playing of patterns that run the length of the body. This holistic approach demands a physical internalization of rhythm that strengthens rhythmic sensibility in other areas, i.e., dance, instrumental playing and general posture and coordination.[*]

Body percussion has been an important medium in Orff-Schulwerk since its inception, mostly performed on four distinct levels—snapping fingers, clapping hands, patting knees and stepping or stamping feet. Keith's work is an excellent extension of this approach, going through the chest to connect claps and pats and through the back of the legs to connect pats and stamps. This creates a more fluid expression that allows for more complex rhythms with less physical exertion. The patterns seem to rest well within the central nervous system, allowing for a more efficient and relaxed physical output.

Carl Orff, with his vision of erasing the boundary between the musician and the dancer, would have been delighted with Keith's work. Body music performances can be alternately viewed as dancers accompanying themselves musically or musicians dancing to their own music. Likewise, body music is elemental, working with the instrument nearest to us—our own bodies, voices and imagination. It can be taught and practiced anywhere and anytime. It can adapt itself to virtually any musical style. It invites the creation of new music. It thrives in the group experience, while allowing for solo expressions as well.

Keith's use of these four patterns (just one aspect of his work) is especially potent for jazz rhythm, allowing for the fluidity and gravitational pull so important to the swing feel.

The learning mode here is kinesthetic and the students must learn to relax and trust the body. We will refer back to Keith's approach in the material to come.

---

[*] For information about Keith Terry's work, CD's and an instructional video, see end of chapter.

13. JUBA

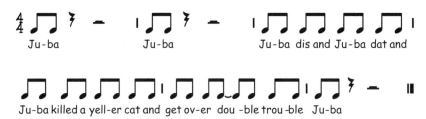

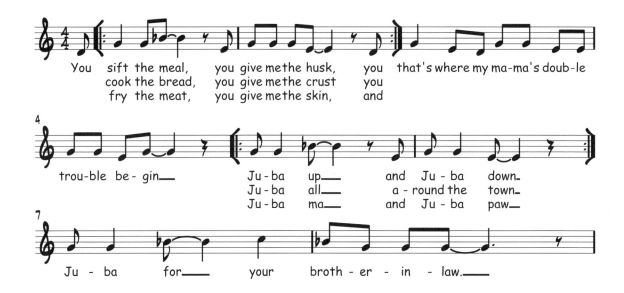

Focus: Traditional African-American body percussion/ rhythmic accompaniment to text

Activity

• This is how I like to teach *Juba*.

> Imagine you are in a rhythm contest at summer camp. Your job is to keep this steady rhythm without breaking the pattern: right hand plays on right knees, left hand on left.

> Everything is going along smoothly when suddenly a mosquito lands on your right hand. You can't break the pattern, but you want to slap the mosquito. Here's how: on the "X" notes, reach across and slap top of right hand with left.

> Now the mosquito flies to your left hand, so you try to slap it with your right hand.

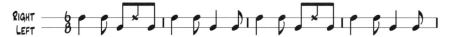

The mosquito goes and gets a friend, so now you have to slap both hands!

You're patting Juba!

- Another approach for those who didn't get it via mosquito slapping:

  Put your right hand over your right knee and make a ceiling over it with your left hand. With your right hand, pat your knee, hit the ceiling and pat your knee again. (The X note indicates coming up to hit the left hand.)

  Do the same on the left:

  Alternate between the two sides, leaving a rest.

  Now try it without a rest, slowly increasing the tempo.

- While patting, all express with their voice or their feet where they feel the beat. Most will choose a 6/8 feel (as shown above).

- Try patting with feet or voice expressing a 4/4 beat. Though this pattern feels so natural in 6/8 meter, the real Juba is in 4/4 time, distributing the accents in unexpected places to give an exciting cross-rhythmic feel. Every three measures, the pattern repeats. (The notation below highlights the accent pattern of each measure.)

- Play the Juba pattern above while speaking the rhyme.

Variations

- Change the pattern to fit more easily into 4/4 time with a 3+3+2 feeling:

- Hit chest instead of back of hand with any of the above patterns.

Comments

This appears complex in print—and it is! With the three's in the hands moving with the 4 beats in each measure and one full cycle of three measures moving with the two measure phrases of the text, this difficult cross-rhythm is typical of African rhythm. If we trust our hands to carry the pattern while we speak the words and don't think about matching the accents, we can do it. Though a short experiment of counting 4 beats while patting Juba may be helpful, the trick is to move right to the text. The phrase *"Juba dis and Juba dat and Juba killed a yeller cat"* is particularly helpful as every syllable matches a pat of the hand. The first variation is also a viable option that is easier to hear.

Juba is one of the most intriguing and complex words in African-American vernacular, at once describing a dance style found in both the Southern United States and the West Indies in the 1800's and 1900's, a popular banjo song, the patted rhythms described above, the stage name (Master Juba) of a dancer named William Henry Lane and more.

This song's text is obscure until the lines *"You sift the meal, you give me the husk"* reveal its meaning—it is about the leftover food given to the slaves after the masters had eaten. This is unusually direct for songs about slavery, but the first part shows the more common veiled reference. Bessie Jones speculates that Juba refers to the giblets, the leftover parts of the meat and that the "yella cat" in the first line is the white folks who would die if they had to eat like this. Like all such songs, the words encourage the slaves to bear up—they will one day "get over double trouble." As you tell the story to the children, they may note that the song and rhythms themselves are energetic and uplifting—it was (and is) one of the strategies for surviving hard times with the spirit intact.

14. HAMBONE

Ham-bone. Ham-bone. Have you heard? Pop-pa's gon-na buy me a mock-ing bird._

> *Hambone, hambone have you heard? Papa's gonna buy me a mockin'bird.*
> *If that mockin'bird don't sing, Papa's gonna buy me a diamond ring.*
> *If that diamond ring don't shine, Papa's gonna buy me a bottle of wine.*
> *If that bottle of wine should break, Papa's gonna give me a booty-ache.*
> *Hambone, hambone, where's ya been? 'Round the world and back again.*
> *Hambone, hambone, where's your wife? She's in the kitchen, cookin' rice.*

Focus: Call and response relationship with speech and rhythm

Activity

- Sing the above song and have the children respond after each line with the following clap:

- Discuss background of song and teach "real" Hambone as follows (all seated):

  1. Hand striking upward on side of leg **(U).**

  2. Hitting chest near shoulder **(C).**

  3. Striking thigh with back of hand (downward motion) **(B).**

Practice two Hambone rhythms

- Practice each after each line in song. All choose one and perform.

Variations

- Practice all patterns with other hand.

- Practice with both hands.

- Practice this pattern:

- Practice a 9 (from Keith Terry's work)with two claps at the end.

All three of these end on the firm cadence of two claps.

- Each chooses one of the practiced variations. All sing with an offbeat clap and perform together chosen variations in the response.

- Improvise or compose new variations.

Comments

There are many variations of this African-American adaptation of an Anglo-American lullaby—*Hush Little Baby.* The lyrics of this one is on the edge of school acceptability—which, of course, is why kids love it! Naturally, if you find it offensive or worry about keeping your job, feel free to use the version with the billy goat, horse and cart. *Hambone* demands loose wrists and a bent body, helping to prepare both mallet technique and a "get down" dancing posture.

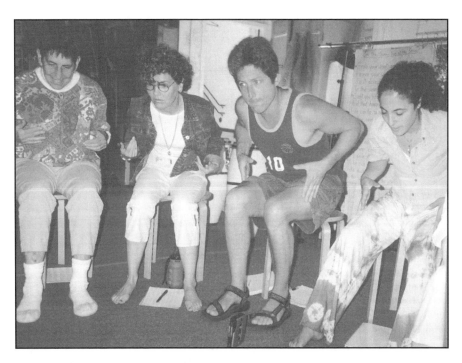

Teachers in Doug's jazz class practicing *Hambone.*

15. THE COOKIE JAR

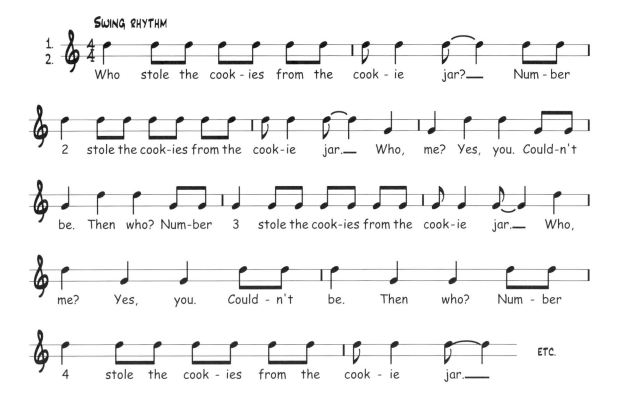

Formation: Seated circle

Focus: Swing rhythm, offbeat clap, call and response, concentration

Activity

- In a seated circle, all keeping a pat clap rhythm. Count off numbers around the circle to the beat.

- Leader speaks number 1's part, next child number 2, whole group recites this part of the dialogue: *"Yes you." "Then who?"* Number 2 calls number 3 and dialogue is repeated as above. Continue in this fashion around the circle.

- Repeat as above, with dialogue only between the two people—the number calling and the number called (caller recites alone the part of the dialogue that the group was doing).

- As above, with callers calling any number: 1 calls 6, 6 calls 3, 3 calls 7, etc. (Three rules: caller may not call the number that called her, may not call her own number and may not call a number not in the circle.)

- Play as a "real" game, with children who make a mistake going out. Possible mistakes:
  –Getting off the beat: starting too soon, too late or missing the basic rhythm
  –Not responding when called
  –Not calling the next number in time
  –Calling the wrong number (see above)
  –Saying the wrong words.

- When someone goes out, recount numbers—children have to remember their new number. Play until there's only one person left. (When there are only two left, they can call the same number back.)

- Kids who are "out" have the following choices: choose one before playing.

  –Sit in the center of the circle (*in* the "cookie jar"—this may help them feel more included than if they were *out* of the circle). They should keep practicing the clapping and help judge who made a mistake.

  –Play at the end of class. Kids who get out are dismissed.

  –Play some rhythmic accompaniment, on the hi-hat, tambourine, or other percussion instruments. (For advanced kids—risky if they're not rhythmically grounded and dynamically sensitive.)

  –Start another game with other "out" kids in the corner of the room for practice.

Variations

- Use different voices—whisper, shout, sing, speak with an accent, etc.

- Increase tempo.

- When a child goes out, the next person to his right becomes the new number one, sets tempo with clapping and begins the chant. (Much more difficult to remember your number!)

- Use names instead of numbers.

Comments

This game is one of my all-time favorites, perhaps because I emerged the champion in my first Orff class with Avon Gillespie at Antioch College! Since coming to The San Francisco School, the annual Cookie Jar contest has become one of the most exciting events of the school calendar. After playing the game all year in the individual music classes, we have a semi-finals play-offs in each class. The winners from each grade go to the finals in the lower division (1st and 2nd grade) or the upper division (3rd, 4th, 5th). There are 12 finalists in each division. We play with the entire school watching: it's as much a challenge for the audience to be absolutely quiet as it is for the participants to play! Each finalist gets a certificate of participation and stays afterward for a small party of cookie eating. The last three get 3rd, 2nd and 1st place ribbons, with first place receiving the coveted award of a cookie jar filled with cookies. I play in the game and if any child beats me, I take them out for an ice-cream sundae. (This has only happened once in 22 years, when 4th grader Michael Canaveral made school history by unseating me. He mysteriously left school the next year.)

Now we are in the world of rhythmic accompaniment, the body percussion *complementing* rather than expressing directly the rhythm of the words. Beyond the obvious reinforcement of the offbeat with the clapping, the syncopation and the swing rhythm of the text, this is an excellent game for developing mental alertness and attention. Every musician needs to develop strong concentration skills, but perhaps the jazz musician most of all.[*] Improvised music means listening at all times and being prepared for the unexpected. *The Cookie Jar* is a fantastic training ground!

We will come back to it in a new form in the next chapter.

---

[*] It was a great pleasure to observe great jazz musicians play this game in the movie *Round Midnight!*

COMPOSITION

We have explored language as a tool for vocal exploration, wordplay, teaching rhythms and creating rhythmic accompaniments, all with an African-American inflection that will lead us to jazz. Now one more possibility remains—the use of poetry as the basis of composition.

When we want to review and assess what we've learned in math, we take a test. When we want to do the same in music, we create something—the act of creation calls forth all our skill and understanding. It also calls on our imagination and powers of observation—the poem itself suggests certain paths to bring it to life. Like a sculptor who cuts away at the stone to reveal the hidden form, the best creators take time to listen to what the poem suggests to further reveal its meaning.

Reflective of their experience, many black poets speak of suffering, death and injustice. They also speak of love, hope, triumph—and music. (See bibliography for a listing of poems specifically about jazz musicians.)

JAZZ POETRY

From: MONTAGE OF A DREAM DEFERRED: Langston Hughes [7]

BLUES AT DAWN
(metered sung vocal)

I don't dare start thinking in the morning.
I don't dare start thinking in the morning.
    If I thought thoughts in bed,
    Them thoughts would bust my head—
So I don't dare start thinking in the morning.

I don't dare remember in the morning.
Don't dare remember in the morning.
    If I recall the day before,
    I wouldn't get up no more—
So I don't dare remember in the morning.

CHILDREN'S RHYMES
(scat and body percussion)

When I was a chile we used to play
"One-two-buckle my shoe!"
and things like that. But now, Lord,
listen at them little varmints!

By what sends
the white kids
I ain't sent:
I know I can't
be President.

There is two thousand children
in this block, I do believe!

What don't bug
them white kids
sure bugs me:
We knows everybody
ain't free!

Some of these young one is cert'ly bad—
One batted a hard ball right through my
    window
and my goldfish et the glass.

written down

for white folks
ain't for us a-tall:
'Liberty and Justice—
Huh-For All.'

Oop-pop-a-da!
Skee! Daddle-de-do!
Be-bop!

Salt peanuts!
De-dop!

HARLEM
(free movement)

What happens to a dream deferred?

Does it dry up,
like a raisin in the sun?

Or fester like a sore—
And then run?

Does it stink like rotten meat?
Or crust and sugar over
Like a syrupy sweet?

Maybe it just sags like a heavy load.

Or does it explode?

EASY BOOGIE
(metered ensemble and speech)

Down in the bass, that steady beat
Walking walking walking, like marching
    feet

Down in the bass, that easy roll,
Rolling like I like it, in my soul.

Riffs, smears, breaks

Hey, Lawdy, Mama!
Do you hear what I said?
Easy like I rock it
In my bed.

16. JAZZ POETRY

Formation: Groups of four to six

Focus: Small group composition using various mediums

Activity

- Each group chooses a suggested medium and goes off to a private space to begin work on the chosen poem. All read the poem together. (The poem must be read, spoken or sung at some point in the performance.) Encourage students to begin by doing something—moving, singing, accompanying on instruments or body percussion—and then discussing afterwards how to shape the ideas generated. Give a time limit (generally 10 to 15 minutes) and the clear expectation that the group will have created and practiced a piece that they will perform at the end of class. Though I prefer not to do it, grading the group as a whole sometimes increase the level of motivation for older students.

- Check in with each group and give various time warnings (5 minutes, two minutes, 30 more seconds, etc.).

- Create a simple A section, as in a body percussion pattern, to be used as the "glue" in a rondo form performance. All perform A, group one performs their piece, all perform A, group two performs theirs, etc.

- Discuss performance afterwards, attending to what worked and what needs further work.

Comments

This process works best when the kids jump in and start trying things and then stop to talk. To aid that, you can make the rule that they can't talk for the first five minutes. On the other hand, if they never stop to talk, the piece won't come into form! Sometimes you need to remind kids to talk with each other!

The teacher's job is to stay out of the way and let the kids come up with their own creative solutions. After they've had enough time to begin work, you can start to circulate and observe the work in progress. When they're stuck, leading questions can be helpful.

> "Show me your idea. Who might come in next? Okay, you've got the middle part, but how are you going to begin? How are you going to end?..."

To keep the performances unified, rondo form works well. (If the set section is A and the groups B, C, D, E, the form would be A B A C A D A E.) The A section can be a short chant, body percussion pattern, movement or song. After the performance, as always, discuss what worked, what didn't and why. You can choose to continue work in succeeding classes, refining, extending or folding into a larger dramatic context or leave it as a one class experience, returning to the structure at another time with different material.

Two rather obscure recordings will give the children an example of adult musicians using this idea (see discography on page 79).

SUMMARY: Language and music

"If you can talk, you can sing. If you can walk, you can dance."
—AFRICAN SAYING

What have we learned about language and music? These two intelligences begin life together in the womb, joined at the ear. Each also forms a vital connection with movement. When sound enters the infant's watery world, whether it be word or drum, the muscles respond.* The trio of speech, music and movement ride into the world together and for years, are carried by rhythm and rhyme. They may stay connected through their mutual love for a lifetime, but each begins to court other suitors. Words move towards *meaning*, concentrate on storing information, interpreting experience and spinning out abstract concepts. Music moves decisively towards more sophisticated rhythm and tone, into a landscape that begins where words leave off. Movement stays tied to music through rhythm, keeps connected to speech through gesture and parts company with words as they make their way into print. If we are to learn the music of language and the language of music, we must begin with both. The strange notion that music and dance are only for some while language is for everyone comes from missing this connection.

We also discover that *what* you speak—your native language—and *how* you speak it—your dialect—makes a difference in the music that follows. From *Mama lama kuma lama* to *Doo wah doo wah* to the poetry of *A Dream Deferred*, African-American speech steps out its unique rhythms and sings its own cadences. As we tune our ear, we find an English language animated by Africanisms and that lead us towards its musical counterparts—gospel, blues, rhythm 'n' blues, soul, funk, rap—and jazz.

Schools struggling to integrate this speech (recently named "Ebonics") in the classroom recognize that it is not "bad" English, but a dialect consistent within its own standards of expression, one that has added color to the palette of American speech. As a recent article made clear, "most Americans, black, white or other, don't have to learn to appreciate black English. They already use it." [9] From its early contributions of "jubilee, jambalaya, banjo, mumbo jumbo, mojo, juke and jazz" to the Be-bop and Beat "lingo"—"hip, cool, square, straight, dig, wig, gig, jump, jive, rock, roll, cook and burn" to the 60's "uptight, outta sight, groovin', gettin' down, funky, far out, baaad, honky" to the 90's incarnations of "rap, cap, yo', bro', homey, dissin', wannabe," black English is an indelible part of the American linguistic soundscape.

At the same time, all American children need to feel at home in the neighborhood of standard English, not only to compete in the job market, but to access the gifts of the European literary heritage and to understand the reflective *meaning* of words. An increased vocabulary and understanding of the power of language to build intellect is beneficial to *all* children. It is true that as language grows more abstract, some of its *music* is lost. But crossing the bridge doesn't mean burning it—we can move freely back and forth between the music and the meaning without diminishing either.

If the cultural mandate is for young African-Americans to begin the journey in one direction, the rest of us hyphenated-Americans can cross in the other direction, towards the music of a dialect that leads us to the music of jazz, our cultural treasure. That journey begins with our new national anthem: *"Oop bop sh'bam, a klook a mop"*

---

* Studies reveal that by the 7th month in utero, the infant is already making precise muscular responses to the phonemes of the mother's speech. [8]

Endnotes

1. Bly, Hillman, Meade: *The Rag and Bone Shop of the Heart*

2. Examples of Wordplay can be found in Jane Frazee's *Discovering Orff*: Schott, pp. 21, 34

   Examples of Teaching Rhythm can be found in *Music for Children, V. I*

   Carl Orff-Gunild Keetman, Margaret Murray Edition, Schott: pp. 50–52

   Examples of Rhythmic Accompaniment on p. 1 of above volume

3. Porter, Lewis: *Jazz: A Century of Change*: Schirmer Books, p. 224

4. Leonard, Neil: *Jazz: Myth and Religion*: Oxford Univ. Press, 1987 p. 95

5. Amoaku, W. K.: *Orff-Schulwerk in the African Tradition*: Schott ED 6376

   Nketia's comments are in the introduction, the speech piece is on p. 22: Mede brebre masi ta

6. Terry, Keith: *Body Music*: Article in the Spring '92 Orff Echo: Vol. XXIV, No. 3

7. Hughes, Langston: *Selected Poems*: Vintage Classics, p. 221

8. Pearce, Joseph Chilton: *Evolutions End*: Harper San Francisco 1992, p. 71

9. De Witt, Karen: *Talkin' black ain't new to America*: S.F. Sunday Examiner and Chronicle: Jan. 5th, 1999

Bibliography

Name Games: Activities for Rhythmic Development: Doug Goodkin: Warner Brothers Publications

A Rhyme in Time; Rhythm, Speech Activities and Improvisation for the Classroom: Warner Brothers Pub.

Play, Sing & Dance : Doug Goodkin: Schott (Chapter 2—Speech; Chapters 9 & 10—Body Percussion)

Heart Full of Grace: A Thousand years of Black Wisdom: Edited by Venice Johnson: Fireside, Simon & Schuster

The Collected Poems of Langston Hughes: Arnold Rampersad, Editor: Vintage Books, Random House NY: Selected Poems: Langston Hughes

Sing to the Sun: Ashley Bryan: HarperCollins

The Jazz Poetry Anthology: Edited by Sascha Feinstein & Yusef Komunjakaa: Indiana University Press

Videography

Body Music Part One with Keith Terry www.crosspulse.com

DANCING: New Worlds New Forms; Program Five—Produced by Thirteen/WNET in association with RM arts and BBC-TV (for an example of Juba)

Discography

Poetry, Prose, Percussion and Song: Charles Williams, Tom Teasley (available from Website http://psong.iuma.com) Includes the following Langston Hughes poems: *Africa: Peace: Since I Laid My Burden Down, Dancer*

Weary Blues: with Langston Hughes, Charles Mingus and Leonard Feather: Verve 841-660-2. Includes the poem *Harlem* included in the lesson and fifteen others besides.

Keith Terry recordings: *Crosspulse: Serpentine* CPCD 002 / *Body Tjak: The Celebration* CPCD 003 / *Professor Terry's Circus Band Extraordinaire* CPCD 004 / *Slammin: All Body Band* CPCD 005 All available through www.crosspulse.com

CHAPTER 4: JAZZ MOVEMENT

"Movement is fundamental to all Orff process. It is the foundation on which all other learning rests."

—Avon Gillespie

"You got to move."

—Reverend Gary Davis

One summer I was teaching at a music camp and decided to offer some group lessons in folk dancing. I had developed a little theory that since the side-close-side step re-occurred in various folk dances, that it would be useful to isolate it, master it and then "plug it in" to various dances. I took my small class up to an outdoor deck, broke down the step into its basic parts and we practiced it without music playing. While we were practicing, some African-American girls came up, watched for a bit and then turned around and started to leave. I asked them if they wanted to join in and they said, "No—we thought you were going to teach some *dancin'*!"

As we enter this chapter on jazz dance, we might pause to inquire what we mean by "dance." These girls had inherited the traces of an elaborate tradition with many layers of distinct meanings—social, emotional and stylistic. I had been trained in a monochromatic abstract view of learning and made the unpardonable error of reducing the *dance* to the *steps*. I was intent on teaching a pattern in the feet and my critics were confused as they searched for some semblance of *style*. Before we leap into the activities with the children, it is worthwhile to look at the chasm that separates these two approaches to dance. If we understand a bit about where we're leaping *from* and have a sense of where we're trying to land, we'll be better prepared to lead the children.

ROOTS OF JAZZ DANCE

Dance in West African culture is an educational and religious institution parallel to the European university and seminary. It tells the stories of the ancestors (both the mythological spirits and historical family origins), teaches social lessons to children, preserves rituals and maintains traditions vital to the community's health and cohesion. Judith Lynne Hanna comments in her article *African Dance As Education*:

"In traditional African cultures, dance is less an 'art' than a 'craft,' functionally entwined with multiple components of *vitae curriculum*. What we perceive as aesthetic factors are intermingled and designed for practical application in the economic, political, social and religious spheres of life." [1]

As is well known, this rich legacy of West African dance was lost in the forced journey to the New World, actively suppressed in the Southern colonies and further dismantled by the mixing of disparate tribes, each with their specific tradition. But the *need* to dance could not be touched by mere laws. New dances rose like tenacious plants growing between the cracks of the concrete, driven by the African spirit's thirst for light.

Deprived of traditional forms, many of these new forms were born from imitating the dances of the Anglo slave owners. I imagine a slave observing the Saturday night quadrille at Massa's house and returning to the slave quarters ready to report the "news." "What are they doing up there?" "Some kind of dance—it looked something like this." But indeed, "something like this" was never quite the way the white folks did it.

Though generations had passed since real African dances were done, the quality of body movement was passed down in the motions and gestures of everyday life—the way one worked, walked, swayed while singing, and gestured while speaking. When an African says, *"Our ancestors gave us these dances, we cannot forget them,"* [2] he may be speaking of the need to continue the tradition, but his words carry a secondary meaning for his African-American counterparts. They may not remember the specific *steps*, but it is impossible to forget entirely the whole weight of their inheritance, preserved in their muscle-memory. So as the slave imitated Massa's dance, his own ancestors rose up and alchemically transformed the dancing into something new—European steps and forms with an African flavor. Soon quadrilles, jigs and cotillions became part of an African-*American* dance repertoire, but always markedly different from their European counterparts.[*]

As general style settled into specific movements, names were given to the new dances—*Ball the Jack, Step It Down, Ranky Tank, Shout, Juba, Buzzard Lope, Snake Hips, Possum-la* and *Pigeon Wing* (see *Step It Down*). These colorful dances are the midwives between the old dances of the African mother culture and their ever-shifting contemporary incarnations. My parent's generation might be more familiar with the *Charleston* than the *Jump for Joy*. My generation might recognize the *Funky Chicken* instead of the *Pigeon Wing*, while my children are unknowingly folding some of *Ball the Jack* into the *Freak*. How exciting for children to learn some of these basic dance steps, tracing the movement from the African dancing ring to the Southern plantation to the urban dance hall!

STYLISTIC CONSIDERATIONS

Just as we begin our musical investigation with the old children's games, so might we come into our dance study with a look at the ring plays—yet with one frustrating difference. With a bit of adjustment and a few verbal guidelines about swing rhythm, ambiguous tones, vocal timbre, etc., we can pass on some game melodies through an approximate notation. Yet dance steps in *any* style are difficult to describe verbally and in the case of African-derived movement, frankly impossible. What we can give is a general description of qualities—and from there, refer the teacher to the oral tradition (specific suggestions to follow).

---

[*] Another quality in the slave's imitated dance was ridicule. As one slave reported: "Us slaves watched white folks' parties where the guests danced a minuet and then paraded in a grand march...Then we'd do it too, but we used to mock 'em every step." [3]

As we enter once again a list of generalized qualities, we must stay alert to the many exceptions. To claim the same characteristics for all African-derived movement is to ignore the remarkable variety of specific dances. Within West Africa itself, the qualities of dance in Ghana are distinct from those in Senegal. Within Ghana, those of the Ewe people are different than those of the Ashanti, while within two Ewe villages, there may be distinct dance "dialects." Telescoping out geographically, Cuban salsa, Brazilian samba and Afro-Haitian dance are separate movement languages, while from a historical vantage point, the Cakewalk, the Twist and Hip-hop seem worlds apart. Within all these permutations, there may be additional differences between the rural and urban expressions. What we're looking for are the general sensibilities that connect these separate dance traditions, summarized in the following three points.

1. *"You've got to get it all over!"* *

One of the girls' frustrations with my "side-close-side" exercise was the lack of animation in the whole of the body. The body is a drum—or rather a drum ensemble, with its various parts playing polyrhythms that echo, accent and complement visually the audible rhythms of the drum choirs. The feet play one rhythm, the hips another, while the back, shoulders and arms may articulate yet others.

"You put your hand on your hip and let the backbone slip." The loose, supple and rippling motions of the back of African dance are particularly distinctive, in marked contrast to European-derived movement. From classical ballet to Viennese waltz to Irish jig to Spanish flamenco, European movement tends towards straight backs and bodies moving in one piece. Rhythms tend to be confined to the feet in European dance, whereas Africans add another rhythmic voice with their back. Another layer enters through the hips and shoulders—the cause of much distress to Victorians shocked by African-American dance and much delight to Edwardians striving to escape their sexual repression!

One word of caution. The invitation to dance with the whole body does not imply a wild flinging of body parts in all directions. The tendency of white middle-class suburban teenagers encountering the liberating rhythms of rock and roll has been precisely this reckless and arhythmic abandonment. The African sensibility is much more controlled and subtle, refined over centuries of practice. A speaker from the Kongo people of Zaire says:

> "You must move your entire body, vibrate the whole, but you must keep the movement self-contained, not go too far out with gestures and thrusts of the arms and legs." [4]

2. *Gettin' down*

Here we encounter one of the most marked contrasts between Europe and Africa. European culture has been obsessed with the vertical dimension—from the religious paintings of eyes gazing upwards towards the heavens to the tall spires of the great cathedrals to the skyscrapers of the cities and the missiles of the space program, we encounter the phallic underpinnings of its patriarchal culture everywhere we turn. The African matriarchal culture has been more grounded in the earth, at home in the horizontal dimension. (See *Soul and Spirit* in the Appendix for an elaboration of these ideas.) Naturally, both manifest in the subsequent dance, the former with its straight, skyscraper backs leaping away from gravity and the latter releasing its weight towards the earth. This horizontal quality of the dance is as important to style in movement as swing rhythm is to the music. *"Give me the kneebone bend"* says the ring play, and one moment of really

---

* Another jewel from the pithy wisdom of Bessie Jones.

feeling this quality of letting go into gravity, loosening what is stiff, relaxing what is rigid, is part of the liberation we experience when we "get down."

Fourth graders "gettin' down."

3. *Gettin' into it*

Bess Lomax Hawes, *Step It Down's* "translator" of Bessie Jones's oral tradition, writes of her confusion when trying to set down the dances:

> "The plays and games were quite carefully formalized for the most part, but the shape of the dances seemed to melt and shift just when I thought I had finally understood them. 'Well, you *could* do it in a circle, or you wouldn't have to if you didn't want to,' Mrs. Jones would remark comfortingly, as I tore up one description after another." [5]

The European concern for form and choreography grows from the entire mind set of its intellectual inheritance. Focused on the abstractions and formal intellect of math, science, philosophy, theology, its dances reflect its concerns. While astronomers studied the movement of the planets, the dancing masters worked out the elaborate geometric permutations of allemandes and galliards, quadrilles and contra dances.

Africans, more interested in intuitive wisdom and heart intelligence, put their energy into the style of the steps. "Gettin' into it" is more important than organizing elaborate spatial structures. Loose improvisational structures serve these purposes better than formal choreography.* (Perhaps this is why the imitation of the white folks' quadrilles proved to be a passing phase, while the ring plays survive to this day in black culture.)

---

* As black dance moved from the street to the stage—Broadway to Motown to Fraternity Step Shows— set steps and formal choreography entered the aesthetic.

We must stay aware of these defining principles of style if we hope to successfully bridge these cultural differences. When white instructors began teaching the African-derived forms of the rhumba, samba, cha-cha, Charleston, Jitterbug, etc., in their ball-room dancing classes, their European aesthetics sapped the vitality of the styles.* The horizontal, polyrhythmic qualities of the original dances rigidified into pale vertical, monochromatic versions. If we are to avoid the same fate in the classroom, we would do well to remember the three "gets"—"get it all over," "get down" and "get into it!"

Ewe dancers in Ghana "gettin' down."

JAZZ DANCE IN THE CLASSROOM

How do we begin jazz movement in the classroom? The first answer is, "We already have—through games." The four games we explored in Chapter 2 and the many more found in the playground and summarized in various books (see bibliography) all have a movement component, from the clapping motions of *Head and Shoulders* to the specific movements of *Soup, Soup* to the improvised dance of *Johnny Brown*. Revisit the games with increased awareness of the movement qualities just outlined.

A second possibility is to **invite the children to share their playground games and dances.** Though I have alluded often to the demise of children's game culture with the rise of TV, computer games and organized sports, they in fact are alive and well in various pockets around the nation, particularly in the African-American community. I was depressed to discover that the children I spoke to during a visit to St. Simon's Island hadn't heard of Bessie Jones and didn't know any of the games in her book, but I was elated when a colleague brought her African-American students from Dr. Charles R. Drew School in San Francisco to my jazz course and they shared a wide variety of contemporary games and dance steps! Though you as the teacher must think about their place in the music curriculum, and in this case, how they may serve to illuminate key

---

* See video *New World, New Forms* for some filmed examples.

concepts in jazz, the children are the "experts" who have the last word on style. Don't forget to ask them!

A third possibility is to move to jazz music keeping in mind the basic qualities we have just outlined. What follows are several such structures, with sample talk-throughs and suggested music. This format tunes into the child's primary learning modes—activity and osmosis. Children learn to feel and express the music through movement and begin to understand the style and aesthetic by repeatedly hearing great jazz music. Don't be surprised if they start humming along with Miles Davis solos while they dance!

The Jazzwalk.

17. THE JAZZWALK

Formation: Single file line
Focus: Offbeat, bounce, basic jazz movement

Activity

• To recorded music (some suggestions to follow), students follow the teacher around the room stepping the "Jazzwalk:" Step diagonally side-to-side beats 1 and 3. The free foot taps the stepping foot on beats 2 and 4. (Step diagonal right on right foot, tap left foot to right, step diagonal left on left foot, tap right foot to left.) Bend the knees and keep a small bounce in the body.

• Teacher talks through variations as follows (a sample model—develop your own):

"When you hear music like this, you have to walk a different way. We call it the jazzwalk. Follow me and gently tap your feet together in-between the steps. Make sure you're going the same speed as me so that it fits with the music. If you take small steps, its easier to keep on time. Pay attention to which foot you start with so that we're all going in the same direction. When we all move together, it's like a giant centipede.

"Now, as you tap your feet together, can you snap your fingers at the same time? Just make the motion if you don't know how to snap. As you tap your feet and snap your fingers, can you make a small dip? You'll have to bend your knees on the dip. It's like you let go of your weight for a second. Now as you tap your feet and snap your fingers and take a little dip, can you give your hip a little twitch? Keep your body relaxed, with a gentle bounce.

"How about the arms? They can switch front and back. Up and down. Keep the snaps. Side to side. Can you do a swimming motion? Find your own way to move your arms. Now move out of the circle and jazzwalk freely around the room in your own style. Look around at everyone's style and try some of their ideas.

"Can you jazzwalk in place? Backwards? Now gradually find your own place facing front and keep jazzwalking in that place. When the music ends, show me a good ending shape. Do you know what to say when you make the shape? With a whispery voice, 'Oh, yeeeaaahhhh.'"

Comments

The Jazzwalk (my own word) helps the children get the feeling of accent on two and four in the body. I generally wait until the children have had repeated experiences in walking, patting or clapping a steady beat before introducing the more sophisticated accenting of offbeats. However, this may be my cultural training, assuming you first learn the beat and then the *off*beat. Perhaps both experiences can grow side by side, each tied to their appropriate musical style.

Developing your own sequence and style of talking through each new motion takes some practice. I suggest going over it alone at home with an imaginary class (or enlist your family) to get the feeling for the pacing. A rough outline on a board or bulletin board in a place where you can see it while teaching might also help you feel less panicked in your beginning attempts. Remember that if you ever get stuck and need to regroup your thoughts, challenging the students to "find their own way to do the motion" will buy you some extra time and give them the ownership of the experience that you're aiming for anyway!

18. ISOLATIONS

Formation: Students spread out throughout the room facing the teacher—mirror image

Focus: Exploring jazz feeling in isolated body parts with recorded music

Activity

- Here is a model of how I lead this activity:

  "Standing in your place, can you find the right place to snap to the music? Can you do a gentle bounce as you snap? Keep that feeling while we try moving different parts of our body. Let's start with the head. Can your head say yes? Can your head say no? Let's see some chicken heads *(neck extends front and back)*. How about the shoulders? They can say, 'I don't know' *(up and down)*. Try one shoulder alone. The other. Alternate shoulders. Can your shoulders say no? What can the elbows do? Say 'move over' with your elbows. Stir some soup with your elbows. Let's see some chicken wings.

  "Can you feel your rib cage? This is a hard one. Try moving from your rib cage to the side, trying to keep the shoulders in place. Other side. Make a circle. How about the hips? Can the hips say no? Can the hips say yes? *(Generally laughter here)*. Can you move your hips in a circle? Try the other way. This is what made Elvis famous. Try moving your knees in a circle with your hands on your knees. That's the 'ball the jack' step. The other way. Can one knee say yes? The other knee? Alternating knees? Can you move your hips in a circle while your knees keep going? That's the snake hips motion. Can your knees open and close in time to the music? Do any of you know how to switch your hands while you do this like in the Charleston dance?

  "How about your feet? Can they open and close without jumping? Try it with your heels glued to the floor. Now with your toes. Try alternating, first heels glued, then toes. Can your feet say no with your heels glued? With your toes? Staying in your place, find two body parts to move to the music. Try switching from one side of the body to the other or facing slightly one way and then the other. Now keep doing your motion, but watch someone else while you do it. Study them carefully. When I say switch, change to the motion that person is doing. Ready? Switch! Now look around. Did anybody take your motion? Go back to your own motion. When the music stops, freeze into a shape and remember what to say!"

Comments

Remembering Bessie Jones admonition, "You've got to get it all over," this exercise helps children discover how each part of the body can express itself. This is essential in any movement class, but particularly in African-derived movement which depends so heavily on the use of the whole body.

The form of each student creating his or her own motion and then having others observe and copy is a different slant on the *Johnny Brown* game. It's always a winning strategy to have kids make up their own motion, not only because it becomes more personal and meaningful, but also because the brain works at its highest level when it has to create.

Taking the next step of copying their neighbor's motion effortlessly expands the range of their movement vocabulary and affirms that we are all students *and* teachers.

19. TOUCHES

Formation: Students facing the teacher as in Isolations, using mirror image
Focus: Weight transfer

Activity

- The following is a model of how I lead this activity:

    "Let's see you bounce lightly to the music. Can you add the snap? Let's practice some touches. That means you touch your foot lightly but don't step on it or put weight on it. *(Demonstrate the difference.)* Remember to copy me mirror image. If I touch to this side *(point)* you also touch to the same side. See if you can keep the bounce while you touch. *(Begin touching to one side—touch on beats 1 and 3 if the music is the same tempo as the jazzwalk— between 132–144 beats per minute).* What does it feel like if the hip goes out while you touch? If the top part of your body turns as you touch? Experiment until you find your own style of touching—but don't forget to keep the beat steady! Try touching to the other side. Try four on one side and then four on the other. Two and two. One touch on each side.

    "Try touching in front. What happens to the weight? Notice how the body tends to lean back to help keep the balance. Try the other foot in front. Two of each. One of each. Now touch in back. Now the body leans forward. Face the direction you're touching. What are we going to do next? Right—the other foot. What next? Two of each. One of each.

    "We've touched to the side, front and back. Can you cross in front? Try your arms and upper body twisting to the opposite side of the touch. Switch sides. One on each side. Now try crossing behind the other leg. This time, the arms move with the touching leg. One on each side. Let's try all the different touches again, one on each side, but twice as fast. Who remembers the secret of going faster? Right—keep relaxed and make everything smaller. Try making your own pattern of touches. Look around. When I say switch, try someone else's pattern."

Comments

The difference between a step that takes weight and a touch that doesn't is crucial to all styles of dance. Once again, the offbeat feel and relaxed bouncing body is reinforced while the mind and body focus on the new task of touching without taking weight. The use of both sides of the body and the spatial changes of side, front, back, and cross, keeps the milk of variety flowing while enjoying the comfort of repetition.

Fifth graders dancing in a play.

20. SIDE–CLOSE–SIDE

Formation: Students facing the teacher, using mirror image
Focus: Weight transfer, steps and touches, patterns

Activity

- Perform side-close-side patterns to recorded music as follows:

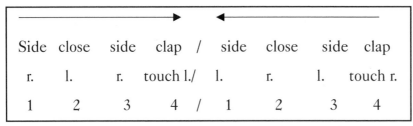

Side	close	side	clap	/	side	close	side	clap
r.	l.	r.	touch l. /		l.	r.	l.	touch r.
1	2	3	4 /		1	2	3	4

- Cross in front or behind on beat two. Touch in front or behind on beat four.

- Perform going front and back (three steps back with a clap, three forward, clap). Keep the feeling of a slight dip on beats two and four.

- Perform a longer pattern:

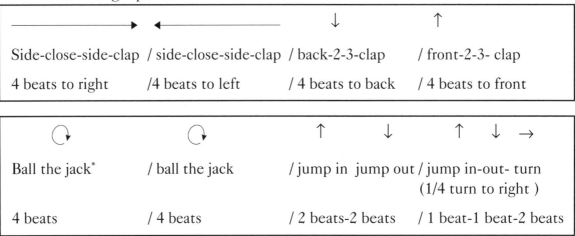

Side-close-side-clap	/ side-close-side-clap	/ back-2-3-clap	/ front-2-3- clap
4 beats to right	/4 beats to left	/ 4 beats to back	/ 4 beats to front

Ball the jack*	/ ball the jack	/ jump in jump out	/ jump in-out- turn (1/4 turn to right)
4 beats	/ 4 beats	/ 2 beats-2 beats	/ 1 beat-1 beat-2 beats

- If first facing is north, repeat whole sequence facing east. South. West. Return to north.

Comments

As told in my story at the beginning of the chapter, this step can be found in many folk dances across diverse cultures, but with markedly different expressive qualities. In the jazz style, the relaxed upper body and supple hips remain a crucial feature. In keeping with accents on 2 and 4, there is a slight release of weight, a dipping and bending of the knees on the close and the 4th beat.

I first experimented with dances similar to the above when *The Hustle* was popular, taking something familiar to the kids but putting into a jazz context. The qualities of movement are similar, but dancing to Dizzy Gillespie's music is a decidedly different *musical* experience. Such group choreography, with everyone moving in unison and changing his or her facing, is still popular in pop dancing—witness the Macarena. Once again, the above is a model. Feel free to create your own, or better yet have the kids make their own choreography.

We will come back to this dance again in Chapter Five with *Step Back Baby*.

---

* See *Soup, Soup* game.

21. 1-2-3-CLAP: DAILY LIFE MOTIONS

Formation: Students facing the teacher, using mirror image
Focus: 4th beat accent, stylized motions from everyday life

Drinkin' juice jazz style.

Activity

• I model a sequence of motions to recorded music as follows:

> "Let's imagine that when you wake up one morning, you find that you simply must clap on the 4th beat in everything you usually do. So you wake-up and stretch *(stretch-stretch-stretch-clap)*, rub the sleep out of your eyes *(rub-rub-rub-clap, etc.—make sure there's the light bounce in all these motions. This and succeeding motions should also be repeated several times. Sometimes this can be humorous, as in putting on your pants. After the 3rd or 4th time, tell them it's a cold day.)* Wash your face. No towel—shake your hands dry. Brush your teeth. Can you brush your teeth with your elbow? Put on deodorant. Let's get dressed. Put on your pants. Put on your shirt. Brush your hair. Put on chapstick. Time for breakfast. Eat your cereal. Pour your juice. Drink your juice. Ooops—you spilled it. Wipe it up with a rag. Wipe it up with your elbow. With your head. Let's wash the dishes. Oh no! You dropped one! Sweep it up. Get the dustpan. Throw it away. No, not in the garbage—in the glass recycling can! Time for school. Wave goodbye.

> "Now we're in the car. *(Pretend you're driving.)* Let's turn one way. The other. I live in San Francisco—let's go up the hill. Down the hill. Shift the gears. It's starting to rain—put on the wipers *(arms become windshield wipers)*. Which way do your wipers go? *(Both*

together, opposite, out of rhythm with each other, one only, etc.) Somebody's in your way—honk the horn. Honk it with your nose. With your belly button. Uh-oh! We're starting to skid! Get the car under control! Finally, we're at school.

"Say hi to your friends with your head. Tell them to come over with your hands. With your shoulder. No—wrong person—tell them to go away with your elbow. We have some time on the yard before school starts—let's play on the swing. On the teeter-totter. Climb the pole and slide down. Play hopscotch. Bounce the ball. Shoot it in the basket. Play catch. Play baseball. Soccer. Show me the game you like to play.

"The teacher is ringing the bell. Come in *(with slumped shoulders)*. Get your work out at your desk. Write your name on the paper. You know the answer to the question *(wave hand wildly)*. You don't know the answer *(slump down and try to hide)*. Time for reading.

"Let's do some writing. Can you write your name on the board? Write your name with your nose. With your knee. With your chest.

"Time for music class. *(Wild enthusiasm.)* Let's play the xylophone. The recorders. Sing like an opera star *(just mime)*. Like a rock star. Play the violin. The guitar. The drums. The bass. The saxophone. Let's show off our best dance. We're getting sleepy. *(Yawn and slowly sink down to the floor, lie down, still clapping on 4th beat, until music ends, give final 'yeah' posture lying down.)*"

Comments

This is a variation of the side-close-side work and can precede it or follow it. The playful quality, the range of movements and the connection to daily life experience make this one of the favorites for my students to do—and for me to teach! This one in particular requires some practice at home. Recently, I discovered that the part "driving in the rain" coincided with a moment in the music I used (*Housed with Edward*—see next section) when the drums and saxophone depart from the basic beat of the bass, creating a rhythmic tension that carries through a 12-bar blues pattern and resolves on the downbeat of the next pattern. This has now become the moment when the car is skidding in my story, righting itself on the aforementioned downbeat. This adds some wonderful color to the experience, but also takes some practice to get the timing right. At the beginning, the music is meant to provide the rhythmic framework without attempting to match other musical events with the movement, but the more the two experiences parallel each other, the richer the experience is. It can be as simple as "going outdoors" when the new soloist begins or as specific as the example just given.

This, and all the preceding activities, can be led by music or classroom teachers with no dance background. Orff Schulwerk and jazz education are both properly music *and* movement education, but as there are very few structures in place for movement teachers in our schools, it falls on the music or P.E. teacher to lead activities. Orff's idea of elemental music and movement steers the beginning experiences away from practicing paradiddles and plies and draws from the world close at hand. This activity in particular is a good example of taking movements that we do every day and bringing them over to the feeling of dance through rhythm, repetition and a stylized movement suggested by the music.

The elementary general music teacher and the middle school band teacher resisting the idea of moving out of the territory of their expertise may be relieved to discover movement activities that do not require dance training to lead. If they take the risk, they may discover at least three unsuspected benefits in their subsequent music teaching:

1. The children will be refreshed by the opportunity to move and the light, playful atmosphere will open their excitement about learning.

2. Key rhythmic qualities will be communicated viscerally that will then re-appear in their playing.

3. They will have had the opportunity to listen to some high-quality jazz music and internalize both general styles and specific rhythms and melodies. This last point leads us directly to the next consideration: which music to play?

Fourth graders dancing to jazz.

SELECTING MUSIC FOR JAZZ MOVEMENT

Choosing repertoire and listening examples is one of those hidden duties of a music teacher that rarely gets discussed. Here are five suggested criteria for selecting music to accompany the preceding movement activities:

1. **TEMPO:** In reviewing pieces I have used over the years, I was surprised to discover the narrow range of tempo that felt comfortable for the children—generally between 132 and 144 on the metronome. (Lest this should seem fast, keep in mind that they are only stepping on counts 1 and 3). This tempo range is slow enough to settle comfortably into the feel and fast enough to keep the energy flowing and the beats accurate. It is surprisingly difficult to find a large repertoire of pieces that fall in this range. The succeeding suggested pieces all fulfill this tempo criteria. Naturally, once children are comfortable with the movements, it is important to extend these experiences into faster and slower tempos.

2. **LENGTH:** The length of the piece will determine the content of the exercise. There must be enough time to settle comfortably into the movement task, yet not so much that it becomes boring. The variations suggested will help keep things interesting, but the teacher must practice beforehand to get a sense of the timing. The pieces listed generally run between 3 and 9 minutes. Taping from recordings gives the flexibility of shortening pieces as necessary (using a fade-out ending).

3. **QUALITY:** Teachers have a marvelous opportunity to affect the lives of children. With opportunity comes the obligation to pass on the highest quality, be it food, literature, ideas or music. This is a chance to begin to introduce the great jazz players. Just as one would not choose Salieri over Mozart in introducing European art music of the late 18th century, so would it be foolish to introduce children to big band music via Glenn Miller over Count Basie or Duke Ellington.

4. **PERSONAL PREFERENCE:** The pieces I list are available as models or jumping off points for the jazz novice. Though finding the pieces that work best for *you* takes a little more energy, it is ultimately more rewarding. Your own pleasure in hearing music you enjoy is picked up by the children in a variety of ways. Though this may be in conflict with the third criteria (you prefer Glenn Miller), it is important to begin with what you love and then move towards other acknowledged masters of the style.

5. **LESSON CONTENT:** The choice of material ideally should reflect other specific goals in the jazz study. For example, if you are learning about Louis Armstrong, move to his music. If you're about to teach *Now's the Time* on the instruments, first move to the recording. If you're focusing on developing a strong internal beat, choose a recording with a drum solo. This kind of integration of material helps the learning on all levels, demonstrating a logical sequence satisfying to teacher and student alike.

How often should one change the music? I suggest using at least one piece a number of times, particularly for a warm-up jazzwalk. Having done this with the tune *Pretty-Eyed Baby* (see below), I found the children beginning to scat sing along with the solo! Whereas children can learn the words and every instrumental nuance to a pop song very quickly, the depth and sophistication of jazz improvised solos invite repeated listening to get closer to the ability to sing most of what is happening in the music. "Familiarity breeds contempt" is the opposite of the musical experience, especially with quality music.

The following is a list of some of the music I have enjoyed using for these movement activities. Keeping in mind the value of repetition, the goal here is not to use all the selections, but to pick and choose according to your individual needs and tastes. However, children exposed to many of these suggested pieces will have experienced a wide range of performing ensembles (from small groups to big band), jazz styles and many of the major jazz artists over a 60 year span of jazz history! Again, teach from what you love and add your own discography to the list.

Recommended Recordings

- *Pretty-Eyed Baby:* Roy Eldridge, Dizzy Gillespie: ***Diz and Roy***: Verve 314-521-647-2

One of my all time favorites to use—great tempo, good length (5:30), fantastic example of how great improvisers can sing what they play, with both Diz and Roy alternating fabulous scat singing with their exquisite playing. Also a nice study in the basic similarities and differences between the swing and be-bop sensibilities.

- *School Days*: Dizzy Gillespie: ***Dee Gee Days: The Savoy Sessions***: Savoy Jazz ZDS 4426

Another fabulous recording to move to from Dizzy Gillespie, with an additional bonus of a fantastic text. I love to give a lecture in my adult jazz classes about the unpardonable sin of taking English nursery rhymes and converting them to jazz instead of using African-American children's games. Everybody nods their head in respectful agreement and then I put this recording on to move to, with Joe Carroll singing snatches of *Humpty Dumpty, Little Jack Horner, Ring Around the Rosy, Little Sally Walker, Go In and Out the Window,* and the title song, *School Days,* all in a 12-bar blues. In jazz, even the unpardonable is permissible if done right! After moving to this music, the lesson might continue into a class based on the above rhymes, games and songs. Unfortunately, this CD has proven difficult to find. I have seen the song included in a few other Dizzy Gillespie recordings. Check with your local store. The length is 3:08.

- *Housed from Edward*: Branford Marsalis: ***Trio Jeepy*** (CD): Columbia CK 44199

I've particularly enjoyed this for the 1-2-3-clap version of daily life motions (this has the section with the "car going out of control"-from about 3:40 to 4:06 into the recording). It's a good tempo and somewhat long (9:27), so be prepared for a long day! Great quality recording and an excellent example of an improvisation beginning simply and building in complexity.

- *Bag's Groove: Gary Burton,* Gary Burton: ***For Hamp, Red, Bags, and Cal*** : *Concord CCD-4941-2*

It's always good for kids playing Orff instruments to hear vibraphonists and Gary Burton is one of our national treasures. Great tempo and foreshadowing of the tune included in chapter 7.

- *Watermelon Man*: Herbie Hancock: ***Takin' Off***: Blue Note 4109

  The rock-gospel feel provides a nice contrast to the swing rhythm of the other jazz pieces while maintaining heavy emphasis on beats 2 and 4. A nice sample of a full jazz quintet.

- *Now's the Time*: Charlie Parker: ***Bird: The Original Recordings of Charlie Parker***: Verve 837 176-2:

  A good example of an easily accessible be-bop blues by the great Charlie Parker. Relatively short (3:07), unusual walking bass solo and good preparation for later ensemble playing.

- *Trio Blues*: Count Basie: ***Jazz Piano: A Smithsonian Collection: V. 1***

  A fantastic live recording, that captures Count Basie's unique style amidst the encouragement of the audience and fellow musicians. (Tell the children the applause on the recording is for their good dancing!) Medium length (4:06) and good moderate tempo, with a few wonderful double-time outbursts by "the Count."

- *Let's Call the Whole Thing Off*: Billie Holiday: ***The Billie Holiday Story*** Columbia-KG 32124

  Another song that children enjoy, sung by someone they have a patriotic duty to know. Slightly on the slow side and fairly short (2:36).

- *Let's Call the Whole Thing Off*: ***The Best of Ella Fitzgerald & Louis Armstrong***: Verve 314-537-909-2

  A good contrast to the above—take time to listen after the movement experience and have the children articulate the differences in feel, tempo, arrangement, etc.

IMPROVISATIONAL MOVEMENT

We can get a feel for the qualities of jazz movement through the jazzwalk, isolations and side-close-side work . Another possibility—and perhaps more interesting from a dancer's point of view—is to discover what natural movement responses arise from the body while listening to a variety of jazz. Rhythmically contrasting styles of music—fast, slow, in the groove, rubato, bossa nova, etc. will evoke a wider range of expression. I like to record excerpts from four to six pieces, with each excerpt lasting from one to two minutes.

Remind students to let all aspects of the music release the movement—not just the beat. The pieces that tend to inspire the most interesting movement are those in which the clichés of jazz dance can't be easily applied. If you find the students bouncing around to Coltrane's *A Love Supreme* with the same quality as James P. Johnson's *Carolina Shout*, review the intent of the exercise! Keep in mind that movement doesn't always have to parallel the music exactly, but can also contrast it—slow movement with fast music, unmetered gesture with metered rhythms, etc. Leave time afterward to discuss what felt right, what worked well and why.

In the context of our jazz study, this is an excellent opportunity to introduce the remarkably diverse repertoire that falls under the label of jazz. These pieces can later be revisited as listening selections (see Chapter 11). As always, the larger the investment, the bigger the return. Making a compilation tape for your class is a labor of love that makes your curriculum more personal and alive. Take the time to draw from your listening repertoire, dancing alone in the privacy of your home to test the movement potential of the pieces. If you don't have an extensive jazz background or jazz recordings collection, *The Smithsonian Collection of Classic Jazz**** is an excellent source for some contrasting pieces. Below are some sample groupings from that collection to get the novice started.

SAMPLE COLLECTIONS FOR MOVEMENT FROM
THE SMITHSONIAN COLLECTION OF CLASSIC JAZZ

HISTORICAL JAZZ STYLES
Early blues: *St. Louis Blues*: Bessie Smith
Ragtime: *The Maple Leaf Rag*: Scott Joplin
Dixieland: *Struttin' with Some Barbecue*: Louis Armstrong and His Hot Five
Swing: *Taxi War Dance*: Count Basie
Be-bop: *Koko*: Charlie Parker
Cool: *Summertime*: Miles Davis with Gil Evans

CONTRASTING RHYTHMS
Slow Tempo: *Blue in Green*: Bill Evans
Fast Tempo: *Shaw 'Nuff*: Dizzy Gillespie
Rubato: *I Should Care*: Thelonious Monk
6/4 meter: *West Coast Blues*: Wes Montgomery
Unmetered: *Alabama*: John Coltrane

TEXTURE
Steppin': World Saxophone Quartet
Enter Evening: Cecil Taylor
Lonely Woman: Ornette Coleman
Diminuendo and Crescendo in Blue: Duke Ellington

---

* You can order this set directly from the Smithsonian Institute.

22. IMPROVISED MOVEMENT: Solo, Mirror, Shadow, Mirror and Shadow

Formation: Students begin spread out throughout the room, each in their own space.

Focus: Movement exploration inspired by diverse musics/ reading other's movements

Activity

- *Individual Improvisation*: Begin with students moving freely to recorded music, moving as the music moves them.

- *Mirroring with partner*: Partners facing each other. First partner moves to music, second immediately copies. Movements must be clear and intelligible, either moving slowly and/or quickly settling into a recognizable pattern.

- At change of music or teacher's signal, partners switch roles.

- Try again without clearly defining the leader.

- *Double-mirror*: Two sets of partners facing as follows: A's mirror A's, B's mirror B's:

$$A$$
$$B \qquad B$$
$$A$$

- *Shadowing*: Group is in a diamond shape, all facing the same direction:

$$4$$
$$2 \qquad 3$$
$$1$$

(in this case, all face 1).

1 moves to the music and all immediately shadow, i.e., copy the movement from behind. The leader should avoid doing arm movements in front of the body that the followers can't see. She can move in place, forward and back and to either side, but the moment she turns, the diamond faces a new direction and a new leader is established at the point of the diamond. Thus, if 1 turns to her right, 2 becomes the new leader. If two turns 180 degrees, 3 becomes the new leader. The goal is to keep the music flowing so that the new leader carries through the energy of the previous one, through continuation or contrast.

- Invite groups to move throughout the whole space, intersecting with other groups while maintaining their diamond shape.

- *Mirror and Shadow*: Form four lines as follows:

```
                A
                A
                A
                A
  B  B  B  B        B  B  B  B
                A
                A
                A
                A
```

A's and B's at the front of each line mirror the person opposite. Those in line shadow leader at front. Leaders choose when they've had enough and go to the back of line. Next people in line become the new leaders.

Comments

These various structures offer yet another opportunity for the untrained dancer to evoke movement from students without having to model specific styles or techniques. The music itself will suggest certain movement qualities and the variety of forms for imitating will both enlarge each student's movement vocabulary and automatically create small choreographies. The first—individual improvisation—is both a warm-up and a chance for the teacher to observe the student's range of expression and ability to respond to contrasting music. The second—mirroring—is intimate, exposed and a great exercise for social as well as kinesthetic reasons. The double mirror lightens the mix and tickles the movement intelligence as one set of partners notices and ultimately seeks contrasting movements to the other set.

Shadow movement presents new possibilities. Now four people are moving in unison and the change of leadership is fluid. Many students report feeling less self-conscious and freer to move with their backs to the group. The combination of mirror and shadow is especially powerful, as the group moves from single improvisation to partners to double partners to groups of four to intersecting groups to the whole group at once. A recording I particularly recommend for this last activity is *Berta* from Branford Marsalis's CD *I Heard You Twice the First Time*.

Truckin'.

JAZZ SOCIAL DANCE

We have used the term "jazz dance" in this chapter, but up to now, have only taken a brief look at qualities of West African dance and how they carried over into an emerging African-American dance style in slavery times. When did the ring plays and quadrilles crossover into a style called jazz dance?

Brief Overview of Jazz Dance

Jazz music and jazz dance came up together. Each new style of music had its accompanying new style of dance—or was it the other way around? By the Ragtime Era around the turn of the century, the plantation tradition of the Cakewalk—a formal dance contest in which the winners won a cake—had evolved to a semi-choreographed prancing strut popular in minstrel shows. The migration to the cities during and after World War I brought the dances from the rural "jook joints" into the city ballrooms. While blacks danced the Shimmy and the Black Bottom to the Dixieland music of the Roaring 20's, the Charleston crossed racial boundaries to become a national craze. By the 30's, the music and the dance had changed yet again. Whites and blacks alike flocked to the Savoy, Alhambra and Renaissance Ballrooms in Harlem to dance to the music of the big bands.

The Lindy Hop was the dance par excellence for Swing band music—smooth, energetic and athletic. Named by George "Shorty" Snowden after Charles Lindbergh's "hop" over the Atlantic, the dance featured "air steps" that must have brought business to the chiropractors—men flipping their female partners over their backs or bringing them under their legs and out the other side, all without missing a beat. This energetic social dance also found its way into some Broadway stage productions and Hollywood movies (the Marx Brothers' *A Day at the Races* perhaps the most famous of them).

Partners Lindy Hopping.

The Swing Era of jazz was the height of the African aesthetic—no boundary between music and dance—transplanted to the urban American culture. The dancers inspired the musicians and the musicians urged on the dancers. As Leon James describes it:

> "Dizzy Gillespie was featured in the brass section of Teddy Hill's screaming band. Every time he played a crazy lick, we cut a crazy step to go with it. And he dug us and blew even crazier stuff to see if we could dance to it, a kind of game, with the musicians and dancers challenging each other." [6]

This intimate connection between music and dance provided a trellis for the music to grow. Yet at the same time that it offered support and direction, it also meant limitation—tempos, length of pieces, degree of improvisation. By the 1940's, the light was pulling the music in another direction. A revolutionary group of New York musicians would finish their big band engagement and go uptown to play in small groups in extended jam sessions well into the morning. Freed from the confines of the big band dance format, they could follow their imaginations and expressive possibilities into new musical territory. While still grounded in the physical rhythmic drive of earlier jazz, phrasing became more obtuse, tempos stretched at both ends of the spectrum and improvisations extended as long as the soloist had something to say. This revolution in jazz, later named be-bop, turned jazz away from the social dance.[*]

Both music and dance come from the same impulse, one channeling the impulse toward motion aurally, and the other visually and kinesthetically. The be-bop musicians internalized the dance rhythms, bringing them from an overt, extroverted form to a subtle, introverted one. The *internal* union of dance and music was kept intact, if not strengthened, by increased complexity of rhythm, melody and form. Be-bop was to jazz dance what Bach was to court dances, retaining the form and feeding the energy of the dance to the intricacies of musical variation. The elaborate variations that Charlie Parker wove within the fabric of the blues and jazz standards were parallel to the complexities of Bach's Courantes and Gigues.

Though the move towards the more abstract and intellectual expression required in negotiating melodic variations within harmonic structures tipped jazz further to the European side of the mix, this internalization of the dance maintained in be-bop kept one foot firmly planted in African soil. Referring to the African-American way of singing, Bess Lomax Hawes points out:

> "All singing was accompanied by swaying, weight shifts, and hand, head, and body movements of greater or less degree, all suggesting a dance that was not yet quite visible. Their 'real 'dances seemed, then, simply broader, more explicit statements of the dances they were already doing while they 'stood still' to sing." [7]

Once be-bop cut the umbilical chord, it was never re-tied again. Jazz music and dance went their separate ways, the former into the small nightclubs and concert halls, the latter, onto the dance concert stage and the theater. The need for social dance moved back to the street with its new musical patrons—Rhythm and Blues and Rock and Roll, later Motown and Disco, still later Funk and Hip-hop. Many dances continued—and continue—to originate in the black community and quickly spread to American youth

---

[*] Another point of view is that be-bop suggested a new kind of dance that the public wasn't ready for. In one of his famous quick-witted repartees, Dizzy Gillespie responded to an audience member who complained that you couldn't dance to bebop, "Maybe *you* can't dance to it."

everywhere. From the Jitterbug of the '50's to the Twist of the '60's to the Hustle of the '70's to the Electric Slide and Break Dancing of the '80's to the Hip-hop of the '90's, the African love for dance has become an indelible part of American culture.

Yet, for better or for worse, they are no longer "jazz dances." We may find a remnant of this term in classes advertised as "jazz dance," but the words are ambiguous at best. Such a class may mean the old social dances or Broadway routines or African-American modern dance or glorified disco aerobics, none of it necessarily danced to jazz music. One of the few places left where people try to express the beauty of diverse jazz styles in movement may very well be the music classroom!

Doug doing the Sugarfoot with fourth graders.

Social Dance in the Classroom

Though Swing Dance has skyrocketed in popularity recently, it is rare to find people conversant with the original Lindy Hop steps or music. Orff colleague and teacher Susan Kennedy was fortunate to study with Nontsizi Cayou at San Francisco State University, who in turn had learned some basic Lindy Hop steps from Pepsi Bethel, one of the early professional Lindy Hoppers. Susan has been a favorite guest teacher in my summer jazz course, leading us through the colorful dance moves of the Lindy Hop with their equally colorful names—*Messin' Around, Truckin', Peckin', Runnin', The Shorty George, The Suzy Q.* After learning some steps, half plays live music while the other half dances—and then, in true Orff fashion, the two groups switch.

Sadly, these dances cannot be taught through the medium of print—and hence, no detailed descriptions for the beginner are given here. For those who have some experience, these drawings may be useful reminders. For those intrigued, research the living archives of your community for a potential Lindy Hop guest teacher and invite them in. Search for workshops on the Internet (but before signing up, ask what kind of music the teacher will be using). Watch the old films on video. Or simply put on some Lester Young and let the music move you. However you do it, you're in for a treat.

SUMMARY: Music, Motion and E-motion

"Out of movement, music, Out of music, movement."

—Dorothee Gunther [8]

Children learn with their bodies. They learn by touching and being held, by moving and watching others move. *All* of their learning—from math to social skills—is built on this foundation, but touch and movement are especially central to *musical* learning. Carl Orff's visionary work suggests that movement leads us directly to music—and conversely, music releases our need to move. Which comes first? Centuries before Orff probed the chicken-egg conundrum, West African culture already understood that music and dance are the warp and weft of a cloth woven in the womb.

> "For people of my tribe, with its rich musical context, exposure to music begins in the womb, when pregnant mothers join in the community dances. From inside the womb, out babies feel the vibrations of the rhythms enter their bodies. Infants are then wrapped onto their mothers' backs with a cloth and taken into the dancing circle with everyone else." [9]
>
> —Yaya Diallo

Note how the above speaker moves seamlessly between the words music, dance and rhythm. In his tradition, the threads of music and dance are not picked apart, but felt as the whole cloth, the same one that ties the infant to the mother's back for its post-natal education. From the back to the ground, the education continues as children help work in the home and the fields, gather at the community dancing rings, massage the legs of an elder storyteller at night. By the time formal learning begins for some at the ripe old age of five or six—specific dance steps or drum rhythms—the child is already brimming over with rhythmic vitality, expressed outwardly in the dance and inwardly in the music.

These are vital lessons for the European-trained mind. So-called "natural rhythm" is not the legacy of a racial stereotype, but the understanding that it is our nature to move, sing and dance and it is natural to move, sing and dance with our children, in the womb and out of it. We in the Western world are finally beginning to understand how important the body's role is in the unfolding of our full intelligence.[10] What neuroscientists are discovering in the research lab and speak about in terms of neural connections, Africans and African-Americans have been trying to tell us in a different language: not only the connection between the body and the intellect, but the direct route between the hand and the heart.

In his article *Music-making Children of Africa,* John Miller Chernoff writes:

> "In describing the act of beating (the drum) alone, Dagombas say that it is the heart that talks and the arm that does what the heart wants; only a child with a 'bright heart' can gain wisdom." [11]

Gospel singer Thomas A. Dorsey says: *"Black music calls for movement. It calls for feeling. Don't let it get away."* [12] and stitches together "movement" and "feeling" without a moment's pause.

The body *knows*, the body *feels,* the body *moves,* and where there is rhythmic movement in the body, we are but a beat away from being moved in the heart. When children touch and are touched, they may *be* touched later by the beauty of a thing learned. When they move, they may *be* moved later by the power of an experience or an idea.

Connecting the hand beating with the heart talking and the mind's wisdom, a new vision of education is revealed, one built on the rhythmic foundation of the body. Cognitive science tells us *why* with the language of intellect while West Africans and their African-American descendants show us *how* —*"Put your hands on yo' hips and let yo' backbone slip!"*

Endnotes

1. Hanna, Judith Lynne: *African Dance as Education*: *IMPULSE: The Journal of Contemporary Dance*: Impulse Publications

2. Malone, Jacqui: *Steppin' on the Blues*: Univ. of Illinois Press, p. 11

3. Ibid. p. 18

4. Ibid. p. 20

5. Jones, Bessie & Hawes, Bess Lomax: *Step It Down*: Univ. of Georgia; p. 124

6. Stearns, Marshall: *Jazz Dance*

7. *Step It Down*

8. Orff, Carl: *The Schulwerk*: Schott

9. Diallo, Yaya and Hall, Mitchell: *The Healing Drum: African Wisdom Teachings*: Rochester, VT: Destiny Books

10. Recent books discussing the body/heart/ brain connection include Damasio's *Descarte's Error*, Berman's *Coming to our Senses*:, Goleman's *Emotional Intelligence*, Pearce's *Evolutions End*: Gardner's *Frames of Mind*

11. Chernoff, John Miller: *Music Making Children of Africa*: Orff Echo Vol. XXI/Spring 1989

12. *Steppin' on the Blues*

Bibliography

Jazz Dance: *the Story of American Vernacular Dance*: Marshall and Jean Stearns: Macmillan Publishing Company

Black Dance: From 1619 to Today: Lynne Fauley Emery: Dance Horizons Book, Princeton Book Company; 1972

Steppin' on the Blues: The Visible Rhythms of African American Dance: Jacqui Malone: Univ of Illinois Press,

Discography

See "Recommended Recordings" in this chapter

Videography

DANCING: New Worlds New Forms; Program Five—Produced by Thirteen/WNET in association with RM arts and BBC-TV, 1993 (for an example of *Juba*)

A Day at the Races—Marx Brothers

Stormy Weather (scene with The Nicholas Brothers)

Lindy Hop with Frankie Manning (Beginning, Intermediate, Advanced)

The Spirit Moves, Part I: Jazz Dance, 1900–1950

Both of the above are available through the Website www.swingdanceshop.com

The San Francisco School Orff Ensemble practicing.

CHAPTER 5: BEGINNING
ENSEMBLE PIECES

We've been pattin' Juba, scattin' "doo-wah," movin' our feet, groovin' with the beat, playin' the games and sayin' the names. The jazz self is waking up, though it will be two more chapters until it earns its proper title. Now is the time to bring out what we can move, sing, feel and hear to the instruments. But if the instrument is a trumpet, saxophone or stand-up bass, there will be a painful gap between being able to sing a phrase and play it with good tone on the instrument. There will need to be dedicated practice and at least a year of putting up with an out of tune ensemble. There will be young children with small fingers who may have to wait. What can we offer in the way of an instrumental ensemble to the children who have been clapping, dancing, speaking and singing and are ready for the next step?

Here is where the genius of the Orff approach comes to the rescue—using the specially designed Orff instruments, simple techniques, simple scales, basic jazz rhythms, familiar songs and games and structures for improvisation, we can create a second grade jazz band! The children can play ensemble pieces that are both pleasing in themselves and a step towards the jazz repertoire.

Orff Schulwerk recognizes that the child comes to us filled with music—our task is to draw it out (the Latin root of the word education is *educare*, to lead forth, to draw out). The material offered thus far invites children to bring out their innate musicality in the ways that suit them best, playing their way into understanding. But this process of education never occurs in a void. Just as a growing vine needs a trellis to twine around and a young tree needs a stake to anchor it, so does the child equally need *instruction*— a built-in structure to wrap her creative potential around. Orff pedagogy is more than fun and games—it is also serious work.[*] It offers clear sequential guidelines for developing musical concepts so that musical hearing, skill and understanding grow together each step of the way. The keyboard-like Orff instruments are ideal vehicles to begin grappling with the melodic and harmonic theory that is needed to progress.

---

[*] Miles Davis once said, "People act like I was born with a golden horn in my mouth. Man, I had to *study*!"

The "pre-jazz" orchestrations offered here serve as midwives between the mother folk culture and the subsequent jazz offspring. Though they are scored for Orff instruments, they are readily adaptable to a variety of instrumental ensembles—concert bands, string groups, keyboard labs, and guitar classes. The particular keys chosen are directly related to the demands of the Orff instrumentarium and may need to be transposed to meet the needs of other ensembles.

Beginning Melodic Theory—The Pentatonic Scale

The pieces in this chapter are all based on the pentatonic scale. Coming from a traditional Western musical training where the major scale is the center of the melodic universe, the pentatonic scale seems exotic and mysterious. It is in fact the most universal of scales, found in all its modal variants and tunings throughout Asia, Africa, South America and parts of Europe, North America and Australia. Though technically penta (five) -tonic (tone) means any five-toned scale, the most common example, and the one referred to throughout this book, is do, re, mi, sol, la, (do). In the key of C, it looks like this:

Do   Re   Mi   Sol   La   (Do)

Looking down from our Euro-centric standpoint, we might say this is a scaled-down major scale, a gap-toothed version missing the 4th and 7th (fa and ti). Seen from another viewpoint, the pentatonic scale *precedes* the major scale, both historically and pedagogically. Why is the pentatonic scale (with variations in tuning) so universal? Why is it used so extensively in Orff and other programs* in the melodic training of young children?

The child's answer is simply that the notes "sound good together" when they improvise. The music theorist might talk about the lack of half-steps and absence of leading tones. The philosopher might discuss the pentatonic as an unconscious sounding of the first five tones (with one maddening exception) of the harmonic series.** Whatever reason you choose, the fact remains that the pentatonic is an ideal tried-and-true vehicle for early (and middle and late!) musical exploration. We will soon see why it is also the scale of choice in any beginning jazz study.

A typical Orff practice is to take a familiar rhyme—say *Pease Porridge Hot*—and orchestrate it for Orff instruments. The first melodies tend to begin with the falling minor third so ubiquitous in children's culture, eventually using (as in this example below) all five tones. They are accompanied by the drone—the open fifth interval that grounds the piece harmonically and adds both color and stability. For the three years—generally first through third grade—that the children play in the pentatonic scale in ensemble, the drone remains the harmonic ground, allowing them to improvise melodically free from concern with changing chords. Rhythmic ostinato ("ostinato" means a short repeated pattern), melodic ostinato and color parts (here played in the wood block, alto xylophone and glockenspiel respectively) are other devices of elemental orchestration that add texture, color and interest. After children sing the melody twice, they may play the melody on a soprano xylophone or take turns improvising over the accompanying parts in the pentatonic scale.

---

* The Kodaly approach also recognizes the importance of pentatonic.

** See Chapter 19 in my book *Play, Sing & Dance* for a more detailed explanation.

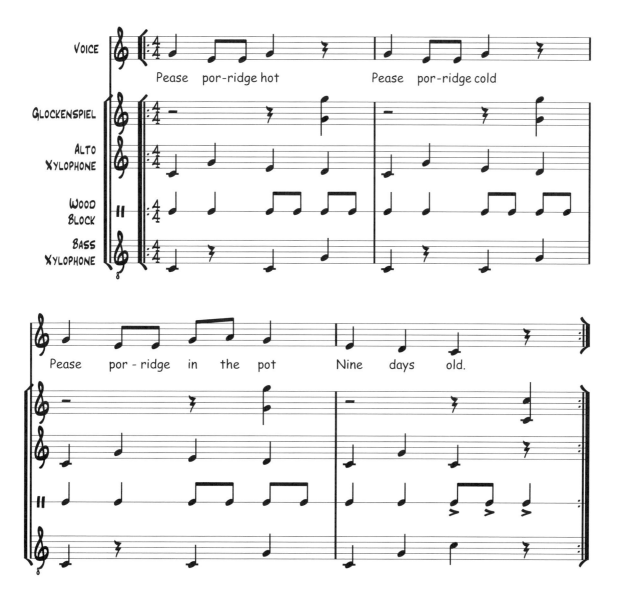

The above is a playable first grade arrangement that gives the children a foundation in elemental melody, phrasing, drone harmony and texture. Since they will continue to play children's games, learn folk dances, explore movement, sing songs (in all kinds of scales) and begin learning simple notation, the instrumental ensemble will be just one strand in the multi-colored cloth they are beginning to weave. By the end of first grade, they may have learned—and helped orchestrate—three or four rhymes like this.

When they enter second grade, they naturally need to review familiar concepts and then learn new arrangements at a higher degree of complexity. But they also will learn something new about the familiar pentatonic scale—that if we chose another note besides C as the home note and reinforce it with a drone on that note, the whole character of the piece changes. Asked to make a new melody with A as the home tone, the children might play something like this:

This new arrangement of tones is a mode of the C pentatonic scale which is rather clumsily named the "la pentatonic mode," referring to the solfege syllable that is its starting note. *This mode will prove to be essential in our beginning jazz work.*

In third grade, transposition is the new concept introduced. Whereas finding the modes of the C pentatonic scale requires keeping the same five notes but changing which is the most important one, transposition means shifting all five higher or lower. Thus, if F is "do," the F pentatonic scale is as follows:

These two concepts placed next to each other can be confusing and that is why we don't introduce them in the same year. But an analogy that I have found helpful is pick five children and line them up as follows:

Andrew   *Juliette*   *Micah*   *Zaina* *Lee*

Imagine it's a hot day and everyone's thirsty and Andrew is the only one who remembered to bring a water bottle. That makes him the most important person—the "do" in the major pentatonic scale. But the next day, Andrew forgets his bottle and Lee remembers hers.

Andrew   Juliette   Micah   Zaina <u>Lee</u>

Now she's the center of attention—we're in the "la" mode. If it was Juliette, it would be "re" mode. Those are the modes.

But now let's say we're back in "do"—Andrew has the water—and the whole group decides to move into the next room where it's cooler. Their relationship stays intact, but the room is different. That's transposition. If Lee has the water when they move to the next room, that's both a modal shift and transposition.

Coming back to the world of notes, the three common pentatonic scales and their *la* mode variants used on the Orff instruments are as follows:

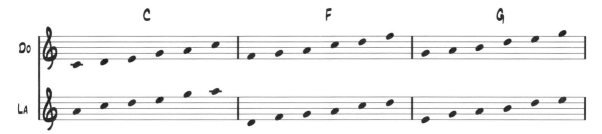

This outline not only introduces the basic theory behind Orff orchestration, but will form the basis of the "pre-jazz" and jazz orchestrations to follow. Those without Orff training may be enticed to investigate this further,* while those with it may be delighted to discover that our jazz study will proceed from familiar ground.

This beginning jazz work is entirely compatible with the Orff pedagogical sequence, but with a few changes in emphasis and vocabulary. To aid the reader, the following is a handy chart that helps us move from one to another.

Orff → Jazz Conversion Chart

Classic Orff Schulwerk		Beginning Jazz
English Rhyme	*changes to*	African-American Game
Beat	*changes to*	Offbeat
Strong beat accents	*change to*	Syncopation
Straight rhythm	*changes to*	Swing rhythm
Rhythmic ostinato	*changes to*	Groove (same principle, different name)
Melodic ostinato	*changes to*	Riff (same principle, different name)
Do pentatonic	*changes to*	La pentatonic (later, Blues Scale)
Drone	*changes to*	Vamp (same principle, different notes)
Triads	*change to*	Tritones

Intrigued? Let's get into the arrangements themselves and see if we can come out the other side with a clearer understanding of how to lead children—or any beginners—into the joys of the jazz ensemble.

---

* The brief summary above takes years of work with children to thoroughly understand, as well as three Levels of Orff training. See information for Orff Training listed at the end of the book.

23. TAA, TAA, YEE

Ghanaian Lullaby

Pronunciation: Taa = tah, Tee = tay, Yee = yay

Focus: African roots of polyrhythm, offbeat, syncopation, pentatonic scale

Activity:

• Teach song echo fashion.

• Practice playing the accompanying rhythms as follows:

• Practice each of the above while singing the song.

- Form three groups, each playing one of the rhythms above for 16 measures. Sing the song twice while continuing to play, then switch parts. Continue as above.

- Transfer all rhythms to appropriate instruments, following the form above.

Variations

- Dancers put imaginary baby on their back and "carry" the baby bent over while dancing.

- Have children bring in dolls, strap them to their backs and dance and sing.

Comments

This and the following song from West Africa show some of the theoretical connections between African and African-American music mentioned in Chapters One and Two.

The African propensity for the offbeat is clear in the first bell part, the inherent feeling for cross-rhythms and syncopation in the second, and the tendency to end a phrase on an upbeat (a primary device in be-bop) in the "wu-sio" of the text. Like *Soup, Soup*, the melodic range is small—in this case, a four note melody with heavy emphasis on three notes of the *la* pentatonic scale they we will use extensively in the material to come.

This piece, from *Orff-Schulwerk in the African Tradition* [1], is a lullaby with a markedly different character than the flowing quiet rhythms of European lullabies. Steady rhythm can be both stimulating and calming, and the baby strapped to the mother's back can be sung and danced to sleep while the mother goes about with her work. Putting the imaginary baby or the baby doll on one's back and bending down to keep it from falling off is a good way to learn how to "get down" when we dance.

Note that the teaching sequence uses two vital principles of Orff process:

- Begin in the body before moving to the instruments.

- Teach all the parts to everyone before dividing into sections.

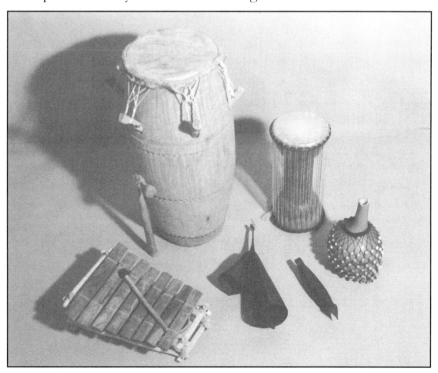

Traditional African instruments.

FUNGA ALAFIA

WEST AFRICA
ARRANGED BY DOUG GOODKIN

– = closed

o = open

24. FUNGA ALAFIA

Formation: Circle with a small circle of percussion instruments in the center (three congas, cowbell, agogo bell, axatse or shaker-see arrangement).

Focus: African polyrhythms, call and response, pentatonic scale

Activity

- Silently teach gestures: Touch head, gesture to the group with both hands outstretched, palms up. Touch lips, gesture to group, touch heart, gesture to group, right hand strokes raised left forearm up and down, left hand strokes right forearm. Each of the preceding gestures lasts for two beats.

- Students echo "a-shay a-shay," one time with voice inflected up, the second time, down.

- Echo again singing both phrases.

- Teacher calls "Funga Alafia," students respond with above phrases.

- Switch. (students call-teacher responds). Half-group calls, other half responds.

- All sing whole song twice through, followed by the gestures twice through (keep song "singing" silently).

- Continue above form, with harmony parts.

- During the gestures, teacher speaks meaning:

    "With my thoughts, I greet you. With my words, I greet you.
    With my heart, I greet you. I have nothing up my sleeve."

- Without losing the flow, teacher teaches body percussion parts (see below) while stepping the beat in place. Students imitate each. Once they seem comfortable, all sing the song twice with the body percussion part and then move on to the next rhythm.

- When all rhythms have been practiced, all return to the first one and teacher silently gestures to one group to begin the second rhythm while all continue the first. Continue in this way until all six rhythms have been played. Sing the song twice more with all the rhythms.

- Teacher returns to each group and has them vocalize their rhythms approximating the sounds (Bell part could be: "Gank gank gank gank gank," a drum part could be: "doom doom doom chak" etc.).

- All continue playing and vocalizing rhythms while teacher plays each part on instruments one at a time and invites one person from each group to come in the center and play.

- Remaining people sing twice with gesture and dance for the length of twice through (Clap-step right-close left foot to right clap/ clap-step-step-clap/clap etc.)

- Leader changes motions teach time on the steps; can also proceed around the circle with each person leading the motion.

- Dancers move towards center and massage musicians for two beats after the claps.

- Leader gestures all to stop after second "Funga Alafia"—sing final "a-shay, a-shay" rubato with leader's direction, with final drum rolls on instruments and massages.

- The entire sequence above should be performed without stopping and without any verbal explanations.

FORM

- Teach the instrumental parts separately from the above sequence. When students are comfortable with both versions, choose how to combine them.

Comments: The Process

The process outlined above is an Orff-Schulwerk tour-de-force, demonstrating in vivid detail everything unique and wonderful about this marvelous practice. Some of its key features include:

- Teaching music by *making* music—no verbal instructions necessary.

- Teaching *musically* by keeping an uninterrupted musical flow so that the teaching of the piece is as musical as the piece itself. A good piece of music has an enticing beginning, connected middle and satisfying conclusion—this process follows that contour.

- Build the piece *one step at a time*, from simple to complex.

- Teach all parts to *everyone* before dividing into parts.

- All rhythms taught in *relation* to other musical elements—below from rhythmic *ostinato* to *beat* in feet, above from ostinato to *melodic rhythm* of sung song, side to side in relation to other *ostinati*. This ensures a deep understanding of each rhythm and its function.

- All rhythms taught first in the *body*, with body percussion mirroring the instrumental *technique*, and in the *voice*, with vocal percussion imitating the *sound* of the instruments.

  When a student comes in the middle to play a part, he or she has been thoroughly prepared, knowing the relationship of the rhythm to all surrounding rhythms, the basic technique and the basic sound to get from the instrument.

- *Play, Sing and Dance.* All participants have sung the song, played the parts on their body and now dance while the instrumentalists accompany them.

- From *imitation* to *creation*. Different people get to invent new dance motions that others copy. Sometimes drummers begin to improvise during the percussion solos.

- Social contact is made not only by playing, singing and dancing together, but by physical contact as well through massage.

The purpose of good education is not mere information, but transformation. Ask the students if they feel better at the end of this experience than they did at the beginning. If the answer is yes, they have been transformed for the moment by the energy, spirit and comradery of both the music and the way of learning it. They have been welcomed into the music class. Some parts may have been difficult (it is hard for most to sing the song while playing the percussion parts) and that will offer a welcome challenge for future attempts to learn all parts of the song. But because the teacher never stopped to correct, laughing with the students when they hit the hard spots, everyone relaxed and kept trying. They know this is a place where social contact matters, where their contribution matters (making up a new motion), where they can make mistakes and laugh—in short, a place where they feel welcome to participate.

How fitting that the song itself is a welcome song. How strange would it be to learn a welcoming song through a non-welcoming process, a joyful song through a boring process, a song with a dubious message through a joyful process. And yet such things happen all the time in school music classes and beyond. Here content and process are wedded together.

Historical background

I first learned this song in an Orff workshop and was delighted to find yet another song to add to my repertoire of welcome songs. No one knew much about its origins and when I finally went to Ghana in 1999, I heard it performed in a concert. The musicians were equally unsure about where it came from, though one suggested that it might be a Hausa song. The Hausa are traveling merchants, mostly from neighboring Nigeria, and since it is clear is that this song had traveled a great deal, this seems a logical explanation.

One student at a workshop once told me that "Alafia" is a greeting of the Hausa people. "Ashay" suggests another connection with Nigeria—a Yoruban word some have translated as "good health," but others insist has a deeper meaning of "spiritual power and force." When I was in Brazil, I heard many people say "Ashay" as an affirmation at a capoeria demonstration and with the connection between West African Yoruban culture and Brazilian candomble religious practices, this potent word is now used on both continents.

The song is a perfect one to teach in a workshop setting because it is much simpler and easier to sing than many similar ones in either Brazil or West Africa. But it turns out that its ease and familiarity is not only because it is a simple melody. One time while singing it, its vague familiarity suddenly became clear-it is almost the same melody as the chorus to the American Folk song, *Liza Jane!*

Oh E - li - za Li'l Li - za Jane, Oh E - li - za, Li'l Li - za Jane.

Had it traveled all the way to the states or was this merely coincidence? I began to look for information about *Liza Jane* and found it equally baffling—most sources simply say "traditional" while one book attributes the song to someone named Countess Ada de Lachau! As a listening exercise, compare the arrangement of *Funga Alafia* recorded on the CD *Poetry, Prose, Percussion and Song* (see Chapter Four) with two other versions of *Liza Jane* recorded by Nina Simone and Linda Tillery respectively (see discography at end of chapter).

Once again, not only is the process welcoming, the melody accessible and the words reinforcing the sense of greeting, but the gestures are as well. The greeting is made yet more powerful by it coming from our thoughts, from our speaking them out loud, from our speaking them from the heart and from our assurance that we have nothing up our sleeve. The latter will need an explanation for the children, a saying that means there is no hidden weapon, that we have no tricks and come in peace. These days, so many people greet each other with an agenda-buy my product, vote for my candidate, convert to my religion-that it is refreshing to encounter a greeting that generously offers the hope to know us and see us and enjoy us, no strings attached.

Musically speaking, the pentatonic scale familiar to the children playing Pease Porridge Hot over drones and ostinati is now given an African character with its syncopated melody, drone and ostinati. (Note that the harmony takes us out of the pentatonic and a mixolydian mode is used in the solo.) The pentatonic scale is quite common in Ghana, as evidenced by the pentatonic xylophone tradition. However, it is by no means the most important scale and it is common practice to harmonize even pentatonic melodies.

Note that the syncopation in the accompanying rhythms and emphasis on the offbeat reveals some of the African roots of jazz rhythm. Note also that by damping the lower bell of the agogo, the offbeat accents on the higher bell mirror the bell part of the previous piece Taa Taa Yee, but are easier to play for the beginning musician. This is a good example of how we can adapt and simplify for more immediate success without sacrificing the integrity of a rhythm.

Finally, teachers are not expected to duplicate the entire process I outlined above—it took me at least 20 years of teaching to be able to do that! Simplify and adapt according to the age of the children and their experience. Teach just one or two of the supporting parts instead of six. Teach just the song to the little ones and have them dance after singing while you play the drums. (And when you teach it to the small ones, don't be surprised if their parents ask you: "What is that song about mushrooms? My child goes around all day singing 'Fungus I love ya!'")

25. SOUP, SOUP (Instrumental arrangement)

Formation: Students are seated at the Orff instruments set up in C pentatonic scale
Focus: *La* pentatonic; instrumental improvisation; hi-hat

Activity

• Find the note they sang (A) on their instrument and play the response. If there are not enough instruments for every child, have the remaining children help sing the call and/or clap on the offbeat, switching roles as time allows.

• Find the note below A (G) and play this response:

• Find the note above (C) and play the same rhythm:

• Choose which they prefer. Inevitably, both will be chosen. Impress the children with your democratic problem-solving skills and suggest alternating:

Review the song with this changing response.

• Sing each phrase of the call ("Way down yonder," etc.) and echo the rhythm on their instrument. (They may choose the pitches—best to limit them to A, C, D).

- Divide into two groups, bass instruments playing the response and alto/soprano instruments improvising for 4 beats on just three notes:

- As above, with E, G, A:

- With all five (A as center):

- Select soloists to improvise the call, four phrases each.

- Create form: (ex.: Sing once, soloists play, sing, and play.)

Variations

- Reverse above, with improvisation in the *response* rather than the call.

- One group improvises in the call, another in the response.

- Select soloists as above. Include recorder, voice and/or other instruments.

Comments

By taking something we've already played as a game and transferring it to instruments, we experience both the comfort of the known and the challenge of the new. The clapped offbeat is now played on the tambourine, the sung song is now played on the xylophones and the game's movement improvisation is now a melodic improvisation. This kind of teaching is, of course, not limited to our jazz study, but it is a universal principle of good, solid teaching: **Move from the known to the unknown.** That's what good jazz soloists do when they improvise on a theme and what good teachers do when they introduce a new idea, activity or piece: by referring to an old one.

This in turn reveals the enormous task of the *spiral curriculum*—organizing the vast world of vital information by breaking it down into its component parts—necessary skills, key concepts, crucial material—ordering those parts into a coherent sequence and building them back up again to an experience of the whole. We need a practice that gives us enough repetition to internalize the skills and concepts and enough variation to keep it interesting and move us up the spiral of learning. That variation takes the following fundamental forms:

- Revisit in a different piece (perform offbeat clap in *Head and Shoulders* and *Johnny Brown).*

- Transfer to a different medium (move the offbeat clap to the tambourine, as in our instrumental version of *Soup, Soup*, transfer our vocal improvisation in scat singing to instruments, etc.).

- Increase the complexity (jazzwalk to music at faster tempos).

As beginning teachers, we may be content merely to hold the student's attention and teach a few good pieces, but as we gain experience, we learn to weave a giant tapestry, storing each experience in a wide-angle memory that can track each strand and know when and where to re-introduce it. Though artistic inspiration doesn't usually travel down neat sequenced pathways, the *teaching* of an art form finds such structure valuable. Few may choose to follow the exact sequence outlined in this book, but it is worth noting that there *is* a sequence, one in which *every new concept and skill introduced in a piece is reapplied in subsequent pieces.* In this way, we build our expertise, getting both the necessary practice to master the material and the crucial variations that move it up the spiral.

In the arrangements that follow, each one reinforces key concepts from the previous piece while introducing the next important concept. If taught in the given order, the children will build from a solid base of skill development and knowledge and gain a deeper understanding of what they're playing. This repertoire sits at the heart of the beginning jazz curriculum, summarizing and integrating the experiences in games, speech, vocal work, body percussion and movement that precede them and preparing the blues pieces, jazz standards and original compositions that follow. It is aimed towards the third through fifth grade curriculum, though it is relevant to *any* age of beginning jazz study.

The sequence given here to develop the improvisation is quite detailed. We begin by echoing the rhythms of the text but creating new little melodies. This helps to build a rhythmic vocabulary and provide a storehouse of ideas from which to draw when improvising. (Higher up the spiral, the same process takes place learning be-bop riffs.) Limiting the improvisation to the three notes both helps to focus it and reinforces the small range characteristic of the song and style itself. The simultaneous group exploration gives the children the group protection that allows them to experiment unselfconsciously. Yet, what group improvisation adds in "protection," it loses in clarity—hence, we later pare it down to duets or solos.

BOOM CHICK-A BOOM

Improvising Scale

26. BOOM CHICK-A BOOM

Formation: Circle of instruments with space between each

Focus: beginning jazz drumming/ beginning jazz arrangement on Orff instruments

Activity

• Review text of "Boom Chick a Boom."

• Repeat third phrase "I said a boom chick a rock a chick a rock a chick a boom" while snapping on offbeat. Ask students what they notice about the relationship between the text and the snap (all snaps coincide with the word "chick" and "said").

• As above, rocking left foot while reciting (foot rocks down on "chick").

• Invite one volunteer to play the above on the hi-hat.

• Test whether he/she can come in correctly after counting in "One, two, a-one two three." (Secret is to say phrase silently and come in on first "chick.")

• With hi-hat continuing, all say and play with one finger tapping the palm of the other hand "Chick a boom, chick a boom." One person plays on ride cymbal.

• Hi-hat and ride continue while all say and play with right foot and clap.

Clap:	chick	chick
Right Foot:	"Boom -boom *	Boom -boom *

• One person plays on bass drum (right foot) and snare drum (clap).

• All three above continue while group plays on knees with alternating hands "Uh-huh."

• "Oh, yeah" in the rest of the bass/snare part. One person plays on the edge of the conga (open sound). The full effect is as follows:

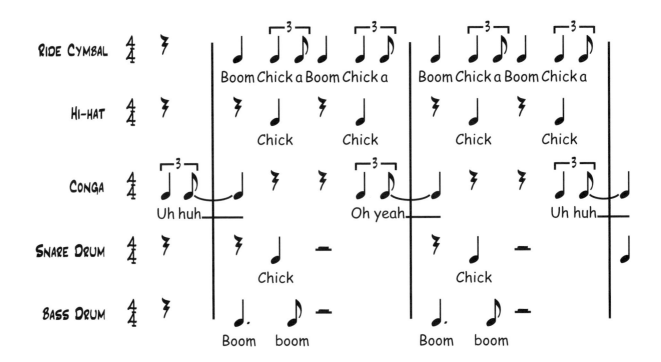

- With all parts continuing above, sing each succeeding part in the instrumental arrangement and invite those who look ready to play on the instrument.

- Using notes in improvising scale given, one person on soprano xylophone improvises a phrase following the text with another on soprano metallophone echoing. Be sure they follow the phrasing: Medium (4 beat) / Medium / Long (8 beat)/ Four short (2 beats each)

- After once through, soprano becomes leader.

- Invite others in the group to fill in the spaces between the instruments. Their job is to study the person to their right and prepare themselves to play. When the leader says "Switch!" all move one space to the right. Those who watched will now play, those who played will now study (or help the person to the left—see Comments). Continue around the circle until time is up or all instruments have been played.

- If the group is large and there are still people left who are not playing or watching, have them perform *Boom Chick a Boom* as a partner clap. At the end of the whole activity or in the next class, switch with the people who got to play.

Comments

There is a lot going on in this activity, all of it worthy of deeper reflection. To begin with, this rhyme seems tailor-made to teach beginning jazz drumming. We have clapped the offbeat in our games and snapped it in our earlier version of this rhyme—now we take something known and try it a different way by putting it in our left foot. Here the rhyme not only helps us understand when to come in and where the offbeat is in the text, but the sound of the "chicks" is precisely the sound we're aiming for on the hi-hat. Technique, relationship to text, sound (like our percussion parts in *Funga Alafia*), all prepare the student to play in a more natural and profound way than simply counting 1 *2* 3 *4* . It is fitting to start our drum set study with the hi-hat, the one instrument of the drum set every music teacher should own if they can't afford the whole set. Remember to insist that the students use their *left* foot and suggest the rocking motion to damp the cymbal so it gets a dry "chick" sound.

Next in order is the ride cymbal and again, language helps us feel the swing rhythm. The "chicks" in "chick a boom" have to line up with the "chicks" of the hi-hat part, again, easily clarifying this important relationship. The bass drum and snare come next and here it becomes clear why the left foot is important to use for the hi-hat—now it's the right foot for the bass drum. Note the resulting "Soup Soup" rhythm in the bass drum. Finally, the conga complements the bass/snare part, filling in the space with what is the most rhythmically subtle of the parts. Keep the player speaking "uh-huh" and it should line up more easily. Keep in mind that you might choose to do a class just with these parts of the drum set and save the instrumental parts until later.

Teachers in my jazz class are often surprised by this simple, effective idea—*split up the drum set into three or four parts*! Don't start with one person playing the whole set, but with four people. When I do this activity in my workshops, I always ask for someone who has never played the drums to come up first. They are so excited to realize that they can do it! If they falter or get off, I always bring them back to the text and that seems to help get them back on track. In general, the whole mystique of feeling the offbeat and knowing when to come in is diffused by all the preparations we have made in the games now made conscious.

Though the drum set is the initial focus of the lesson, students are also introduced to the bass vamp, melodic ostinati, color parts and improvising scale and structure that will continue throughout the next pieces. The improvisation is particularly challenging, as students often lose touch with the form of the phrasing. Another way to do that is have each sing a phrase and then try to play what was sung, or vice-versa.

There is another notable feature of this lesson and that is the form of putting instruments in a circle with students between each one. This accomplishes much at once:

1) It solves the problem of classes that don't have enough instruments for every student. If the student-instrument ratio is one to three, there can also be two students between each instrument.

2) It reinforces our notion that we should teach all parts to everyone and gives everyone a chance to experience the piece from markedly different angles.

3) It puts the responsibility on the *student* to prepare for playing by watching closely and figuring out the part *before* getting on the instrument.

4) Most importantly, the very structure of the lesson encourages children to *help each other.* Please take note—I never suggest to students that they help each other out, but just watch what happens when a student arrives at an instrument and can't get the part right away. 9 times out of 10, the student who has just played generously turns back and offers help, even at the risk of missing his or her own preparation for the next part.

That last point cannot be emphasized enough. I believe that we all have the impulse to help, *without expectation of punishment or reward.* Helping is its own pleasure—by helping, we feel needed and useful and happy to lend a hand. It also feels good to be helped, especially when help comes from a generous, spontaneous gesture. In the music class, we're all happier when the music works and sounds good and students helping each other helps the music sound good. These are all *intrinsic* motivations set up by the very nature of the exercise.

Why don't we always help? My belief is that just as this structure implicitly suggests that we help each other, other structures explicitly suggest that we don't. For example, if I was grading kids on the curve about their performance and their grade was essential to some future reward (getting into a "good" school, pleasing their parents, boosting their self-esteem, etc.), I imagine many kids would not be motivated to help. They might think, "The worse my neighbor plays, the better my grade." And they would be right. Don't we do this all the time to children? And then we wonder why they don't grow up with a habit of helping.

One of the deep contributions of Orff Schulwerk is the way in which it purposefully sets up structures to bring out the best in us—our musical best and our humanistic best. *Boom Chick a Boom* has proved to be a fabulous way to awaken children's jazz potential, but, as many teachers have reported, the model given here goes much further and helps us all reflect on how powerfully the way we do things can influence who we might become.

THE BLACKBIRD'S PARTY

Words by Ashley Bryan
Music by Doug Goodkin

Birds like to party. I party too. But not the way those blackbirds do.

Why all the fuss? They party like us.

2. Oh, blackbirds flap, They strut and peck, Right claw forward, Left claw back.
   How many in all, Having a ball?
3. Ten in the pool, Six on the grass, Cawing so cool, Like a birdland jazz.
   School of fish, Pool as a dish.
4. Five dive under, To fish and sup, Smack their beaks, When they come up.
   So many to treat, What else did they eat?
5. After the fish, Ate worms for a snack. Right claw forward, Left claw back.

27. THE BLACKBIRD'S PARTY

Focus

• Bass vamp

• Recorder section

• Break

Form

A—Bass for four bars/ spoken text with bass
B—Recorder with movement
Break
B—Recorder with glockenspiel improvisation

Comments:

This poem comes from Ashley Bryan's wonderful book of poetry and paintings titled *Sing to the Sun.* [2] It introduces a steady bass part (in contrast to the bass response in *Soup, Soup)* reinforcing the Orff Schulwerk experience of a one-chord drone accompaniment to support pentatonic (here again *la* pentatonic) improvisation. Yet this and succeeding jazz-style bass parts are distinct from their Orff cousins in that they move through all three upper notes of the *la* pentatonic scale rather than sit squarely on the 1 and the 5, the distinction made earlier between Orff drone and jazz vamp.

One way to introduce the jazz vamp is to invite the children to make up their own vamps using E G A, with A as the final tone.* You may choose to use one of their ideas instead of the vamp given in the arrangement.

Note that the recorder riff centers on the notes A C D to complement the bass's E G A.

The students on the glockenspiels and chime bars now get to "stretch out" for a 32-bar solo over the bass with the recorder riff backing them.

This poem begs for some movement and I like to have a group of children do both the speaking parts and the movement. This is a perfect 3rd or 4th grade piece, integrating speech, movement, recorder and Orff instruments. Consider folding it into a play about birds.

---

* See discography *Mali toMemphis* for many examples of this kind of bass vamp.

STEP BACK, BABY

Improvising Scale:

2. I went down to let them in.
Step back, baby, step back.
I hit 'em in the head with a rollin'
  pin.
Step back, baby, step back.

3. I picked up a fryin' pan.
Step back, baby, step back.
You should have seen how those
  robbers ran.
Step back, baby, step back.

4. Some ran East and some ran
  West.
Step back, baby, step back.
Some flew over the cuckoo's nest.
Step back, baby, step back.

28. STEP BACK, BABY

Focus
• Body percussion, partner clap and dance

• Multi-media performance

Form
Intro.—Body percussion, cymbals, bass
A—Partner clap with song and ensemble
A1—Improvisation, dance
A2—Ensemble, drama
Coda

Comments:
When I taught this piece to my students in 1985, it was my first attempt to transfer the excitement of an Orff-style integrated performance to the jazz medium. "First thought, best thought" has held true, for in spite of all my intentions to create new pieces like this, *Step Back, Baby* has become a jazz class classic, continuing to hold up in workshop after workshop. It has traveled to Taiwan, Australia, Greece, Scandinavia, Spain and all around North America, returning from each trip invigorated by the enthusiastic response of teachers discovering their "inner jazz musician."

Preparing the "event":
The full realization of this orchestration is an Orff "event" combining singing, dancing, body percussion, drama and instrumental ensemble. The model is flexible—shortened (or lengthened) versions can be adapted as need. Teach each of the components to everyone before dividing into parts. Encourage the children's input, particularly in the area of creating their own dance, drama and body percussion.

This way of working requires a good deal of time to prepare the separate parts—possibly months! Having already laid the foundation through the activities in Chapters 1-4, an entire class might be devoted to learning the body percussion, another class the dance, another class the instrumental parts and yet another the drama. (You might consider teaching the parts separately to different classes in the same grade—i.e., one group works on the body percussion, another on the dance, a third on the instrumental parts, a fourth on the drama—or divide it in a similar way *between* grades.) Putting the sections together, setting the form and practicing the transitions require two or three more classes. In some ideal world (and here I confess I've rarely done this!), we would perform it all again with everyone doing a different part (dancers play, actors dance, etc.).

I find these kinds of experiences essential to the excitement of the music experience. *Performance* completes *process* by setting things into form. The play of discovery takes shape through the work of practice. The family of song, instrumental ensemble, dance and drama, separated to receive special instruction, is reunited again. The community of the class comes alive through teamwork and the culture of the school is enriched by the sharing. Work and play, individual and group accomplishment, process and performance, song and dance, music and drama, all hold hands and bow together at the curtain call.

We know too well the danger of performance-oriented music programs. The show becomes the chopping block on which understanding, exploration, creativity and the child's contribution to the learning process are sacrificed. At the other end of the spectrum, overly process-oriented programs shortchange the child's motivation for disciplined focus, pride in accomplishment, and joy in sharing. Music is, after all, a *performing* art and finds its completion in the special demands of performance. The model given here embraces both process and product in their proper order.

Partner clap: Though you may choose to begin teaching any of the various components, it is often best to start with the song.

• Leader sings verses, students sing response while playing pat-clap pattern on body.

• Select one of the basic partner claps (see *Mama Lama*, Chap. 3) or have the students create their own patterns. Repeat singing with partner clap.

• After much repetition, find out who can sing all the words.

• Teach the bass and xylophone parts to all.

• Ask students to find the *Step back, baby, step back* refrain on the xylophone.

Body percussion: Following the models already given, teach the three body percussion parts to all the children before dividing into groups. These patterns combine Keith Terry's approach with some simplified steps from the Lindy Hop. These are loosely aimed for upper elementary students. You can adapt them to your the needs of your situation by simplifying, changing or having the kids create their own.

• Prepare the first pattern through introducing the "new seven." Instead of hitting the back of the thighs, go directly to the feet. Begin with the right hand.

• For a "neurologically correct" approach,* repeat the pattern leading with the *left* hand.

• Alternate leading hands in each repeat of the pattern.

• Teach the following three patterns to all:

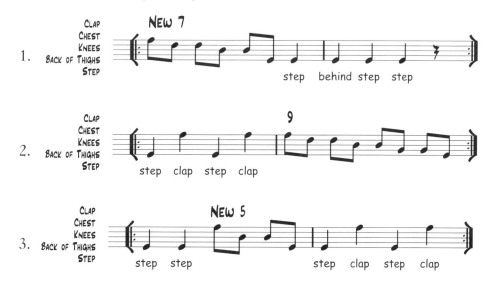

• Each chooses one of three patterns, faces partner and practices.

---

* It is excellent for both body and brain to work on *both* sides of the body.

- As above, in two lines facing each other about ten feet apart. One pattern begins, the next comes in and then the third. After the third, all begin to move towards each other on the step part of the pattern.

    Dance: Formation: Two lines facing. (They will move in opposite directions.)

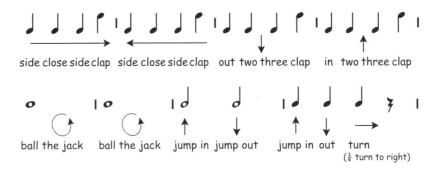

Repeat facing new direction. After 3 repeats, dance returns to starting position.

You may recall this dance was introduced in the Side-Close-Side activity in Chapter 4 (and is given again above for your convenience). Keep in mind that this is only a model— feel free to invite the students to integrate some of their own social dance knowledge. The main rule is that it be clear and follow the form of changing direction every 16 or 32 beats.

Teach Instrumental Parts

- Review hi-hat and ride cymbal parts.

- Teach bass part and have students note similarities and difference with *Boom Chick a Boom* and *Blackbird's Party*.

- Have students play response by ear ("Step back, baby, step back").

- Speak the new version of the call ("Not last night, night before") and play.

- Practice improvising in la pentatonic scale.

    Drama: After thinking for years that this would be fun to dramatize, I finally took the leap and asked the children to use mime, rhythmic movement and restraint to enact the story (the precursor to the movie *Home Alone*!). The result was wonderful! It added just the right touch to complete this multi-faceted performance art. In this particular case, I had the dancers responsible for the drama also, but you might choose to involve a different group entirely and have the dancers resume their initial clapping play and singing.

Final form:

- Divide students into the separate groups.

- Two lines facing 10 ft. apart. Begin body percussion parts one at a time until all three parts are in.

- Keeping body percussion parts, two lines move towards center on steps when ensemble begins.

Ensemble parts enter in the following order: BB/BX, hi-hat, ride cymbal, AX, glocks.

- At cue from leader, 2 lines switch from body percussion to partner clap. Leader sings solo parts, group responds.

- At the end of the song, AX/glocks drop out, selected soloists improvise and 2 lines perform dance.

- At the end of dance/improvisation, dancers enact drama (or resume clapping play while another group dramatizes). AX/glocks re-enter and all sing all the words.

- After last *"Step back baby, step back"*, musicians stop and dancers/actors perform one pattern of 9 "clap clap" (as experienced in *Hambone*—the new "shave and a haircut!"). Musicians re-enter on the last claps.

9 ⟶   Clap   Clap

Fifth graders playing *Step Back Baby.*

LIZA JANE

WORDS: TRADITIONAL
MUSIC BY DOUG GOODKIN

INSTRUMENTAL PARTS REPEAT

29. LIZA JANE

Focus
• Layered melodic riffs

• Transposed *la* pentatonic

Form
Intro—Layering parts
A—First verse and chorus A1—Improv.
B—Second verse and chorus B1—Improv.
C—Third verse and chorus C1—Improv.
End—All play bass 4x

Comments
This piece began its life as an instrumental version of *Boom Chick-a Boom* and ended up as yet another version of *Liza Jane*. The bass vamp extends the *Step Back Baby* idea and includes a *Soup, Soup* rhythm. (I originally introduced just the first half of the vamp and credit 4th grader Brian Furney with the idea of alternating the high and low D's.) The alto parts came directly from the "Uh huh" echoes in *Boom Chick-a Boom*. Once we began playing it, the idea of creating a melody to *Liza Jane* surfaced and a new piece (and bass riff) was born.

Because the melody didn't sit well in the *la* mode of C, we used our transposition skills and knowledge to change to F pentatonic. It was a great exercise for the kids to find the F pentatonic scale, then find its *la* mode (starting on D) and then find the parts they had already learned in the transposed version.

The call and response of the melody make it an ideal vehicle to feature some strong solo singers on the call and the group on the response. It also suggests the form for improvisation, with a soloist improvising the eight beat of the call and an instrumental group playing the melody of the response. The soloist may create a feeling of call and response within her own improvisation, as my 4th grade student Chloe Jury-Fogel did in the following example:

Note that the hi-hat and ride cymbal parts are not notated in the arrangement—from here on, these patterns are assumed and will not be indicated in the score.

THE COOKIE JAR (instrumental)

TEXT: TRADITIONAL
MUSIC BY DOUG GOODKIN

Group:
"Who stole the cookies from the cookie jar?""Sally stole the cookies from the cookie jar."

"Who, me?" "Yes, you!" "Couldn't be!" "Then who?"

(SALLY IMPROVISES 8 BEATS ON LA PENTATONIC SCALE
IN KEY OF C; EXAMPLE ABOVE)

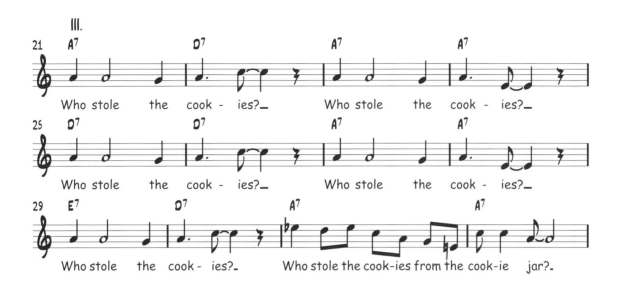

30. THE COOKIE JAR (instrumental)

Focus

- Descending bass

- Composed vocal riffs

- Improvisation over blues chord changes

Form: Part I

- Review "Cookie Jar" game (see Chapter 4)

- Change form as follows:

> A: *"Who stole the cookies from the cookie jar? B stole the cookies from the cookie jar."*
> B: *"Who, me?"* A: *"Yes, you!"* B: *"Couldn't be!"* A: *"Then, who?"*

B improvises a 7 beat[*] body percussion pattern (one beat rest at the end)

- Continue as above until all have had a chance to improvise (can be done in partners or in groups of four)

Part II

- All practice descending bass on the barred instruments.

- Only bass and bass bars play the pattern. With instruments set up in C pentatonic, follow dialogue above with each improvising in the break on one of the three-note groups in *la* pentatonic (E G A or A C D). Recorders may improvise as well.

Part III

- All learn by rote the riff melody, including basses. Divide woods and metal or barred instruments and recorders and echo the first two phrases, joining on the third. Play three times.

- Continue as above with teacher playing the blues chord changes on piano or guitar (see Chapter 7 for guidance).

- Select soloists to improvise over the chord changes.

Part IV

- Students divide up into small groups and make up a melodic riff based on their favorite cookies (some examples given in score above—no product placement intended!). Share one at a time and then "stack" ostinati over piano/guitar accompaniment.

- All sing final section: "Who stole the cookies?"

Final Form

Create with students a final form. One example:

A. Text with descending bass, with four select soloists playing during "break."

---

[*] Truer to style is to end on the upbeat just before the 7th beat. (See "rhythmic phrasing" at end of the chapter.)

B. Riff melody over blues changes—first time one group leading, the other responding, second time reversed.

C. One or two soloists over blues changes.

A. Return to first part with four different people.

B. As above.

C. One or two new soloists.

D. Stacked "cookie riffs." One group sings verse over the riffs. Slow down at the end—dramatic tremolo finish.

E. Celebrate with milk and cookies.

Comments:

In 1998, my students and I had the thrill of a lifetime when the legendary jazz vibraphone player Milt Jackson came to visit our school. The 5th grade had been working on this newly formed instrumental version of the familiar game and were setting up to play when Milt arrived. He looked rather tired, but the moment the first student soloed in the break, he sat up and smiled. By the end of the tune, he had joined in and the 5th graders listened with their mouths wide open, amazed by what he could play in a mere seven beats!

Years later, the young jazz vibraphone wizard Stefon Harris also came to school and we initiated him with the Cookie Jar piece as well. (I must say that both Milt and Stefon needed a little work with the words!)

This multi-dimensional arrangement has all the ingredients for a hit. It revisits a known game, changing it just enough to keep it fresh and interesting by adding the break for improvisation. It introduces the versatile descending bass pattern found in Spanish Renaissance music, the song *Greensleeves*, the pop tunes *Hit the Road Jack* and Thelonious Monk's jazz tune *Friday the 13th*. The simple riff is ideal for both xylophone and recorder players, once again reinforcing the three-note groupings of the la pentatonic scale. The opportunity to make up vocal riffs based on cookies makes the theme of the game come alive, allows the students to share their favorite cookies, and prepares them for Count Basie.

Perhaps the most important experience is the ability to hear how the shifting chords underneath change both the quality of the melody in each repetition and the feeling of the improvisation. This prepares the ear for the blues soon to come and lights up curiosity about what the piano or guitar played. When I tell my students that they will soon be able to play what I did, the excitement is palpable. Enjoy! And don't forget the cookies and milk party at the end!

Milt Jackson playing an Orff instrument at
The San Francisco School.

GREEN SALLY UP

African-American Game
Arranged by Doug Goodkin

31. GREEN SALLY UP

Focus

• Transposed pentatonic (from C to B♭)

• Chord tones—introduction of tritone

• Ambivalent 3rd

Form

Intro.—Layering parts
A—Sing three verses of song
A1—Improv. 12 bars
A—Sing

Comments

I have a special affection for *Green Sally Up*, as it was the first arrangement I tried in this style in 1983. Little did I suspect that it would help open up the entire world of playing jazz with children!

Though it was the first such piece I did, it later became clear that it is further up the sequence of melodic/harmonic theory. Most of the previous pieces are in the *la* mode of the familiar (to Orff teachers) C pentatonic, with one (*Liza Jane*) in F pentatonic. *Green Sally Up* transposes it to a rather obscure pentatonic on the Orff instruments—B♭*— and its corresponding minor mode beginning on G. Though it may appear an odd choice, it will prove to be the key of choice as we move into jazz blues. (For those who want to know why, you'll have to patiently wait until Chapter 7 to find out.)

The following sequence for teaching will help make the connection with previous experiences and introduce the new key concepts.

• Teach the bass part. Notice how it extends the feeling of the bass in *Step Back, Baby* with added rhythmic momentum and how moving to the key of G changes the sound.

• Up until now, we have relied on the essential structure of melody, bass line and rhythmic ostinato. Now we can add the harmonic color of other chord tones—the 3rd, 5th and ♭7th. The brief excursion to the neighboring tones adds color and movement. Play these chord tones with the bass part:

---

* Orff instruments are diatonic, but come with three extra bars—two F♯ and one B♭. In this arrangement, altos are set up with B♮, sopranos with B♭.

- Add the ♭7th to the chord voicing.

Comparing the two above, the latter clearly sounds more "hip."

The above experiment introduces a vital piece of jazz harmonic theory: **The funda-mental jazz chord is a four note chord—1, 3, 5, 7.** In this case, it is a chord known as *the dominant seventh* because the 7th is flatted (F is normally F♯ in the key of G). (We will explore other types of seventh chords in Chapter 8.)

The root is the most important note in the chord, followed by the 3rd and the 7th. The 5th is the last in the hierarchy. A chord built on the root, 3rd and 7th gives a character markedly different from the triad of 1, 3, 5 and distinguishes jazz harmony from English folk songs. The interval between the third and ♭7th is three whole steps—a tritone.* From here on, we will use the term tritone to conveniently label the 3rd and ♭7th of a given chord. *Green Sally Up* introduces the tritone buried in the full chord of 1-3-5-7.

You may notice an apparent contradiction in the arrangement—the dominant chord in the harmony has a B♮ while the melody and improvising scale has a B♭.

---

* The tritone, so vital to the jazz and blues sound, was once called "the devil's interval" by the church.

Is this a mistake? (An Orff colleague once surprised me by secretly teaching my arrangement to our class and playing it for me—with the B in the chord "corrected" to B♭! She simply assumed I had made a mistake.) Our ear can best answer that question. Not only does it sound good, but it adds a flavor that tells us we're in the world of jazz. Why is this so?

One explanation is that the combination of the chord with the B♭ melody note creates a harmonic extension of the basic 4-note chord commonly used in jazz—the ♯9th.

Yet that begs the question—why does the ♯9th chord sound right for jazz? If we return to the early African-American folk singer, we remember the ambiguity of the 3rd and ♭3rd being a crucial part of the expressive repertoire. A guitar player can achieve this by pushing on a string, a trumpet player by half-valves and a mute—but what about a piano player?* The natural 3rd of the chord sounding with the ♭3rd of the melody is the *harmonic* expression of this ambiguity. (However, this does *not* work in the other direction, with the B♭ below B!)

Form: Keeping to the form that will continue into jazz, sing the song with all accompanying parts, follow with select soloists and return to the song at the end. Now the improvisations will take on new character underpinned by the bass *and* chord tones.

---

* The great jazz pianist Thelonious Monk actually *could* bend that note through an ingenious pedaling device. Listen to *Monk's Point* on *Solo Monk* CS9149

HAMBONE

AFRICAN-AMERICAN GAME
ARRANGED BY DOUG GOODKIN

32. HAMBONE

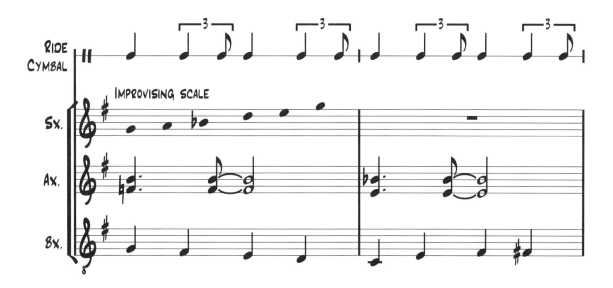

Focus

• Altered pentatonic scale

• IV chord

• Changing tritones

• Walking bass

Form

A—Song with accompaniment

B—Improvisation over I-IV chords

A1—Song over I-IV chords

Comments

Here is yet another piece revisited from an earlier chapter. Begin by reviewing the song and body percussion parts before moving to the instruments.

Key

Hambone, like *Green Sally Up*, is in the key of G, as will be most subsequent tunes. This is entirely determined by the available accidentals on Orff instruments, B♭ and F♯ (any accidentals are available, but as mentioned, these two come with all diatonic instruments). As in *Green Sally Up*, we will need both B♭—for the improvising scale—and B—for the tritones in the middle register. (A parallel need for both F and F♯ will be explained in our next piece, *Zudio.*)

Altered scale

Just as we are settling into the notion of *la* pentatonic as *the* scale in our study, *Hambone* throws us for a loop and introduces a new scale!:

What is this? It has three of the notes of our B♭ *la* pentatonic scale—G, B♭, D, but E and A replace C and F. It looks like a G major pentatonic scale

but with a B♭ instead of a B. Reinforcing the notion of the ambivalent 3ʳᵈ, I call this an altered (major) pentatonic scale. This provides an "alternative" foundation scale that we will encounter again in many of the jazz blues pieces (see *Centerpiece*, *Jumpin' with Symphony Sid* and *Now's the Time* in Chapter 7). Since this scale is in the song, we will use this in both the bass pattern and the improvisation.

IV Chord

While the first part of *Hambone* stays in our familiar one-chord realm, the second part moves us to the next most important chord in the sequence. Our Anglo-American training would lead us to suppose that in any two chord song, the second chord (after the I) would be the *V* chord. Here we are in for a surprise and a first departure from standard harmonic practice: **In the African-American tradition that led to the blues, the *IV* chord is the next most important chord after the I.** We will get some affirmation of this idea when we move to the blues itself.

• Briefly practice playing the roots of the I and IV chords in the following pattern:

Changing tritones

The next move is a crucial one in jazz theory practice. Pay attention!

• Play the I chord with its root and accompanying tritone of ♭ 7ᵗʰ and 3ʳᵈ, then play the IV chord root with its tritone of 3ʳᵈ and ♭ 7ᵗʰ. Compare the two tritones.

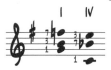

What have you discovered? A vital rule that we will visit throughout the rest of our study: **The tritone of the I chord shifts down a half step to become the tritone of the IV chord.** The 7ᵗʰ of the I chord is pulled to the 3rd of the IV chord and the 3ʳᵈ of the 7ᵗʰ chord gravitates to the ♭7ᵗʰ of the IV chord.

We can also invert the initial tritone and the same laws will hold:

This is an exciting moment when students discover there *is order in the musical universe!*

The mathematically inclined will really perk up here as we show the paperwork, the kinesthetic players will delight in the ease and beauty of the half-step pattern on the xylophones, the ear musicians will hear the movement of the tritones, the feeling musicians will enjoy the resulting music and all will join hands in the place where the four paths cross.

This pedagogical "aside" is indicative of the Schulwerk's contribution to music education. We don't just show the abstract theory—we make it concrete on the xylophones (or keyboards). We don't just play the physical pattern—we sing the half-step changes to make sure we can hear it. We don't just sing it—we do the math of why it "works" and name the rule. We don't just explore these as pedagogical exercises—we apply them to real musical literature and flesh out our intuitive enjoyment of music. This four step recovery program—hear it, play it, understand it, and feel it—offers a much needed healing of the fragmented curriculum.

- Briefly practice the changing roots and tritones, both singing and playing.

Orff teachers without chromatic instruments can position B *and* B♭ as follows:

C D E F G A B♭ B C

Walking Bass

- Play the root note of each chord on the downbeats of each measure.

- Fill in the notes between the two roots using stepwise motion going down and a skip going up.

- Now add the tritones in the alto range using our familiar "*Soup, Soup*" rhythm.

- Add our new altered pentatonic scale for improvisation in the soprano instruments.

Notice how the solo over the shifting chords has a refreshingly different quality from the drone bass improvisations with no extra effort on the part of the soloist. Since all the notes in that scale are compatible with either the I or IV chord (including the ambivalent B/B♭ mentioned in *Green Sally Up*), beginning players do not need to be consciously aware of the chord changes during the improvisation. This allows them to continue to develop rhythmic/melodic ideas and skills without concern for changing scales.

When students realize they *sound* good, they *feel* good. The mystique barrier is broken and they're encouraged to continue. The good news is that they'll continue to sound good over the next few years as we develop the harmonic foundation without changing the scale. By the time they've "hit the wall" and discover that they have to learn how to improvise with *changing* scales, they'll be determined to go on—or not. In either case, they've had the joy of experiencing jazz from the inside and developed a respect for the sophistication required to continue.

Having prepared the understanding of the new elements of *Hambone*, set it into form. Consider integrating body percussion and a movement/dramatic interpretation of the words. (Remember the option of using the gentler version as described in Chapter 3.)

8th graders performing "Jumpin' at the Woodside."

33. ZUDIO, ZUDIO

Focus

- V chord

- Changing tritones I-V

- "Ragtime" bass

Comments

Zudio, Zudio is the next-to-last piece in the puzzle that almost completes the harmonic picture we need. Though not included in the Games chapter, you may wish to first play it as a game (once again, refer to *Step It Down*).

Changing tritones I-V

- Repeat the process described in *Hambone* of discovering the relationship between the tritones of the I chord and the V chord.

Musical order persists! In the I-IV progression, the tritones went down a half-step, while in the I-V progression, the tritones go *up* a half-step, with 3ʳᵈs and ♭7ᵗʰ still functioning as neighbors. (Orff teachers, stay calm! Don't forget that you have the accidental F♯. You can set up your instrument like this: C D E F F♯ G B C, etc.)

G⁷D⁷

Ragtime bass

The character of *Zudio, Zudio* calls for a ragtime-style bass instead of a walking bass, the bass notes alternating with the tritones. Here are two possible approaches:

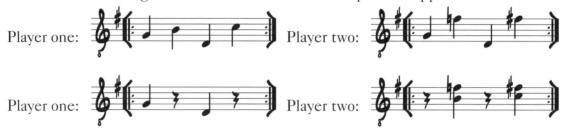

Form

Improvising in *la* pentatonic over a I-V bass will naturally give a different quality than over the I-IV bass. Try also improvising in the altered pentatonic scale introduced in *Hambone.*

34. READY FOR THE BLUES

Focus

• V-IV-I progression

Form

• Melody, improvisation, melody

Comments

We need one final step to prepare us for the 12-bar blues. We've moved from I-IV and from I-V. Now we have to feel the movement from the V chord to the IV chord. Unable to find any folk song using this progression, I composed this little piece to fill in this pedagogical gap.

• Teach the melody echo fashion.

- Accompany with the chord progression on piano or guitar while students sing or play the whole melody.

- All practice the roots and tritones of a V-IV-I progression in the following pattern: (Note the movement of the tritones down a *whole* step from the V to the IV chord.)

- Divide into parts and select soloists to improvise in *la* pentatonic scale.

SUMMARY

Let's review the main points covered in this chapter.

1. Orchestrating the games already played in their traditional form builds a child-sized bridge to jazz, taking them from the familiar—games already played—to the unknown—beginning jazz pieces on Orff instruments, instrumental improvisation and theory.

2. The orchestrations use familiar Orff principles of elemental composition—drones, rhythmic and melodic ostinati, pentatonic scales and improvisation—but alter them as follows:

   - Tonal center is *la* pentatonic divided into two equal halves—A, C, D and E, G, A

   - Drone bass patterns can be composed using A, G, A with melodies accenting A, C, D

   - Rhythmic ostinati proceed from the games: claps transferred to hi-hat, swing rhythm patterns derived from the text (*Step Baby, step*) on ride cymbal

3. The sequence offered here teaches one or two new concepts in each new piece:

   - Drum set parts (*Boom Chick a Boom*)

   - More complex bass vamps. *(Liza Jane, Green Sally)*

   - Improvisation over chord changes played by the teacher. *(Cookie Jar)*

   - *La* pentatonic transposed to D or G starting note. *(Liza Jane, Green Sally)*

   - Layered melodic riffs. *(Liza Jane)*

   - Inner voice movement. *(Green Sally)*

   - Tritones shifting between I and IV chords. *(Hambone)*

   - Walking bass. *(Hambone)*

   - Altered pentatonic scale (alternative improvising scale)/ *(Hambone)*

   - Tritone movement in I and V chords. *(Zudio, Zudio)*

   - Tritone movement in a V, IV, I progression. *(Ready for the Blues)*

   This forms the basis for the theoretical principles that lead us to jazz. We can play them, hear them and understand their logic while still enjoying the *music*. We've experienced the pleasure of our first jazz instrumental ensemble while continuing the work with our body and voice. While each step of our journey is a delight unto itself, it's also taking us somewhere—to the doorstep of the blues. But before entering, one more excursion will help prepare us.

Tips for Improvisation

All of the above pieces give children the opportunity to improvise. Besides being a cornerstone of the jazz experience, there is a pedagogical reason to include so much improvisation—it clearly reveals what the player understands about the style. I find it works best to refrain from giving advice at the beginning. Simply let the students play and observe their natural musicality. After hearing the improvisations, discuss what happened, both successes and failures. This creates a context for discussion based on the children's contribution. The successful example then comes from the student rather than the teacher and helps involve the students in the process—a crucial factor in the success of any class!

What makes a "good" improvisation? As always, it helps to know what we're aiming for.

The following are some general criteria appropriate in any style and some particular considerations in jazz.

Tonal Center

There must be a sense of the "home" note (my term—tonal center or tonic in standard vocabulary). Melodic ideas at the beginning should be confined to a limited range. Starting with A, C, D and then trying E, G, A reveals a crucial element of the *la* pentatonic scale that we've noted many times—its division into two equal halves with the same interval structure—minor 3rd, whole step (4th). Naturally, you can and should explore other combinations—G, A, C, for example—and ultimately use all five notes.

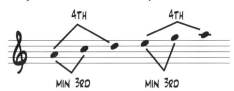

Repetition and Variation

Rather than think of four completely original phrases, think of one. This opening statement prepares the ground for subsequent variations based on repetition and contrast.

From this, you can extend the phrase:

You can keep the melodic shape and vary the rhythm:

You can change both:

Rhythmic qualities and phrasing

Some jazz musicians have remarked that they tend to think rhythmically when improvising, the rhythmic ideas preceding (by a split-second?) their choices of melodic tones. This makes sense in the light of the origins we have already explored—the rhythmic genius of jazz's African parent and the intimate connection with language. While Bach and Beethoven, whose formal constructs are more mathematically based, can keep a rhythmic motif moving through constant variations of melody and harmony, Charlie Parker and Dizzy Gillespie take a different approach.* The stories they tell require rhythmic variations akin to the natural cadences of speech. (Refer back to scat exercises.)

Another way to repeat and vary is to keep the rhythm, but change the melodic shape. Yet this rarely happens in jazz improvisation, just as it rarely happens in real conversation. If we imagine the different words as parallel to changing melodic shape, we can feel how strange a conversation like this would be: *"How are you?" "I am fine." "Is that so?" "Yes it is." "I must go." "So must I." "It's been real." "Likewise, dude."*

A four-phrase musical improvisation built on the same principle might sound equally stilted:

The rhythmic feeling in any improvisation must match the qualities implicit in a given style—in this case, swing rhythm and syncopation. Also of note is the ending of phrases on upbeats. As noted in the footnote to the Cookie Jar game, an eight beat improvised break often ends on beat 6½. This is implicit (and explicit!) in the phrasing of the parent songs:

---

* Two extreme examples: Bach's *Prelude No. 1* is built entirely on this rhythm: 𝅘𝅥𝅮 𝅘𝅥𝅮 𝅘𝅥𝅮 𝅘𝅥𝅮 while the 2nd Movement of Beethoven's 7th Symphony is based on the rhythmic motif: 𝅘𝅥 𝅘𝅥𝅮 𝅘𝅥 𝅘𝅥

Comparing the rhythmic variation of a Charlie Parker tune (*Billie's Bounce*, for example) or a Dizzy Gillespie solo reveals these two distinct sensibilities.

Articulation

The articulation of the notes is as important as the notes themselves. The expressive range of our voice—especially the African-Americanisms already noted—should sing out on our instruments. Here is where we feel the limitations of the Orff instruments. It's hard to get that varied, soulful dynamic expression on a glockenspiel! However, even here we can work on the dynamics of attack. We can use the pedal on the metal instruments and begin to use chromatic passing notes and ornamental neighboring notes.

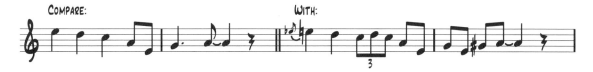

An excellent improvisational exercise for all instruments is to solo on one note only, varying dynamics, accent and articulation.

Play what you sing; sing what you play

As noted in Chapter 4, when Roy Eldridge and Dizzy Gillespie play trumpet solos and then scat sing on *Pretty-Eyed Baby*, they show at a high level what kids can learn to do with two or three notes—singing what they play and playing what they sing. If you listen carefully to recordings of Bud Powell, Oscar Peterson, Keith Jarrett and others, you will hear them singing what they're playing *while* they're playing it. For a simple exercise, have each child sing a short phrase on the notes A C D and then play back what they sang. Have them play a short phrase and sing back what they played. Have them try playing and singing at the same time. This is a habit that will serve them their whole life in any style of music and keep the music honest. When I approach my own jazz improvisation at the piano as a digital exercise or an excursion into mathematical variation, the result is invariably disappointing. When I remember to sing, the results are instantly more coherent and musical.

Improvise from a given song

This is the fundamental principle that frames all of the preceding suggestions. If we begin with a song, we find that the children's subsequent improvisations are generally successful because **the crucial elements of the improvisation are already contained in the song.** The rhythmic qualities, the phrasing, the melodic shape and contrasts present in the song *Soup, Soup* are intuitively transferred to the improvisation. If the improvisation is presented to the students abstractly, out of the context of the song, the result would be dramatically different. Simply put, what comes *out* in the improvisation is directly affected by what goes *in*. Hence, the strong emphasis on the prior experiences of immersion in the African American musical culture.

Understanding the character of good improvisation gives us a feeling of what to aim for. It helps break through the mystique of improvisation as "inspired from above" and gives shape to our efforts. However, analysis always works backwards from the music and never works in the other direction—i.e., the creation of music solely from analytical rules. As we introduce the "rules" of improvisation and style, we should remember be-bop trumpeter Red Rodney's sage advice in the following story:

> The University of Cincinnati brought in Jamie Abersold and Red Rodney as co-clinicians. Abersold spoke first. He articulately parsed what the students had played, analyzing the music in exhaustive detail. When he turned the lecture over to his partner, Red said: "The only thing I would say is, God gave you these," and he pointed to his ears. "That's what guys like me use. And learn the melody, because the melody is never wrong!" [3]

Endnotes

1. Amoaku, W. K.: *African Songs and Rhythms For Children*: Schott, ED 6376

2. Bryan, Ashley: *Sing To the Sun*: HarperCollins

3. Crow, Bill: *Jazz Anecdotes*: Oxford University Press

Discography:

Liza Jane: Nina's Choice: Collectables: Rhino Entertainment Co. COL-CD-6308

Liza Jane: Hippity Hop: Linda Tillery and the Cultural Heritage Choir: Music for Little People, R275951.

Mali to Memphis: An African American Odyssey: Putumayo World Music: Putu 145–2

Now's the Time: A Collection of Jazz Pieces Performed by The San Francisco School Orff Ensembles www.sfschool.org

Gandayina: Xylophone Music of Ghana: SK Kakraba Lobi: Pentatonic Press www.douggoodkin.com

CHAPTER 6: THE VOCAL BLUES

"I'm goin' down to the river, sit down and begin to cry
I'm goin' down to the river, sit down and begin to cry
If the blues overtake me, I'll drink that old river dry."
—WILLIE B.

"You ain't nothin' but a hound dog, barking all the time
You ain't nothin' but a hound dog, barking all the time
You ain't never caught a rabbit and you ain't no friend of mine."
—LIEBER & STOLLER

When Elvis Presley's version of *Hound Dog* hit No. 1 on the charts in 1955, the underground stream of the blues burst into mainstream America like an erupting geyser. But the water had already been flowing through the backyards of African-American culture for over 80 years. Many black musicians had received their baptism in its healing waters and soon the gospel began to spread, traveling upriver from the Mississippi Delta and feeding all the tributaries of the African-American genius—rhythm 'n' blues, rock 'n' roll, boogie woogie—and jazz.

Within a century of its inception, the blues had irrigated the entire national landscape, not only watering the crops of American culture, but exporting its abundance to feed people abroad as well. The river that sprang from the land of Southern blacks kept flowing to become the most influential musical form in American—and possibly, world—history.

As we prepare to move from African-American folk music to an authentic jazz repertoire, the vocal blues is both the river that feeds that repertoire and the bridge that helps us cross over. In this chapter, we will look at the poetry of the sung blues as the foundation of the scales, harmonies and forms that followed. A brief look at the origins of this potent musical style will help make clearer yet the connecting thread between the rural African minstrel singing his people's tradition and the urban African-American jazz musician spinning out the changing story of 20th century America.

BRIEF HISTORY OF THE BLUES

When Samuel Charters journeyed to West Africa to search for the roots of his own African-American musical heritage, chronicled in his book and recording *A Search for the Roots of the Blues*, he concluded:

> "I'd come looking for a kind of song, and even if I hadn't really found it, I'd found the people who sang it." [1]

The blues as a musical *form* cannot be found in Africa—this was the child of the African/European marriage. Its grandparents can be traced to the griot traditions of Senegal, Gambia and other West African cultures. The griot is an oral historian of kings and important people in the tribe's history. The kora, a harp-like instrument and the halam, the predecessor of the American banjo,* accompanies the singer with rhythmic/melodic ostinati and often answers the voice in a call-and-response relationship. This sensibility directly carried over to the bluesman with his guitar. In some cases, parallels can be made with technique—the alternate thumb-forefinger style of the kora surfacing again in some blues guitar practices, for example. Another accompanying instrument of the griot tradition is the xylophone (sometimes called balaphone), whose American counterpart became the blues piano players of the urban tradition. (Suggestions for recorded examples of these parallels are given at the end of the chapter).

Though some African traditions managed to emerge in altered forms relatively early in the history of slavery, the griot ancestors would have to wait. The slaves sang ring plays, field hollers, shouts, spirituals, work songs and more, but they did not sing blues as we know them. Why? One factor is the role of instruments in the development of the blues. Slaves simply did not have access to the European instruments that would become the companion to the blues singer—first the guitar and later, the piano and horns.

Perhaps a second ingredient was *leisure*—something that slaves also didn't have in abundance! The blues sprang from the lives of the unemployed, the culture of African - Americans traveling and searching for work. From the 1870's through the turn of the century, there was a great deal of movement by the newly-freed slaves, people with time to learn instrumental technique and time to reflect on their predicament. The bluesman with his guitar strapped to his back (affectionately nicknamed "Easy Rider") traveled up and down American roads, taking on the role of the West African griot telling the story of his people.

Yet *this* story was markedly different. Where the griot sang to preserve his people's inheritance, the bluesman sang of his people's *disinheritance.*** Likewise, the *need* to hear the story had a different meaning for African-Americans than West Africans. While the latter listened to affirm their place in society, the former tried to *find* their place. Paul Oliver writes in "The Meaning of the Blues":

> "One may wonder why there was such a market for the blues when the records of Mamie Smith first appeared on the stands. It was not for the music alone. It was because the music had meaning not only for the singer but for every Negro who listened. In the blues were reflected the effects of the economic stress on the depleted plantations and the unexpected prosperity of the urban centers where conditions of living still could

---

* It is a little known fact that the banjo, one of the few original instruments from the United States, is an African-American adaptation of this West African instrument.

** As Julio Finn writes: "Africans, whose gods were never suppressed, didn't have the blues—they had no reason to have them. But a people deprived of religion, language, customs and human dignity *did.*" [2]

not improve. In the blues were to be found the major catastrophes both personal and national, the triumphs and miseries that were shared by all, yet private to one. In the blues were reflected the family disputes, the upheavals caused by poverty and migration, the violence and bitterness, the tears and happiness of all. In the blues an unsettled, unwanted people during these periods of social unrest found the security, the unity and the strength that is so desperately desired." [3]

The blues came up from the South —the Mississippi Delta, Texas and the Southwest, and the Atlantic Coast from Richmond to Atlanta (sometimes called the Piedmont). Each of these areas had a distinct style until the era of the radio and phonograph arrived and regional differences diminished. Blues in the country was played on back porches, at house parties, work parties or in the infamous "jook joints"—the Saturday night gathering place for entertainment. As described by Zora Neale Hurston:

"Musically speaking, the jook is the most important place in America. For in its smelly, shoddy confines has been born the secular music known as the blues, and on the blues has been founded jazz". [4]

Thanks to recordings, we now know some of the countless singers who traveled the countryside, stopped by in the jook joints, sang on city street corners, and even found their way into some clubs. Some were blind and dependant on singing for their livelihood—Blind Lemon Jefferson, Blind Blake, Blind Boy Fuller, Blind John Davis, Blind Willie McTell. Many were colorful characters who walked on the shady side of the street. Their names tell their story. Where they came from—Mississippi John Hurt, Memphis Minnie—what they ate—Pigmeat Pete, Catjuice Charlie, Barbecue Bob—their size—Big Bill Broonzy, Big Mama Thornton—their character—Ramblin' Thomas, Sleepy John Estes, Laughing Charlie—their animal totem—Cow Cow Davenport, Howlin' Wolf—their natural quality—Leadbelly, Lightning Hopkins, Muddy Waters. Very few became famous, fewer still rich, yet they influenced some of the most well-known names in contemporary popular music. The colorful poetry of their adopted identities light up the namescape of our American cultural ancestors.

As African-Americans migrated to cities during World War I, the rural blues turned urban. The wandering musician with his single guitar gave way to four or five piece blues bands playing in nightclubs, their music spilling out into the Chicago, Kansas City and Memphis nights. In the 1940's, Muddy Waters amplified the blues with his electric guitar and began to catch the ears of white audiences and performers. At the same time, the mournful blues story joined boogie woogie and rhythm 'n' blues (also called R & B) was born, delivered by black artists like Louis Jordan.

By the 1950's, R & B hit mainstream America when performed by white musicians, once again, affirming Bessie Jones's perception, *"The blacks make it; the whites take it."* Jerry Lee Lewis took Ray Charles's *Whud I Say?*, Bill Haley and the Comets transformed a Trixie Smith '20's blues *My Daddy Rocks Me With One Steady Roll* (the source of R & B's new name—"rock 'n' roll!") to *Rock Around the Clock* and Elvis began his climb to the status of an American god with the song first sung by Big Mama Thornton—*Hound Dog.** Later, the Rolling Stones (who's name came from a Muddy Waters song) recorded blues singer Robert Johnson's *Love in Vain* and Reverend Gary Davis's *You Gotta Move*. While every American knows of Elvis, the Beatles and the Rolling Stones, most know little or nothing about the blues singers who founded their careers.

*Actually written specifically for her by two white songwriters, Lieber and Stoller.

None of this is to disparage the singers themselves, whose imitation was mostly a sincere form of flattery. When the Beatles first came to New York, a reporter asked them what they most wanted to see. When they replied, "Muddy Waters and Bo Diddley," the reporter asked, "Where's that?" The Beatles' answer hit the nerve of our cultural shame: "You Americans don't seem to know your most famous citizens." [5]

Now's the time to hear their story. Put their pictures up on the wall of the Graceland tour, redistribute the rock 'n' roll royalties, put their work in the American poetry anthologies—and bring their music into the school classroom.

The author with eighth graders, playing the blues.

WHAT IS THE BLUES?*

We've briefly looked at where blues came from and where it has gone, but we still haven't entirely answered our question, "What is the blues?" Ask a music teacher and you're likely to get a technical answer—"It's a 12-bar progression with I, IV and V chords." Ask a blues singer, a gospel singer or a jazz musician and the replies are markedly different:

Blues singer Alberta Hunter: "To me, the blues are-well, almost religious. They're like a chant. The blues are like spirituals, almost sacred. When we sing the blues, we're singin' out our hearts, we're singing out our feelings. Maybe we're hurt and just can't answer back, then we sing or maybe even hum the blues. Yes, to us, the blues are sacred. When I sing: 'I walk the floor, wring my hands and cry. Yes, I walk the floor, wring my hands and cry'...what I'm doing is letting my soul out." [6]

Gospel singer Mahalia Jackson: "Anyone who sings the blues has a broken spirit—they are burdened and they sing the blues to relieve the feeling they have. You get relief from spiritual songs, but you don't get real relief when you sing the blues because the spiritual song has divine power behind it and lifts man up, but the blues makes you feel moody and sad and makes you cry." [7]

Blues singer Etta James: "It's not all sad 'woe is me, o lordy, my hog's got cholera.' The blues that I sing, basically I feel it's just some kind of experience. It's like living, dying, breakin' up, fightin', happy. It's everything all mixed up. It's funny, some of it. I'm not saying every time I sing a song, that it's funny. Because some of those songs I sing I get pretty damn mad in there... It's life." [8]

Country blues singer Son House: "Mighty near every record where they sing the blues is made up about a woman. That's what your mind is on... your woman. You want her and she don't want you. That's what the blues is made up about." [9]

Pianist Art Hodes: "The blues heal you. Playing the blues is like talking trouble out. You have to work the blues out of you." [10]

Jazz trumpeter Red Allen: "The blues is a slow story. The feeling of the beautiful things that happen to you is in the blues. They come out in the horn. You play blues, it's a home language, like two friends talking. It's the language everybody understands."[11]

Jazz trumpeter Wynton Marsalis: "The blues is a very deep form in the myth of America. It's like a mythic story: it can be taken as something nice and entertaining on the lowest level, or it can be taken as something that addresses the depths of people's consciousness. Blues is like a tonic, a home base; it's always there waiting for you, providing you with the strength and the sense of direction that you need to address the complexities of life." [12]

Jazz pianist, composer, bandleader Duke Ellington: "The blues ain't nothin' but a dark cloud markin' time." [13]

---

* "What is the blues" may seem grammatically incorrect, but the blues as a musical form like sonata, rock or country is indeed singular.

35. INTRODUCING THE BLUES

Focus: Quotes from musicians who play the blues

Activity

• Without any preparation, students write down their answers to the question "What is the blues?" based on what they already know. Have them include any examples of blues pieces they know.

• Share some or all of the answers.

• Students take turns reading the quotes from "What is the Blues?" out loud. (If you can play some simple blues guitar, this would be a nice backdrop to the above.)

• Discuss the variety of points of views expressed in the quotes.

Comments

I enjoy beginning any new study by taking a survey of what students already know. At the end of the study, we compare what we have learned with what we started out knowing—and the results are often impressive!

   We move from the students' thoughts to the voices of the musicians themselves. The students will notice the variety and even contradiction in these quotes. Though the gospel singer, blues singer, blues pianist and jazz musician all drink from the same blues fountain, they come to it with different thirsts and leave with different degrees of refreshment. The blues means many things to many people and it is large enough to contain them all. The students now get the hint that our study of the blues will not allow for a simple definition to be spewed out on the test—they will have to bring their own life experience to it and discover their own answer.

   The poet Langston Hughes has another child-sized definition of the blues.

"When the shoe strings break
 On *both* your shoes
And you're in a hurry—
That's the blues.

When you go to buy a candy bar
And you've lost the dime you had—
Slipped through a hole in your pocket somewhere—
That's the blues, too, *and bad!*" [14]

36. THE POETIC FORM OF THE BLUES

> "I hate to see, that evenin' sun go down
> I hate to see, that evenin' sun go down
> Ever since my baby, done left this town."

—THE ST. LOUIS BLUES: W. C. HANDY

Focus: Analyzing the blues structure

Activity

Sing a version of "The St. Louis Blues" accompanied by guitar or piano and analyze with the students as shown below.

Comments

The blues is poetry on the wings of song. Following our emphasis on beginning with the music itself and moving towards the "rules," we begin by singing some blues. After singing them, we reflect on their meaning, structure and poetic devices. Below is one model of how I discuss these things with my older students.

> "Like all good poems, these words move the mind. We wonder why the sunset evokes such strong emotion. Did we hear right? The line returns, assuring us that we did. The final line reveals the reason, but it doesn't stop our imagining. We now must backpedal to the first lines and put the two images together. What does 'my baby leaving town' have to down with hating to 'see the evenin' sun go down?' Without that good lovin', nights are going to be lonely. When the darkness falls, we'll be sitting at home with the blues.

> "The first two lines are the call, the last one the response. So the blues begins with this kind of skeleton structure:

a	a	b
call_____		response

> "On the page, the words run together. But when we sing them, we leave some space for the images to sink in. We issue the call and leave some room for a response. While we're chewing them over, it's my guitar or piano that makes a comment.

a	Interlude	a	Interlude	b	Interlude
	Instrumental				
call	response	call	response	call	response

> "The first two lines are alike when read or sung alone. But when the piano or guitar joins in, something changes. The second call sounds completely different. The sunset is still the same, but we move to a different place to watch it. When the last phrase comes in, the instruments make sure we know it by moving to a completely new place.

> "What's going on down there? We'll find out in the next few classes. For now, let's sing it again and listen for all these levels of call and response."

37. BLUES LYRICS I
Focus: Writing blues lyrics, with attention to rhyming and phrasing

Activity

• Share the *a* phrase of a traditional blues lyric (this one by Muddy Waters) and have the class improvise the capping *b* phrase. Afterwards, volunteers share their solutions.

Example: "Brooks run into the ocean, the ocean run into the sea"
The children might sing: "I run to the candy store and buy everything that I see."

Or: "The tree drops the acorn and the acorn grows a tree."
Or: "I can't think of a rhyme and I hope you don't call on me!"

The emphasis here is on coming up with a line that rhymes with, matches the phrase length and completes the meaning of the opening line. Most blues phrases end on an upbeat of the 8th beat and tie over into the next beat .

• Discuss which solution works best. (In above examples, the first responds to the first line by keeping the image of running—"brooks run ocean, ocean runs sea, I run candy store." The second maintains the image of the natural world, of brooks growing to oceans and acorns growing to trees. The third offers a humorous contrast.) All sing, with or without piano/guitar accompaniment.

Comments

This opening lyric continues our water image—brook, ocean, sea, written by Muddy Waters.* Why so much water? Water is fluid, moves with the changes, symbolizes the creative fountainhead in dreams, flows in our tears and its associated color is—blue!

Back in the classroom, both our linguistic and musical intelligence get some good exercise. Getting the phrasing and rhyming down gets us through the door of the blues (though there's more to come). Encourage students to practice creating verses on long car rides, or while waiting for the bus. They can play a partner challenge game—one starts a verse, the other must rhyme it. (For the clever student hoping to win by ending with "orange," I share the brilliant repartee of my student, Jordan Wisner—"I'm feeling kind of hungry, I wish I had an orange (2x); but before I take a break, I have to finish fixin' this door hinge."

---

* The original capping verse—"If I don't find my baby, somebody sure gonna bury me."

38. BLUES LYRICS II
Focus: Personal story
Activity: In class or for homework, students write their own blues lyrics

Comments

In entering any subject matter, it's a good idea to start from what's closest—our own life experience. Though it is crucial to understand the historical and cultural origins of the blues—not just *any* suffering, but the *particular* suffering of African-American people— it's equally important to bring each subject into the reality of each student's life. Though we may wince at the "suffering" of lyrics like "I felt so bad when my Nintendo didn't work," we're still obligated to begin with the situation at hand.

While the last exercise focused on getting the feeling for rhyme, phrase and meaning by completing a given first line, this one asks the students to write a few verses on a theme of their choice. One possible beginning point to help focus this exercise is to give everyone the same first half of the opening line: "When I woke up this morning,..." Some examples from my 8th grade students are as follows:

1. "When I woke up this morning, I was feeling oh so tired, (2x)
   Then I found out that my brother had just been fired."

2. "When I woke up this morning, I didn't feel too good inside, (2x)
   I had just found out my poor little cat had died."

3. "When I woke up this morning, I had some gum in my hair, (2x)
   By the time I cut it out, my poor little head was bare."

This written assignment makes clear precisely who understands the form, phrasing and rhyming schemes. Here are some examples that needed work:

4. "This morning I was depressed, (2x)
   I remembered I had a history test."

The student was challenged to add more words to fill out the phrase and managed to solve the initial problem without changing the basic ideas:

4a. "This morning when I woke up, I started my day depressed, (2x)
    I remembered that today was the day of the history test."

These activities offer wonderful opportunities to work with the language arts teacher.

39. BLUES LYRICS III

Focus: Metaphor, imagery and sexual innuendo

Activity

- Play a chorus or have students read a verse of Bessie Smith's *Empty Bed Blues:* [14]

  > "When my bed gets empty, I feel awfully mean and blue
  > When my bed gets empty, I feel awfully mean and blue
  > My springs are gettin' rusty, sleeping single like I do."

- Discuss the meaning. (This should be reserved for older students and folded into the health/values/sex education curriculum.)

- Discuss the historical experience of masking and poetic experience of imagery and metaphor (see comments).

- Re-work the blues verses already created with an eye towards imagery.

  > "This morning when I woke up, I started my day depressed.
  > This morning when I woke up, I started my day depressed.
  > I remembered that today was the day of the history test."

might change to:

  > "Columbus on the Mayflower, Napoleon begged him to stay
  > Columbus on the Mayflower, Napoleon begged him to stay
  > History test, won't you wait for one more day?"

Comments

The blues at its finest is sheer poetry, employing metaphor, simile, imagery and other poetic devices. But because it's an oral tradition, it is rarely acknowledged as poetry. (Some exceptions: the Anthology *America: A Prophecy*[15] includes blues lyrics.) Bessie Smith's classic, *Empty Bed Blues*, is a masterful example of sexual innuendo framed in poetic images. Instead of the blunt, unimaginative approach of many contemporary pop songs, she doesn't say, "I want to make love," but implies it in a poetic image.

This indirect approach comes directly from the slavery tradition of masked language. Whether it was making fun of Massa, communicating information for the Underground Railroad or simply sharing feelings with those who've "been there," metaphor carried the message, safe from interception by the uninitiated. This sensibility naturally carried through in life after slavery and is characteristic of much African-American music.

Beyond its historical value, it offers an educational value as well. It pays tribute to the smarts of the audience, elevating the listener to an active role of trying to decode the imagery. Those who get it feel the satisfaction of having passed the test. Those who think that the singer can't afford WD-40 on a single person's salary have missed the punch line.

This particular listening example brings in another pet theme of the blues—love in all its joy and failure (and in the blues, mostly failure!). The problems—and delights—between men and women occupy as much (if not more!) space on the blues library shelf as the conflicts between blacks and whites. Just as it was a revelation to my generation that sex was not invented in the 1960's, so are today's adolescents surprised to hear this theme being sung about at the beginning of this century!

40. BLUES LYRICS IV

Focus: Improvising blues melodies

Activity

• Accompanied by the teacher (or other students) on guitar or piano, practice singing select blues verses from the homework assignments.

• As above, with kids improvising both melody and words to something that happened to them that day.

Comments

When W.C. Handy first wrote down and published *The St. Louis Blues* in 1914, literary America took it literally that he had "invented" the blues. But the oral roots of the blues, with loosely structured melodies and improvised responses, resisted print. As a solo form (the literature of choral blues is virtually non-existent), the singer not only can choose the melody, but also change it from verse to verse. (Listen to Joe Williams sing *Every Day Have I the Blues* for one example).

When kids sing their own verses, they don't write down melodies, but improvise them over the guitar/piano accompaniment. Because the blues are so pervasive in American musical culture, most children have an intuitive feeling for how to sing them. Kids generally quickly develop an ear for these improvised melodies, especially when accompanied instrumentally. In some cases, the words themselves suggest certain contours to the melody. As described by Al Wilson:

> "This is the thing about words, why they are important in singing the blues melodies using those four or five notes in the standards blues mode... You pattern the words to rise and fall in a way similar to the way that you would speak them, and construct the words not just any way but so they flow naturally with the flow of the melody." [16]

When students both improvise the text and the melody, they are re-creating the world of the blues singer. *

---

* For a chance to see the process of improvising blues on the spot, there is a wonderful scene in the movie *Adventures in Babysitting*, in which white suburban kids being chased in downtown Chicago inadvertently stumble onto the stage of a black blues club. The place goes silent and as they beg everyone's pardon and try to leave the stage, the guitarist tells them that no one can leave the club without singing the blues. With the musician's help, they improvise a blues on the spot. This is well worth showing to your students!

41. BLUES LYRICS V
Focus: Instrumental improvised response

Activity

• Still accompanied by the teacher, select soloists sing verses and other soloists play or sing improvised responses on Orff instruments, guitars or other instruments in the key of E.

• Listen to the interplay between voice and guitar in *Blues Roots*: V. 10: (See discography).

• Listen to *Empty Bed Blues* again and focus on the improvisations in the response.

Comments

We've already spoken of the dialogue between the African singer and his instrument—particularly his stringed instrument. Now we can hear how the guitar became the singer's companion in the blues, commenting on, extending, supporting and sometimes replacing, the words themselves.

The interplay between singer Bessie Smith and trombonist Charlie Green in the *Empty Bed Blues* carries this relationship into the group setting. The trombone responses are musically inventive, varied, humorous, and comment directly on the text. They remind us that we're listening to a *story*, not a *math lesson*. Charlie Green is not practicing interesting note combinations based on scales he learned in theory classes. He's commenting on Bessie's text the way a congregation responds to the preacher with their "Amens" and "I hear you's." He translates her thoughts from words to horn so we hear everything *twice*. When she sings *"He's a deep sea diver, with a stroke that can't go wrong"*, the trombone plunges to the bottom of the register. *"Bought me a coffee grinder, got the best one I could find"* and the trombone grinds it up. *"He knows how to thrill me and he thrills me night and day,"* and the trombone skips up high like a child opening a birthday present. Through listening, the children begin to hear what to aim for in their own responses.

For all these versions of sung blues, the key of E is an excellent choice for three reasons:

• For teachers accompanying on guitar, the three chords in the E blues are: E7 (I chord), A7 (IV chord) and B7 (V chord), three of the easiest chords to play on the guitar.

• It is a good range for the singing voice.

• The improvised instrumental responses are easy to set up on the Orff instruments—the *la* mode of G pentatonic.

HAVE YOU EVER BEEN MISTREATED

JOE HUNTER
ARRANGED BY DOUG GOODKIN

Have you ev - er_____ been mis - treat - ed_____

Then you know what I'm talk - in' a -

bout.

RIDE CYMBAL
HI-HAT
SNARE DRUM
BASS DRUM

42. HAVE YOU EVER BEEN MISTREATED: Joe Hunter
Focus

- 6/4/ meter

- I chord blues in C

Activity

- Play the bass line to *Have You Ever Been Mistreated* while singing the first line twice.

- Invite the students to create the "capping line." Select those that work well.

   The following two examples came from my 8th grade class:

      Have you ever been mistreated, then you know what I'm talkin' about, (2x's)
      When you're livin' on the street and, you can't seem to find your way out.

      Have you ever been mistreated, then you know what I'm talkin' about, (2x's)
      When your baby's lied and cheated, it just makes you want to shout.

- Compare with the original capping line:

  I worked five long years for one woman, she had the nerve to throw me out.

- All play descending *la* pentatonic scale on words *know what I'm talkin' about*

- Divide up parts and choose soloist on *la* pentatonic scale. Soloist can play after the singers and/or in the responses between each phrase.

Comments

This adaptation of a blues from St. John's Island [17] is a fantastic first ensemble blues. It revisits the *la* pentatonic scale in C and the I chord sensibility of our early pieces *Soup, Soup* and *Step Back, Baby* while introducing the blues poetic form and a new meter—6/4.

Historically, it is valuable because it gives us a taste of a blues poetic form *before* it settled into the now familiar 12-bar blues chord progression. It is likely that the need for that set progression arose from the ensemble blues that grew in urban settings—group playing always demands more formal structure than solo playing. Those early blues musicians singing duets with their own guitars—like Joe Hunter on the recording—had considerable freedom of form and used it.

Culturally, it is likewise a perfect introduction to the blues, setting the tone of the basic theme of most blues lyrics—suffering *("Have you ever been mistreated")* and communicating suffering *("then you know what I'm talkin' about")*.

Many West African songs favor descending melodies (another example of the energy moving downward?) and this example, falling down the octave through the *la* pentatonic scale, echoes that practice. Indeed, its clear logic and easy playability was the impetus for orchestrating it for my students. It's a wonderful companion piece to a blues by Sonny Rollins titled *Sonnymoon for Two* (not included in this collection for copyright reasons), which also uses the same descending idea in a different rhythm.

43. PREPARING THE BLUES "CHANGES" *

Focus: Harmonic structure of the blues

Activity

- Create three distinct spaces on the floor as follows, with each student on the I as space permits (hula hoops work great, carpet squares, string, and floor tiles are all possibilities):

    (I)   (IV)   (V)

- Sing one of the original blues verses to teacher accompaniment, jumping into the hoops on the first beat of each phrase in the following pattern:

    a   a   b
   (I)   (IV)   (V)

- Sing again and jump inside the (I) hoop during each downbeat of the response:

                                          (I)   (I)
    "Columbus on the Mayflower, Napoleon begged him to stay,
                                          (I)   (I)
    Columbus on the Mayflower, Napoleon begged him to stay,
                                          (I)   (I)
    History test, won't you wait for one more day?"

- Review the two rules above:

    Jump in a different hoop at the beginning of each phrase—first (I), then (IV), then (V)

    Jump inside the I hoop during the response, once every 4 beats: (I) (I)

- Sing the song again, combining the two rules above. The pattern is now as follows:

        a   a   b

    call   resp. call   resp. call   resp.

    (I) (I) (I)(IV)   (I) (I)(V)   (I)   (I)

    1   2   3   4   5   6   7   8   9   10   11   12

---

* The term "blues changes" is the vernacular for the standard blues chord progression.

- Practice the last rule: always jump to the IV chord in the missing downbeats (at the beginning of the second measure of each phrase):

"Columbus on the Mayflower, Napoleon begged him to stay,

Columbus on the Mayflower, Napoleon begged him to stay,

History test, won't you wait for one more day?"

- Combine all three rules (still singing with accompaniment):

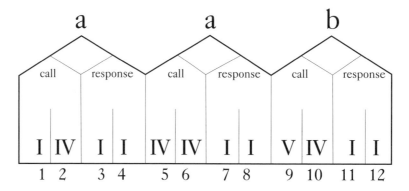

I sometimes describe the blues form as three condominiums side by side, each with four rooms. Each one shares certain qualities with the others, but no two are exactly alike. If we look at them from a different angle, we note that the last three rooms (chords) are the same in each.

I IV I I
IV IV I I
V IV I I

When you enter the front door of each house, you step into a different room and that's what makes each house feel different. The most important room in all three houses is the front room of the second house (the IV chord—as we live for a while in these homes, we can re-arrange the furniture and change some of the rooms, but that room bears the supporting wall that cannot be torn down.

To say the same in more concrete musical terms: The a a b form of the lyrics divides the 12 bars into three groups of four measures. Note that the last three chords of each pattern are the same. **Remember that the above is the most basic beginning pattern.** As we move through the blues, we will experience many variations of the above chord pattern, but the IV chord in bar five will always stay in place.

- As above, sitting on the floor and patting left knees for I chord, right knee for IV and outer side of right knee for V, four beats per measure:

I I I I / IV IV IV IV / I I I I / I I I I / IV IV IV IV / IV IV IV IV / I I I I / I I I I /
V V V V / IV IV IV IV / I I I I / I I I I

- As above, singing with eyes closed and patting while teacher plays and observes.

- As above, patting neighbor's knees on each side.

- Students write out progression individually. Select one to write it out on the board.

- Students review pattern one more time (looking at board or not) while singing the root notes with their number and proper pitch. (Teacher sings or plays blues instrumentally.)

Comments

Finally we arrive at the moment where most blues lessons in music classrooms begin—the chord changes. What have we gained by waiting? First, we now should have a thorough grasp of the poetic structure—its form, phrasing, rhyming pattern, content, linguistic devices, melodic possibilities and call-and-response structure. We have listened to many examples and our ear has absorbed some of the basic relationships between chords and texts. We should have a *feel* for the way the chords change with the phrases—now it's time to find out specifically what's going on down there.

Here some unorthodox ideas—jumping in hoops, patting chords on knees, etc.—are used to help us master the blues progression. What is the thinking behind these approaches?

- Connecting the chord change with a physical response roots it in the body as well as the ear. Placing the hoops as indicated gives a feeling for the space and order later transferred onto the keyboard. Two other bonuses: 1) landing on downbeats (jumping slightly before) demands a physical understanding of preparation on the upbeat—a vital rhythmic skill in any style. 2) It's fun, imaginative and channels children's abundant physical energy.

- Singing while performing the above helps cement the connection between the text and the chord pattern. **This is the fundamental point of this approach**—by understanding how each chord relates to the words, students begin to understand the deeper structure and have a means of correcting themselves when they get off. In contrast, students who merely count and memorize the chord pattern minus the melodic layer often can't *hear* when they get off and if they do, don't know how to get back in.

- Performing the above while internalizing the melody (while teacher plays) roots it further in the ear and body.

- Transferring it to the knees prepares it more precisely for the xylophones.

- Closing the eyes while singing helps some children's focus and helps the teacher see who really has it independently and who is just watching and copying others. (This last tactic is okay and necessary for some as a starting step, but the final goal is independence.)

- Writing the pattern out individually locks it in yet further and makes even clearer who still needs work and where the problem is.

- Writing it out on the board and practicing will be a moment of profound relief for some. Though I believe it's crucial to come to music first through the ear, notation often offers a vital clarification of what one hears. It serves the visual learners who feel lost in the aural world or can only come to it through the eyes. It helps process theory by lifting the music out of the heat of music-making into the cool light of reflection. So by all means, write it down. Just don't do it at the beginning of the first blues lesson.

- Singing the intervals brings it squarely back into the musical world—now eye, ear, hand and intellect work as equal partners.

At the end of all this, some students *still* won't get it. The answer for some will be more practice, for others, figuring out where their understanding breaks down in the loop of learning. But experience bears out that the above approach helps children feel, hear, understand and play the basic blues progression.

Milt Jackson enjoying an eighth grader playing the blues.

44. PLAYING THE BLUES CHANGES
Focus: Playing the bass on instruments

Activity

• Find the root notes of the I, IV and V chord in the key of C (C, F, G).

• Repeat a shorter version of the above on instruments in the key of C. Singing or to teacher's accompaniment, play at the beginning of each phrase (C, F, G), in the response (C C)and in the middle of each phrase (F), ending with the full sequence:

• Add the 5th above to each chord and practice sequence:

• Alternate between the 5th and 6th of each chord and practice:

• Play as above in the following rhythm:

• Play in the basses only, others sing a select blues and/or improvise responses.

• Repeat above in the key of G, with students figuring out how to transpose.

   G (I) C (IV) D (V)

Comments

This exercise should be sheer delight to the Orff teacher. Remember that by the end of third grade (see Chapter 5), the students have played in the keys of C, F and G pentatonics, accompanying each with the following drones:

Now all three are reviewed in a chordal context. Such inspired spiral curriculum teaching! To make it even more exciting, the next step of moving to the sixth is parallel to the next step in the Orff progression—the moving drone. Finally, the rhythm adds a variation that extends the old familiar drones into their jazz counterpart.

Remember that every student should try all the parts, but all are welcome to ultimately stop at their level of comfort. Rather than drop out, the student who hits the wall at adding the 5th can just continue to play the roots and still contribute to the ensemble. At the other end, the whiz kids can stop complaining about being bored and take it to the highest level of the rhythmic variant. If they're still bored, have them sing the solo *while* they play. If *that's* still too easy, have them play the offbeat on the hi-hat at the same time! From there, it's up to them to come up with more challenges (a time-step with tap shoes on?).

SUMMARY

We began our instrumental excursion in Chapter 5 with A as our home tone (the *la* pentatonic mode of C)—*Soup, Soup; The Blackbird's Party; Step Back Baby* —and a I chord accompaniment. We then transposed to G—*Green Sally Up; Hambone; Zudio; Ready for the Blues*—and moved from the I chord to I-IV, I-V, and V-IV-I. We began this chapter in the key of C, learned a classic 12-bar blues pattern using all three chords—I, IV, V—and by the end, after one piece in E, have transposed back to G. We spent a great deal of time with the poetic form and learned a particular style of bass to accompany the vocal blues.

Like much of our work, this style is both valid unto itself and a stepping stone. As a musical form, the vocal blues moved from the rural solo singer with guitar to the urban band with singer, piano (or guitar), drums and horn and also evolved into a distinct instrumental style for solo piano—boogie woogie. In terms of jazz history, this proved to be a dead end, but the cul-de-sac of boogie woogie built some houses on suburban lots and resurfaced as a rhythm and blues style in the 50's and 60's. (The piano playing of Jerry Lee Lewis is clearly indebted to his African-American predecessors). We don't want to spend too much time here, but boogie woogie bass patterns transfer reasonably well to the Orff basses and are fun for kids to practice on their own on piano.

Where do we go from here? Six chapters into the book, we're finally ready to enter that music of jazz itself! Those tritones we so meticulously prepared in Chapter 5 that seem to have mysteriously dropped out in this chapter will make their reappearance. We'll stay in the key of G for a while, grow a bit on the drum set, learn some new bass patterns, explore some chordal variations and re-trace the thread of the blues as it enters the big band jazz group. On to Duke's Place!

THE HEALING POWER OF THE BLUES

The blues is the story of the African-American experience in the United States, reinterpreted anew by each geographical region, generation and economic class. Playing the blues and hearing it means something different to the black Southern sharecropper, urban factory worker and young rock musician, but each will recognize the common thread of being on the outside looking in. When it entered the reservoirs of mainstream culture and came out the taps into white middle-class homes, it changed again. Processed in those water treatment plants, some of its vital natural minerals were sapped. But there was clearly a *thirst* for its quenching tonic, especially as young people questioned "the Establishment." The current proved strong and as the blues river flowed out into the sea, it spread its influence far beyond the American shores, *directly* affecting music styles and music-making throughout the world. American blues are being sung in Japan, Australia, Germany, Argentina—and even back in some countries in its motherland, Africa.

The specifics of the blues as a musical form are undeniably African-American, singing out the suffering of disenfranchisement, alienation and oppression. But the *Blues* is universal—suffering recognizes no national boundaries or racial ownership. The Spanish sing the pain of life in passionate gypsy blues, the Bauls of India wander the land with their one-string blues ektara telling their story, while the mournful shakuhachi bends Japanese blue notes. Even the English have their haunting minor ballads about death and disaster. Those who accept that suffering is the dues we pay to be a member of the human race are open as listeners and creators of blues-based music. Naturally, there is no reason to expect that this music from different cultures will parallel the blues in *musical* ways (though in some cases, there is a remarkable parallel musical quality apparently independent of acculturated influence). But singers across musical and geographical borders will recognize their companions in the cry and exultation of the voice behind the words and notes.

What is the place of the blues in the classroom? Is it appropriate to share so much pain and suffering with children in schools? There are various lobby groups who petition schools to remove songs like *Go Tell Aunt Rhody* or *Cock Robin* because they sing of death, and death is too depressing for young children. (Though one has to wonder if those same children are sheltered from the image of Christ on the cross, the evening news or the latest shooter video game.) The blues is neither about wallowing in our pain nor swallowing our pain. It's about facing our troubles, singing them out and putting them out there in the community for everyone to recognize *("You know what I'm talkin' about")*. As Branford Marsalis says:

> "The true purpose of blues music is triumph in the face of adversity. Blues music serves as a means of overcoming an oppressive situation. Having the blues is one thing, playing the blues is quite a different matter." [18]

Children need the blues, not just for the hidden history they hold, but for the lessons they teach in emotional intelligence. *"Birthing is hard and dying is mean,"* says Langston Hughes, and when children discover that truth at Grandpa's funeral or when they find the stiff hamster in the cage, they're going to need some help. Writing stories, creating art and singing blues helps them to bear the pain and help it grow from *personal* suffering to connect with a *universal* suffering. It teaches them how to *grieve*.

America also needs the blues. We need the blues to grieve our historical atrocities—Native American genocide and African slavery, for starters—and heal our contemporary disgraces—the abandonment of our children to television, the erosion of the arts in the schools, the strip-malling/mauling of the land, the corporate invasion of every corner of the world and more. If I were Secretary of Culture, this would be my platform: *Blues for Yesterday* sung next to the national anthem. New meaning when we salute the Red, White and *Blue*. "Triumph in the face of adversity," our new national motto. Poetry instead of Prozac, ritual instead of Ritalin, creativity in the classroom instead of crack. B.B. King in the Therapists National Hall of Fame.

When we learn to *sing* the blues as a nation, when we learn to hear the whole story they tell, then we can move beyond *having* the blues. For, as Robert Johnson reminds us:

> The bluu-u-u-u-ues is a low-down shakin' chill,
> You ain't never had 'em, I hope you never will.

Endnotes

1. Charters, Samuel: *The Roots of the Blues: An African Search*: Quartet books

   African Journey: A Search for the Roots of the Blues (Recording): Vanguard Nomad Series SRV-73014/5

2. Finn, Julio: *The Bluesman* p. 5

3. Oliver, Paul: *The Meaning of the Blues*: Collier Books, 1960 (p. 32)

4. Leonard, Nancy: *Negro Anthology Characteristics of Negro Expression*

5. Lomax, Alan: *The Land Where the Blues Began*: p. 402

6. Shapiro, Nat and Hentoff, Nat: *Hear Me Talkin' to Ya'*: N.Y. Dover

7. Feather, Leonard: *The Book of Jazz*: Dell Publishing: p. 29

8. L.A. Times: 12-27-92

9. Marsalis, Branford: *I Heard You Twice the First Time* (CD liner notes): Columbia CK 46083

10. Balliett, Whitney: *American Musicians: 56 Portraits in Jazz*: Oxford Univ. Press, p. 151

11. *Ibid.*: p. 40

12. Marsalis, Wynton; liner notes to recording *The Majesty of the Blues*: (LP) Columbia OC45091

13. Feather, Leonard: Liner notes to *Symposium in Blues*. RCA PRM-235. (LP)

14. Hughes, Langston: *The Collected Poems of Langston Hughes*: Vintage Press, p. 608

15. Rothenboerg, Jerome: Quasha, George: *America: A Prophecy-John Lee Hooker's Black Snake*: p. 150

16. Roberts, John Storm: *Black Music of Two Worlds*: Original Music

17. Hunter, Joel *Have You Ever Been Mistreated BLUES MASTERS: V. 10 Blues Roots*: Rhino R271135

18. Marsalis, Branford: *I Heard You Twice the First Time* (CD liner notes) Columbia CK 46083

Bibliography

The Sanctified Church: Zora Neale Hurston: Turtle Island Foundation, Berkeley

The Roots of the Blues: Samuel Charters: Quartet Books, London

Born With the Blues: Perry Bradford: Oak Publications, NY

The Meaning of the Blues: Paul Oliver: Collier Books, NY

Stompin' the Blues: Albert Murray: Da Capo Press

Blues People: LeRoi Jones; Morrow Quil Paperbacks, NY

The Land Where the Blues Began: Alan Lomax: Pantheon, NY

The History of the Blues: Francis Davis Da Capo Press

R. Crumb's Heroes of Blues, Jazz and Country: Abrams, NY

Discography

Southern Journey:Volume 3—61 Highway Mississippi: Delta Country Blues, Spirituals, Work Songs & Dance Music: The Alan Lomax Collection: Rounder CD 1703

Blues Masters: The Essential Blues Collection—Volume 10: Blues Roots: Rhino Records R2 71135

Mali to Memphis: Putumayo World Music: Putu 145-2

Mississippi Blues: Putumayo World Music: Putu 196-2

The Blues: Smithsonian Collection

Roots of Jazz: Collected by Doug Goodkin; www.douggoodkin.com

CHAPTER 7: JAZZ BLUES

"The blues is the single element that connects the jazz musicians. Why is that? Because blues has the emotional, harmonic and technical depth to inform whatever you do in this music."

—WYNTON MARSALIS

July 4, 1776 marked the beginning of a new chapter in American political history. A testament to the ideal of political freedom was declared and a force set in motion that would change the world. July 4, 1900 marked the beginning of a new chapter in American *cultural* history. A declaration of musical freedom was set in motion that would also reverberate around the world—Daniel Louis Armstrong was born.*

Raised by his single mother in a poor New Orleans neighborhood known as "The Battleground," singing on the streets for money at an early age, arrested at 13 for firing a pistol in the air, sent to a reform school for two years, Louis Armstrong's early life reflected the status of many African-Americans in the society. He learned cornet at the reform school, hung around the "tonks" (neighborhood bars) listening to the music of the early jazz musicians, hung on the coattails of the great King Oliver, and played in clubs and riverboats inbetween delivering coal, unloading banana boats or selling newspapers to support his ailing mother. From these beginnings, Louis (alias "Satchmo" or "Pops") rose to become America's "Ambassador of Jazz" and the first great exponent of the art form.

While Louis Armstrong was performing around the world on an official U.S. State Department tour in 1961, Wynton Marsalis was born into a middle-class family in Louis's hometown of New Orleans. The young Wynton received his first musical training from his father (a jazz pianist and educator) studied classical music in high school, and attended the prestigious Juilliard School of Music in New York. He began performing and recording both classical European music and jazz, receiving accolades in both fields. He is currently Artistic Director of Jazz at Lincoln Center in New York and receives commissions from that institution to compose large-scale jazz works.

---

* There is now some evidence to suggest that he was born on August 4, 1901, but here is a case where the mythological truth is truer than the factual—his birthday indeed was a "Declaration of Independence" and his work set the tone for the 20th century's most vibrant new music. I'm sticking with July 4, 1900.

Separated by time, education, economic class, performance opportunities, social climate, and musical style, Louis and Wynton played jazz trumpet across opposite ends of the century. The meeting ground of their music is the ever-present refrain of the blues.

THE BLUES IN JAZZ

When Scott Joplin published the *Maple Leaf Rag* in 1899, the ragtime craze was in full swing. 30 years after "emancipation," African-Americans had more opportunities for formal and informal study and access to a wider range of instruments. This new marriage of two worlds, with its incorporation of European harmonic theory, compositional form and formal technique, moved African-American folk feeling a step closer to jazz. Ragtime also expanded the European piano music vocabulary with its African-Americanised offbeats in the left hand, syncopation in the right and percussive technique.

However delightful the ragged bass ("ragtime" derives from "ragged time") and the sparkling syncopations, it wasn't potent enough to conceive jazz as we know it. It needed more of the African Soul—swing rhythm, improvisation and the blues. Jelly Roll Morton brought all three into his piano playing (almost justifying his outrageous claim that he "invented jazz" in 1902) and the embryo was formed. Simultaneously, European brass bands in New Orleans were inspiring African-American counterparts, and the inevitable alchemical transmutation of Spirit touched by Soul took place. Midwived by Louis Armstrong's masterful improvisations combining advanced technique and theoretical complexity with the deep expressive power of the blues, jazz was fully born.

Each change in the evolution of jazz style interpreted the blues anew. The thread linking Armstrong and Marsalis passed from the New Orleans-style blues of Jelly Roll Morton and King Oliver to the Swing blues of Count Basie and Duke Ellington to the Be-bop blues of Charlie Parker and Dizzy Gillespie to the Cool blues of Miles Davis and Sonny Rollins to the funk blues of Horace Silver to the modal blues of John Coltrane to the avant-garde blues of Ornette Coleman to Wynton Marsalis's contemporary compositions.

Though a listener new to jazz would have a hard time hearing how pieces like Ornette Coleman's *Bird Food*, John Coltrane's *Pursuance* and Charlie Parker's *Billie's Bounce*, relate to Bessie Smith's *Empty Bed Blues*, the link can be made clear if we follow each step of its changing face in the history of the music. Having firmly established the aesthetic foundation of jazz, from its African roots to its African-American folk and popular incarnations, we are now ready to examine the details of its evolution. This means listening, analyzing, and most importantly, playing the music itself.

JAZZ BLUES IN THE CLASSROOM

Just as we preferred authentic African-American folk material to jazzed-up English nursery rhymes, so must we now go directly to the literature itself. Not only do we strengthen the connection to the "real" world of music, but we also allow the voices of the great musicians themselves to enter the classroom through their music.

Our approach of recreating the historical progression would suggest that we begin with New Orleans-style blues, but there are both historical and pedagogical reasons to reconsider this. If ragtime was a dead end, New Orleans-style was a rough gravel road needing to be paved over before jazz could really start moving. In those early formative years, there were still many elements that were discarded as jazz searched for more efficient ways to swing. The bass shifted from a jumping 2/4 oompah to a smoother walking 4/4, the piano (thanks to Count Basie) added both harmonic outline and rhythmic punctuation without duplicating the bass and drums, the drums kept it all moving with the ride cymbal—the modern rhythm section was born and it was swinging! Away with the tuba and banjo, more saxophone than clarinet, and trumpet replacing cornet. No more freewheeling improvised polyphony—enter tightly controlled written ensemble parts with more space for soloists. The Swing Era had arrived and would thrive until the mid-40's, when a new generation added the next story to the house of jazz.

The motto of the new sensibility was first spoken on Count Basie's piano—*get the maximum swing from the minimum notes.* This is music to the ears of the music teacher in the classroom. It means beginning students can play a simple riff here, a well-placed tritone there, a few well-chosen notes for their solo and contribute beautifully to the ensemble sound. Ragtime and Dixieland, by contrast, demand advanced technique and facility with changing scales and arpeggios. The music of the Swing Era leads the student towards modern jazz, not only setting the foundations of the style, but also teaching a repertoire of tunes that jazz artists are still re-interpreting.

This is where we'll begin our formal entry into real jazz, and there's no better place to start than in Duke's Place—with the classic statement of swing and simplicity of one of the art form's greatest: Duke Ellington's *C-Jam Blues.*

A San Francisco School parent and student playing the blues.

DUKE'S PLACE—C-JAM BLUES (IN G)

Words by Ruth Roberts, Bill Katz and Robert Thiele
Music by Duke Ellington
arranged by Doug Goodkin

If you've never been to Duke's Place.
Get your tootsies down to Duke's Place.
Life is in the swim in Duke's Place.

45. DUKE'S PLACE—C-JAM BLUES (IN G): Duke Ellington

Focus

• Riff blues melody

• Blues scale improvisation

• 12-bar blues progression

• Inner voice (shifting tritones)

Comments

C-Jam Blues summarizes all the preparation we have done for six chapters! The music teacher or experienced band student could look at the notes and play this piece by following the score. The younger student could learn the parts by rote. But in both cases, there might be no understanding of nor appreciation of how the structure evolved. By contrast, we can trace the hi-hat offbeats to *Head and Shoulders*, the ride cymbal ostinato to *Step Back Baby*, the syncopation to *Soup, Soup*, the swing rhythm to *The Cookie Jar*. We improvised in the G blues scale in *Green Sally Up*, learned about shifting tritones in *Hambone*, *Zudio* and *Ready for the Blues*, learned the blues chord progression and call-and-response form in *The 8th Grade Blues*, learned to scat and get a feel for soloing in our various games and exercises. We've also been steeped in the power and beauty of the pentatonic scale and gotten a good feeling for improvising in many styles through our experiences in Orff Schulwerk. We've been fully involved in the learning process, can hear the historical connections and feel the cultural background, can understand the basic theory and are starting to learn enough to orchestrate our own instrumental blues without dependence on an outside arrangement. We've landed squarely on two feet in the world of jazz.

As we enter our first authentic jazz piece, let's come in through the door of a familiar Orff process. The following activity is a miniature summary of the Orff-jazz connection that eloquently demonstrates their similarities and differences. It can be used in a variety of ways, as follows:

1) As a "coming attractions" for young children (1st to 4th grade) to give them the pleasure of being inside a "jazz blues" and get a sense of their feel for jazz rhythm and phrasing as they improvise.

2) As a quick review for the older children (5th to 8th grade) beginning their jazz study.

3) As an introduction to the joy of the blues for the general beginner of any age. I have done this in workshops with businessmen who have never played music, Orff teachers who have never played jazz and my own teachers in my school and the look of amazement on their faces as they effortlessly play such great-sounding music is a delight to behold!

Activity

- Sing a two-note melody as follows:

- With xylophones set up in the C pentatonic scale, invite the students to find the melody on their instrument. (Note that wood xylophones should tremolo to sustain the last note of each phrase.) This is also easily playable on recorder. For a little variation in the repetition needed to master the melody, all play the melody three times on the low E and A, repeat on the high E and A, repeat playing in octaves.

- Add drones in bass. Create simple form:

  - Metal plays melody three times

  - Wood improvises for length of three times

  - Wood plays melody three times

  - Metal improvises

  - Both wood and metal play melody

  - Select soloists

  - End with melody, singing while playing

- Discuss the aesthetic value of the piece, with its minor pentatonic melody and long, legato tones. (Many people answer, "Soothing, mysterious, pretty, etc.")

- Repeat the melody using a percussive technique and a new rhythm. Basses now play melody instead of drone.

All play melody three times (once through) alone. Next time, teacher joins in playing walking bass and tritones on piano and hi-hat (optional).

Watch the look on the students' faces when they hear themselves with the piano!

- Select soloists improvise with this new swingin' rhythm while all tap mallets on the offbeat. Repeat melody at the end, all end with the familiar piano tag (see measure 25 in arrangement—transpose to A). All end with a tremolo on G.

- Discuss the aesthetic value of the piece. ("Fun! Exciting! Exhilirating!") At this point, I ask: "Why did the soloists sound so good?" Students might reply:

  - They were playing with swing rhythm.

  - They had a good sense of phrasing.

  - They were playing notes in the pentatonic scale that always sounded good.

I continue, "All of this is true and of course, these are stellar musicians! But there was one thing that made them **really** sound good."

Students: "**You** playing the piano!"

"That's right! So if you want to repeat this experience, you all have to buy my CD of piano back-up!" (At this moment in workshops, many teachers start reaching for their wallet! But being an educator and not an entrepreneur, I continue.) "Or—I can teach you what I did on the piano. In 45 minutes and with a little practice at home, just about everyone can do what I did. More importantly, we'll learn these parts on the bass bars and bass xylophones, so you can be a completely independent jazz ensemble and I can go out for a coffee break. Shall we go on?"

I hope the reader can imagine their exuberant, "Yes!"

Pedagogical comments

Along with *Funga Alafia, Boom Chick a Boom* and *Step Back Baby*, I count this little sequence as a model of everything I care about in education. The activity begins with a simple sung phrase that students must find on the xylophone, activating the needed-connection between the voice and the hand. The simplicity of the phrase ensures success for even the most beginning of musicians. The drone, also simple to play, adds the ground that gives a pleasing texture and the pentatonic scale guarantees some measure of musicality in their improvisations. My guiding principle of "Do it first—discuss it next—do it again," is at play here. We begin with an active experience, discuss how it sounds (and perhaps *why* it sounds so good) and then prepare for the next experience.

Equally important is that there is some sense of mystery. The students don't know where we're heading with all of this, but are willing to trust me, especially as they get immediately satisfying results. It's as if I'm leading them step by step through a forest in which every step along the path is pleasant, but they don't know what they'll find at the end. When the piano comes in, it's like arriving at a spectacular vista that is made all the more beautiful by its surprise.

Motivation is a crucial component of successful education and when the students hear how good they sound playing over the piano harmonies, they are motivated to move on to the next step—how to play those harmonies themselves. And of course, another part of what makes them sound so good is the piece itself, a brilliant Ellington masterwork, and the musical form of the blues, that genius expression of the African-American culture. Success, surprise, sequence, motivation, quality music—these produce a palpably different atmosphere in a class from the usual dry, "Sit down, get ready, we're going to learn a piece called the *C-Jam Blues* from your book on page 182."

Now the students are ready to begin their study of an authentic jazz repertoire. The following is a review and elaboration of the key concepts that will help them understand more clearly what they are playing and why.

The Riff

The riff is the jazz term for melodic ostinato—a short, repeated melodic pattern lasting two to four bars. Used extensively in big band music, it is generally in the background, giving rhythmic energy and encouragement to the music the way the congregation responds to the preacher in the black church. The riff can also be in the foreground as the main melody itself. Riffs can answer each other (as they often did in the brass and reed sections of big bands), overlap and layer over each other. They usually make generous use of silence to further pronounce their syncopated accents.

Riff blues are an ideal way to begin an exploration of the jazz instrumental blues literature. Though the riffs may be rhythmically challenging, they can be simple melodically and undemanding technically. They assure a place in the ensemble for students who are not ready for the improvised solo or are having difficulty with the bass progression. Most importantly, they invite the possibility of students creating their own riffs after a period of sufficient imitation.

The riff in the *C-Jam Blues* is a masterpiece of effective simplicity. It consists of two pitches and two rhythmic motifs: ♫ and our old familiar *"Soup, Soup"* ♩. ♫. How is it possible that such a simple idea can be the basis for a whole piece? First, we must remember that the riff has replaced the vocal melody and has the same relationship to the underlying harmonic progression. That is to say, each time the riff is repeated, it is redefined by the chords underneath and feels like a new melody. If we imagine the riff as a noun—say, *pepper*, the chords underneath are the adjectives—*green* pepper, *red* pepper, *yellow* pepper—that give the riff a different flavor each time.

It is worth noting that this is a central principle of the European harmonic system. To further demonstrate, have the children sing a repeated single tone—say G—while you play different chords on the piano: G C Eb Gm Cm Em A7 Dsus4 G7 C. Each new chord re-defines the sound of the sung G. Extend this idea with some key listening examples: Chopin's *Prelude No. 4*, Dizzy Gillespie's *Con Alma*, Antonio Carlos Jobim's *One Note Samba*.

The Blues Scale

We're now ready to drop the *la* pentatonic terminology and call our by-now familiar note series by its jazz name—the blues scale. We have played it over a I chord bass, a I-IV setting, a I-V progression and a V-IV-I pattern. Now that we are in jazz and playing it over the I-IV -V blues changes, it has earned its new title.

Basic Blues Scale in Key of G

Why have we bothered with this pentatonic route? Why not just call it the blues scale from the beginning? And why is this blues scale different from most found in music textbooks and jazz theory books? These questions deserve consideration—pedagogically, historically and theoretically.

In the first instance, the *la* pentatonic terminology has served to connect us with the melodic development as outlined in Orff Schulwerk. It supports our emphasis on the pentatonic as the scale of choice for improvisation freed from harmonic restraints. Its foundation in the overtone series qualifies it as an excellent *starting* point.

This approach is likewise supported by the cultural origins and historic evolution of African-American music.* Many of the field hollers, work songs, prison songs and early spirituals from which the blues came are pentatonic-based (with some ambivalent tones) and draw their musical energy from rhythmic, melodic and expressive devices rather than harmony. They tend to have a limited melodic range, centered around the three-note clusters we've practiced in our early improvisation.

*Thorough documentation of this theory is beyond the scope of this book—a ripe field for a doctoral dissertation!

It was ear-ly one Sat-ur- day_ morn-in'   When I went to Lou - isi -an - a

Early in the Mornin': Prison Work Song

Free at last____ free at last_____ thank God a' might-y I'm free at last_

Free at Last: Spiritual

Wade   in the wa - ter__   Wade   in the wa - ter child-ren oh

Wade   in the wa - ter.__   God's gon-na troub-le   the wa - ter.__

Wade in the Water: Spiritual

Coming into jazz from a Western approach, many well-meaning music educators miss this foundation. Textbooks and jazz books alike commonly describe the blues scale as a major scale in which the 3rd, 5th and 7th degrees are sometimes flatted to make "blue-notes."

To cite but one example published in a reputable music education journal (whose source will remain anonymous to protect the guilty):

> "Blues melodies often have 'blue' notes in them (pitches one-half step lower than pitches
> of the major scale, especially on the third, sixth, and seventh degrees of the scale). Thus,
> a melody based on the C scale might have these pitches: C, D, E♭, E, F, G, A♭, A, B♭, and
> B."

This way of thinking comes from the ethnocentric notion that the major scale is the center of the musical universe. It's as if the author imagined the early blues musicians sitting in the juke joint with the major scale written on the board. *"All right,"* says the leader, *"We've got seven notes here. I'm going to point to them one at a time. Now we've got to keep the first one, so I'll move right to the second. How many vote to flat the second one? Come on, raise your hands... Okay, how many votes for the 3rd?..."*

By contrast, our historical approach acknowledges the tendency towards the pentatonic in early spirituals, work songs, ring plays and, eventually, folk blues. As the music moves out into the jazz repertoire, the pentatonic scale is extended—ultimately, the blues scale will use all 12 notes of the chromatic scale.* But the skeleton that holds it all together is pentatonic, and this is where we should begin.

This serves a practical purpose for beginning students, allowing them to improvise rhythmically and melodically without changing scales with every changing chord. Every

---

* Charlie Parker's *Bloomdido* is an example of a blues melody that uses all 12 tones.

note of the scale "works" with every chord in the progression. The student enjoys the success of sounding good and is motivated to continue.

Most students work too hard when they improvise. The beauty of this form is the changing chordal foundation that will do much of the work for them by redefining the quality of each note. If they stick to short, riff-like figures within the small ranges of the partial pentatonic, they'll get a better sound with less effort.

The changing scales approach is ultimately necessary for those who want to continue to develop their jazz improvisation, but in the early stages inhibits success. By shifting the energy to the intellect and abstract combinations of notes, the *music* of the blues is lost.

Once again, we can make this point strongest by looking at what does *not* work. A well-known book on jazz improvisation (again, anonymous) introduces the blues to the student with this chord progression (in itself, an odd starting choice with the Major chords in bars 1, 3, 7, 8, 11, 12) and the accompanying scales:

Improvise following this model, and then with our model of our pentatonic blues scale over shifting tritones. Which sounds better?

Does our choice hold up theoretically? For the mathematically inclined who want to know "why" this scale works, we can define each note in relation to the chord tones of the I-IV-V. Isolate each note of the scale and play with the accompanying root/tritone.

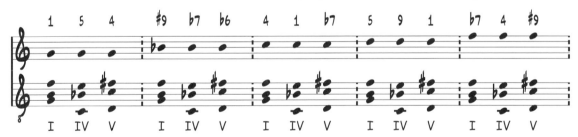

This brief analysis reveals that most of the tones match the stated or implied chord tones—1, 5, ♭7 —while others state the extensions of the chords—9, ♭9, ♯9, ♭13, 4, a non-chord tone, appears three times, creating some tension. But even if we were to only play that note the whole 12 bars, the underlying progression would resolve the dissonance after two bars.

Improvisation

The children have been well-prepared to improvise, not only from a constant diet of pentatonic improvisation over drones in their Orff training, but also from all the pieces they have played from Chapter 5. Now their improvisations will take on a new character because of the shifting chords beneath them (see next section). Without any extra effort on their part, they will suddenly sound good! If you doubt this, watch their faces as they fly over the blues chords, exhilarated with the power of their expression.

As mentioned earlier, I generally leave the students to their own imagination and simply enjoy listening to how they are thinking musically. Are they swinging? Thinking in short, riff-like phrases? Using repetition to build tension and variation to release it? Is there a shape to their melodic flight? After listening to them, I sometimes suggest adjusting according to some of the guidelines above. I also have them listen to each other and try to articulate what they liked about their fellow students' solos—and then invite them to shamelessly steal every idea they can!

One idea related to the chart above that has proved fruitful is to solo five choruses of the blues, each one starting with a different note in the scale. Try it yourself on the piano and notice how each note suggests different ideas when used as a starting point.

Tritones

Now we pick up the thread from Chapter 5 and revisit the tritones introduced in *Hambone* and *Ready for the Blues* within the blues progression. On the Orff instruments, the tritones are played on the altos, using the inversion that is lowest in range, i.e.,  instead

of . Those who don't have chromatic instruments can set them up like this:

Now it is clear why we have chosen the key of G. With the accompanying accidentals of F♯ and B♭ that come with Orff instruments, G is the only key that allows us to play the tritones of all three chords—I, IV, V. The tritones can also be played on the upper part of the bass xylophones (see our next piece, *Blues Legacy*, for an example). Traditionally, these inner voices played on the piano and root notes played on the bass are in the next octave down:

Key of G: G⁷ tritone   C⁷ tritone   D⁷ tritone

One of the things that make the blues played by the Orff ensemble sound a bit strange is that everything is transposed up an octave. Playing the bass on contrabass bars and the tritones on the bass xylophones helps give weight to the sound. Naturally, piano or band teachers introducing these ideas need not worry about the ranges of xylophones and are free to transpose to the keys of their choice—they need not stay with G. (Coincidentally, G is the preferred blues key for saxophones—however, that means playing in concert B♭).

The fact that the blues ends with a tritone deserves some notice. Jazz theory is the same as Western classical theory, but with a twist. Note that a G7 chord in a Bach piece would most often function as a V7 chord cadencing to a I—the B is the leading tone pulling to the C, the F, the 4th degree, falling to the E.

I ask my Conservatory students if they could imagine a piece ending with a G7 without resolving and they firmly say no. Imagine their surprise when I play the 7th chord at the end of a blues progression. Given the right context, we can live with the tension of the tritone without resolution.

Chromatic Orff Instruments

Although the following arrangements of the blues in the key of G can mostly be played on diatonic Orff instruments, we have reached a level of harmonic sophistication where chromatic instruments are preferred. I particularly recommend the model created by Periople-Bergerault,* that features tubular resonators, stands with wheels, removable bars, and sustain pedals for the metallophones. Now is the time (middle school especially) to add piano, keyboards, and/or professional vibraphone or marimba.

Form

Following the basic form we've established in previous pieces, we play the melody twice, have different soloists improvise for one or two 12-bar cycles and then return to the melody played twice. This tune also introduces a signature ending. In jazz parlance, the melody is called the **head** and one cycle through the 12 bars of the blues is called a **chorus.** This shorthand is useful in reviewing the form with the students—"We'll play the head twice, Maria solos for one chorus, Nick for one chorus and then back to the head." Likewise, pointing to your head during a performance will remind the initiated students what's coming next. Because the form of a jazz piece is open-ended, such non-verbal signals are crucial. When someone's improvising well, rotating your finger in a circle can indicate that he should take another chorus. Moving your finger across your neck in a throat-slashing gesture tells everyone the end is near.

The music student may notice a parallel with the Western classical sonata form—"head-improvisation-head" is a similar concept to "exposition-development-recapitulation." Both begin by stating the theme, proceed to develop the material and return to the theme at the end. But whereas the European composer mostly re-works the themes harmonically, the jazz soloist keeps the harmonic structure intact and improvises *melodically*.**

---

* For further information, see www.peripolebergerault.com

** Some European compositional forms also concentrate on melodic variations within a constant harmonic structure—Pachelbel's *Canon* and Bach's *Passacaglia and Fugue in C Minor* are two of the more well-known examples. Likewise, some jazz soloists venture into harmonic variations of the theme—Art Tatum in one genre, John Coltrane in another.

How can you create more formal interest in the head-solo-head structure? Some beginning possibilities are as follows:

- Be aware of *timbre*, dividing the band into sections. (In the case of the Orff ensemble, xylophones, metallophones and glockenspiels). Create different colors in playing the head and accompanying riffs through isolating or mixing different sections.

- Be aware of *texture*, adding or deleting instruments in different sections.

- Add *set riffs* behind solos. (In this case, repeating the head riff lightly under the second chorus of a soloist.)

- Assign *contrasting soloists* (as in voice, recorder, drum, glockenspiel).

BLUES LEGACY

Milt Jackson
Arranged by Doug Goodkin

46. BLUES LEGACY: Milt Jackson

Focus

• Walking bass

• Snare drum with brushes

Teaching the parts

Now that we have a grasp on the component parts, we can decide the order in which each is introduced. In general, it's a good policy to start by teaching the melody, but for variety, it can work equally well to practice the chord progression or the drum parts. In all cases, make sure at least one other layer is sounded in the music; i.e., the students can scat-sing the melody while practicing the rhythm, or the teacher can play the chord progression while students practice the melody or play the bass while the students practice the chords. Working this way, the ear is absorbing the next part of the lesson while the hand is practicing the first part.

At this point in our unfolding progression, let's pause and review some general principles for teaching these pieces. I stress the word *general*—there are many exceptions and situations that invite different approaches:

• Teach all parts to everyone before dividing—including the chance to solo.

• Change parts on different pieces so that children experience the music from all angles. (The child who played bass plays melody next time, the drummer on one piece plays the chords on the next, etc.).

• Teach the melody first and/or keep at least two layers of the music going while practicing.

• After sufficient experience changing parts, ask students to notice which they prefer—bass, rhythm, background riffs, solos, etc. Equally vital to beginning with a generalist approach is settling on a specialty in the middle stages.

Riff Melody

This piece, like most that follow, is a riff blues—one pattern repeated three times over the blues changes. It confirms the basic blues scale that we have established, with one exception—the E in the opening triplets. Note the use of the repeated Bb and encourage students to include such repetitions in their solos.

Walking Bass

This piece extends the work with the walking bass begun in *Hambone*. Each fragment is as follows:

When the IV chord moves to the I, play:

The whole walking bass pattern is as follows:

The walking bass adds forward drive to the ensemble while simultaneously explicitly stating the basic four beats per measure. We start with a set pattern, but in the real world of jazz, the bass player improvises bass patterns derived from an expanded repertoire of stock phrases. Playing the root note of the chord on the downbeat of the appropriate measure is the given—the path taken to arrive at each root is up to the player. Mostly my students stick with a set pattern, but sometimes they "hear" some connecting notes and start to add them in.

Trying the walking bass on the contra-bass bars.

Snare Drum

Our introduction to the drum set began with the hi-hat playing the offbeat. We then added the ride cymbal to underline the swing rhythm. Now we bring in the snare drum played with brushes to reinforce both. The right hand duplicates the ride cymbal pattern while the left creates a background "swishing" sound with a slight accent on the offbeat. For a beginner's brush technique, swish the brush in the left hand from right to left across the middle of the snare drum to a quarter note beat. When the left hand goes to the right, the right hand crosses to play the "chick" of the "chick a boom" ride cymbal pattern. When the left hand goes to the left, the right hand uncrosses to play "a boom." As students improve, they might try the more sophisticated technique of moving the left hand brush in a clockwise circle, with an acceleration between 12:00 and 6:00. This technique is difficult to describe in print—consult your local drummer!

You will have noticed that we have separated the parts of the drum set in our preliminary work. Now we can consider trying two parts together. The three combinations are:

• The hi-hat and the ride cymbal.

• The hi-hat and the snare drum.

- The hi-hat with the ride cymbal pattern on top. (This was first introduced by Jo Jones in the early 1930's and produces a markedly different quality from the ride cymbal alone because of the muffled timbre when the cymbal is closed.)

For the next few pieces, nothing new needs to be taught on these three instruments. You may simply ask, "Who wants to play the hi-hat/ride cymbal/snare drum?" and the students should know what to do. Naturally, those who are ready to try two at a time (hi-hat and ride cymbal/hi -hat or snare drum) should do so.

Comments

The late, great vibraphonist, Milt Jackson, composed this tune, along with four other blues included in this chapter. Milt's work is ideal not only because of the vibraphone/ Orff xylophone connection, but because so many of his melodies reinforce the notion of the *la* pentatonic as the center of the blues scalar universe. Milt often begins his improvisations as well with this basic blues scale before radiating out into the chromatic variations characteristic of the be-bop era in which he came up.

When Milt came to visit our school, my 8th grade students began playing this piece for him. Sometime during the second playing of the head, he stopped and tipped his ear towards the music with a puzzled look on his face. Suddenly, a big smile broke out as he realized what it was—he had composed so many blues, he had forgotten that this was his own tune!

Milt Jackson playing the vibes.

SKJ

MILT JACKSON
ARRANGED BY DOUG GOODKIN

Tritone with walking bass during solos:

(NOTE: Once the students—and teacher—understand the basic blues progression with accompanying tritones, it is not necessary to write out all the parts for each arrangement. For most of the succeeding pieces, we will use a short-hand notation, as above.)

47. SKJ: Milt Jackson

Focus

• Bass drum kicks

• Riff tritone accompaniment

• V chord on turnaround

The Bass Drum

The bass drum in the drum set came directly from the bass drum of the New Orleans marching band at the turn of the century. Marching to the cemetery in the funeral procession, the bass drum was carried and played by one person, the snare drum played by another. When the emerging syncopated marching music settled down in the club or dance hall, one person played both bass drum and snare in an alternating 2/4 oompah beat. The invention of the foot pedal for the bass drum, credited to Baby Dodds, freed the hands to play the snare and cymbals. By 1925, two cymbals held vertically close to the floor (called "Low Boy") were played by a foot pedal. This design evolved to a horizontal set-up high enough to be played on top by the hands—hence the name hi-hat. By the Swing Era, the basic drum set* was established.

As the one-two punch of Dixieland changed to the 4/4 of Swing, the bass drum in the Swing Era was often played in "four to the floor" style—keeping a steady beat to underpin the ensemble sound. The immense sound of the horns in the big bands made this both possible and necessary. The smaller groups of the Be-bop Era changed the bass drum function from time-keeping to rhythmic punctuation. In jazz vocabulary, such accents are called "kicks." (Be-bop drummer Max Roach called them "dropping bombs.")

The delicate dynamics of the Orff ensemble preclude the "four to the floor" approach. In this piece, the bass drum accents the last two notes and the rest of the riff melody. It now becomes clear to the students why we insist they play the hi-hat with the left foot—they need the right foot for the bass drum.

Tritones

In the previous two pieces, the tritones played a steady beat—four to a bar. This allows the students to concentrate on the logistics of changing tritones with the bass. Once they're comfortable with the changes, a more rhythmic approach is possible. In an advanced jazz ensemble, the piano player improvises the rhythmic punctuation of chords. Because we are dealing with beginners and have several students playing the tritone part at once, the rhythm here is set and continues throughout the piece. You may notice our familiar *Soup, Soup* rhythm yet again. Its syncopated punch over the steady walk of the bass gives the piece a stronger rhythmic drive than the chords and bass playing together on every beat.

This shift has a parallel in the history of jazz. In Count Basie's band, guitarist Freddie Greene almost always played chords four to a bar. As jazz moved from Dixieland through Swing towards Be-bop, the search for efficiency of swing was a driving force. By the mid-40's, each instrument's role was streamlined to give maximum swing with minimum duplication. The bass gave the basic quarter-note pulse while outlining the harmony, the hi-hat played the offbeat and the ride cymbal announced the underlying swing, the

---

* Also called the "trap set." When people first saw it, they asked, "What is that contraption?" This was later shortened to "trap."

piano filled out the chords that the bass implied and both punctuated the melodic accents and filled the spaces in the melody in company with the snare and bass drum. The bass, drums, and piano (or guitar) are called the **rhythm section** because they each have a rhythmic role in the overall time feel, the ground over which the melody of the horns soars. This is useful vocabulary to introduce to the students during rehearsal time (as in, "rhythm section, stop talking!"). In the Orff ensemble, the bass and/or bass bars naturally corresponds to the bass, the drum set is, of course, the drums, and the "piano" is either the alto or bass xylophones, depending upon where you choose to play the tritones. It goes without saying that a real piano, keyboard or guitar can either replace or supplement the alto/bass parts.

It should be clear that as we introduce the next level of jazz blues arranging in each new piece, we can revisit old pieces—like *C-Jam Blues*—and apply the new learning. Each blues arrangement presented here is not fixed, but is a stepping-stone to increased understanding of the options. A second rhythmic figure that could be used in this and subsequent blues is as follows:

Turnaround

You may have noticed a change from the blues progression we've used so far—a V chord in bar 12. Since the blues is a cyclical form, the V chord serves to "turn it around" back to the I chord of the beginning—hence the name **turnaround** to describe the last two (and sometimes four) bars of the cycle. Note the increased harmonic density of the last four bars—a different chord for every measure. As we progress from simple to complex, we will continue to add chords that change more often than in our basic progression. Note that the V chord should *not* be played in bar 12 at the end of the piece—naturally, we must end on the I.

Comments

This is another winning blues by Milt Jackson, not only affirming the basic blues scale, but also echoing the descending pattern from *Have You Ever Been Mistreated* in Chapter 6. Like *Blues Legacy*, it has a built-in feeling of call-and-response, this time with three calls and one response filling the entire four bars.

The arrangement here suggests a solo melody with the rhythm section accenting the downbeats of measures before moving into the walking bass pattern with the tritone riff. During class, it is good for everyone to solo to gain experience and develop ideas. For performance though, two or three soloists is a more musical solution. I usually set the number of choruses, but more advanced students can do as real jazz musicians often do—solo for as long as they feel they have something to say.

JUMPIN' WITH SYMPHONY SID

LESTER YOUNG
ARRANGED BY DOUG GOODKIN

Gotta get hip and flip to the latest, people who love to swing with the greatest,
There is a Deejay show at the station, spinnin' the hottest tunes in the nation,
Symphony Sid a jive talkin' daddy, Jumpin' with Symphony Sid.

Better tune in this prince of the platters, playin' 'em all and that's all that matters,
Dizzy and Duke and James with a killer, Ella and Bing or Basie and Miller,
Get on the move, it's gonna be groovy, Jumpin' with Symphony Sid.

48. JUMPIN' WITH SYMPHONY SID: Lester Young

Focus

- Changing pentatonic

- Parallel harmony

- Creating riffs

Changing Pentatonic

This tune is clearly in the world of our second blues scale, the altered pentatonic, with one important exception. On the I chord, the B is natural (making it a major G pentatonic scale), but on the IV and V chords, it is flat. This is our first step in the direction of changing scales with changing chords. B is available in our improvisation over the I chord, but it must change over the IV and V chords. A simple ear test will reveal why—the dissonance is too much.

Other jazz blues tunes that follow the formula of changing the B in the riff to B♭ at the IV chord include *Bluebird, Buzzy*, *Cool Blues* (Charlie Parker), *Tenor Madness* (Sonny Rollins), *Blues for DP* (Ron Carter), *Turnaround* (Ornette Coleman) and *Blues in the Closet* (Oscar Pettiford).

Parallel Harmony

A parallel melody line adds another possibility to our expressive palette. Though the students can learn it by rote, this is an opportunity to lead them towards our goal of independence through hearing and analysis. Here is a possible sequence:

- Figure out and play the same melodic rhythm and similar melodic shape starting on a different note of the pentatonic.

(This should be played on alto instruments below the soprano melody.)

- Try each possibility with the melody, deciding by ear which sounds best.

- Going slowly, one note at a time, analyze the troublesome dissonant intervals in each case. You can now decide to use one of their solutions or lead them toward the parallel melody given, adjusting notes as necessary.

Creating Riffs

- Keeping to the altered pentatonic scale, have the students experiment with creating their own riffs using a limited range and their understanding of jazz rhythm and phrasing. It is easy enough for them to come up with something, but tricky to come up with a riff that really swings. As always, have all students improvise riffs simultaneously (you may wish to provide a rhythm section), listen to one at a time and choose autocratically or democratically one or two to incorporate into the piece. The second riff given in this arrangement was created by my student, Jorge Miranda.*

The other riff in this arrangement uses only two notes and suggests a tritone response.

The Snare drum—kicks and fills

This piece features two other important roles of the snare drum—to further accent other parts in the same way the bass drum did in our last piece and to fill in the spaces left by the melody and/or soloist with improvised rhythms. These latter accents—simply called "fills" in jazz—provide a running commentary in the midst of the musical flow. At our beginning level, we begin with a few set rhythmic riffs and move towards the ultimate goal of listening closely to the overall texture and improvising our contribution to that texture. In this piece, the snare drum can reinforce the accents shown in the melody.

Color, dynamics, form

By this point, we have considerably enlarged our expressive vocabulary of the basic jazz ostinati on the drum set. Now we can give our attention to the color and dynamics. As beginning drummers, we think simplistically in terms of beating out rhythms, but the jazz drummer uses the drum set like a giant palette from which to paint the aural canvas. Each chorus of the 12-bar blues offers a possibility for a slightly different color and dynamic. Again, though this is improvised at its higher level, it should be set in the beginning stages. The choice to play with quiet brushes for the glockenspiel solo and change to sticks for the piano solo is a step in this direction.

The Tom-toms

The tom-toms are the last members of the drums we introduce to the children (though historically, they were part of the drum set from the beginning). They are Chinese in origin, as were the early cymbals, adding an interesting twist to this already multi-cultural music. The tom-toms give a tonal color more precisely pitched than the dull thud of the bass drum or metallic buzz of the snare. They offer a melodic voice to the drum set, particularly effective in drum solos.**

---

* One day when I was unexpectedly late for my jazz class for teachers, the movement teacher, Susan Kennedy, spontaneously begain teaching a modern African-American game, *Jig-a-lo*. The refrain on the game is "Jig-a-lo, jig-jig-a-lo." Later that morning, I taught *Symphony Sid* with this accompanying riff and Susan exclaimed "That's *Jig-a-lo*!" That day, the spirits were present!

** One of many fine examples of a tonal drum solo can be heard on Art Blakey's version of *Doodling*.

Eighth grader playing drum set.

The Drum Solo

Drum solos were rare in Dixieland ensembles and uncommon in early swing bands. It was Gene Krupa's lengthy solo in the Benny Goodman Band's 1937 version of *Sing, Sing, Sing* that helped catapult the drums into the foreground. Though a white drummer, Krupa acknowledges his indebtedness to the black drumming tradition of making drums sing. Early on, we spoke of the deep connection between speech, song and drum found in the West African talking drum and the tuned-drum choirs. Now with an entire drum set at his disposal, the drummer could sing in his own language, using the mixed timbres of cymbals, snares, toms and bass drums as his choir. As Krupa describes it:

> "Baby Dodds taught me more than all the others. Not only drum playing, but drum philosophy. He was the first great soloist. His concept went on from keeping time to making the drums a melodic part of jazz. Baby could play a tune on his drums and if you listened carefully, you could tell the melody... Most white musicians of that day thought drums were some things you used to beat the hell out of... few of them realized that drums had a broad range of tonal variations so they could be played to fit into a harmonic pattern as well as a rhythmic one."

Drum solos were firmly established as a part of ensemble play by the be-bop era in the mid-forties. Kenny Clarke, Roy Haynes, Art Blakey and Max Roach were some of be-bop pioneers extending both the rhythmic complexity of soloing and the expressive range.

In addition to playing extended improvisations following the form of the song, many drummers "traded eights" with the melodic players—improvising for eight bars responding to each other's ideas. The children in Orff classrooms are already familiar with this format in question-answer exercises—now they can extend it to improvised conversations between drums and xylopyhones.

In the Classroom: How can we develop the art of drum soloing with our students? For a start, we need to make the entire drum set available to one student and to introduce the idea of using all four limbs at once. Keeping within the beginner's scope of this book, here are some suggestions for non-drummer teachers:

John - ny works with one ham - mer, one ham - mer, one ham - mer.

John - ny works with one ham - mer, now he works with two.

- Sing the above song up to "four hammers," playing on the drum set as follows (Others can practice in the air):

1—right hand	2—add left hand	3—add right foot	4—add left foot
play ride cymbal	on snare drum	on bass drum	on hi-hat

- Create a pattern using all four limbs, thinking in shapes. A circle: r.f., r.h., l.h., l.f.; reverse: l.f., l.h., r.h., r.f.. An X: r.f., l.h., l.f., r.h. (reverse). Two parallel lines: r.h.&r.f., l.h.&l.f., etc *

- Play a tune on the drum set, treating each separate part as one note. (Ex: *Hot Cross Buns*)

Ride Cymbal
Snare Drum
Bass Drum

- Play a jazz tune on the drums, as in the melody to *Symphony Sid*.

- Play a riff and develop it through repetition, contrast, extension, etc.

- Listen to a variety of classic drum solos.

Form

For contrast, begin this piece with the solo line implying the harmony.

1st chorus: Melody and hi-hat alone.
2nd chorus: Bass roots on downbeats, parallel melody, ride cymbal enter.
3rd chorus: Bass roots every beat, first riff, tritone response with snare drum accent.
4th chorus: Riff repeated, some parts a 3rd above.
5th chorus: Solo on altered pentatonic. Brushes on snare drum.
6th chorus: Drum solo.
7th chorus: Second riff.
8th chorus: Second riff with melody.
9th chorus: Second riff, melody and parallel melody, offbeat on rim of snare drum.

---

* This approach is thoroughly developed in a book by drummer George Marsh titled *Inner Drumming*, self-published 1983.

Final Exam

Having followed the sequence and played four riff blues, the students have enough information about rhythm, melody, harmony, texture, orchestration and form to create and perform their own riff blues. If you found a Lindy Hop teacher (see Chapter 4), have one group play music and another group choreograph a swing dance. This can take place across classes, across grade levels and over many class periods. In keeping with the Orff aesthetic, have select dancers and musicians switch places in the middle of the performance.

Comments

Symphony Sid was the nickname for Sid Torin, a disc jockey in New York who was one of the few to play be-bop on the radio in the 40's and 50's. One set of lyrics mentions some of the great players and singers of the day—Dizzy Gillespie, Duke Ellington, Harry James, Ella Fitzgerald, Bing Crosby, Count Basie and Glenn Miller—but oddly omits the man who wrote the tune, the great tenor sax player, Lester Young.

Doug's adult jazz class playing a mixture of chromatic and diatonic Orff instruments.

CENTERPIECE

Harry "Sweets" Edison
Jon Hendricks

2nd verse

I'll build a house and garden somewhere, along the country road apiece.
A little cottage on the outskirts, where we can really find release.
"Cause nothin's any good without you, 'cause baby, you're my centerpiece.

49. CENTERPIECE: Harry Sweets Edison and Jon Hendricks

Focus

- Three-measure riff

- ABC poetic form

- Parallel thirds

- Flatted fifth

- Altered turnaround

Expanded blues scale—the flatted 5th

Perhaps many have been wondering—"I thought the blues scale had a flatted fifth?"—and finally, here it is! Why have we waited so long to introduce it? First, because this note (D♭) is not present on the standard Orff instrumentarium*(here we sing it) and secondly, because it tends to function more as an ornamental passing tone than a bona fide scale tone. From here on, we can add it to our definition of the blues scale and use it when improvising on chromatic instruments. You may choose to use it earlier in your program without fearing investigation from our Jazz Sequential Curriculum Committee! Note how the D♭ neatly divides the two equidistant halves of our scale:

Those with chromatic instruments can now include the ♭5 in the subsequent solos.

The Turnaround

We have worked with a so-called "standard" blues progression, but as jazz evolved, the possibilities for harmonic routes through the 12 bars expanded. In small group performance, these will be somewhat improvised in each chorus, with the players listening closely and responding on the spot to the routes taken. To make it more confusing, the bass, piano or horn player can each be the driver! (Now we're getting close to the heart of jazz, the intense *listening* necessary and subsequent immediate response.) As always, we must first set the possible routes before improvising our way through them.

This arrangement of *Centerpiece* introduces an expanded turnaround. A simpler beginning version substitutes II and V for V and IV in the last four bars as follows:

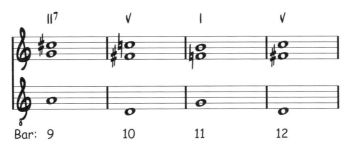

---

* We can create the blues scale with the flatted fifth on Orff instruments in the key of E (E-G-A-B♭-B-D-E)—see *Bag's Groove* in this chapter. *Birk's Works* by Dizzy Gillespie (not included here) is an excellent tune for introducing the ♭5th.

The next example gives a lot of energy to the turnaround by increasing the harmonic rhythm in the last two bars. If we look closely, we perceive a satisfying structure—the last two bars echo the progression of the preceding four in a condensed form.

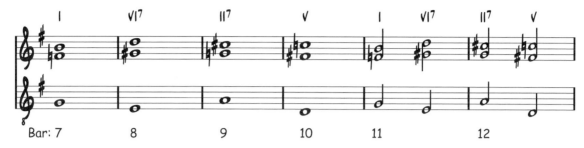

Finally, we can begin the turnaround in bar 8 by using the VI⁷ chord to lead us to the II⁷. This kind of harmonic motion comes from the circle of fifths and will be explored more thoroughly in the next chapter.

Comments

This delightful piece, popularized by Lambert, Hendricks and Ross, begins with a singable and easily playable three-measure riff. This is the only example in this chapter of a sung blues and a good opportunity to both involve the school choir (with proper attention to jazz vocal style!) and select soloists. Unlike its vocal blues predecessors, it changes the form from a repeated first line to three distinct phrases. The opening melody clearly outlines our secondary blues scale, while the harmony of verse two introduces the ♭5th. (Note that the top melody is usually sung alone for the first and the second melody joins in on verse two.) Either scale or a combination of them now can be used in improvisation.

From Orff xylophone to professional vibraphone.

NOW'S THE TIME

50. NOW'S THE TIME: Charlie Parker

Focus

• Through-composed blues melody

• #IV diminished chord

• IIm^7 chord

Additional chords

Moving on from *Centerpiece*, we continue to enlarge our harmonic vocabulary. This arrangement features a passing diminished chord, suggested by the melody when the C in measure 5 changes to the C♯ in measure 6.* We will look at diminished chords more closely in Chapter 8, but mostly they are chords that carry a lot of tension—they contain not one, but *two* tritones!

This tension helps push the harmonic movement along—hence, it's function as a passing chord. In our situation, only the bass need change (and here you must either use piano, a real bass or buy a C♯ bass bar) while the tritone can stay the same. For a smoother transition, play the 5th rather than the root in the bass in bar 7 as shown below:

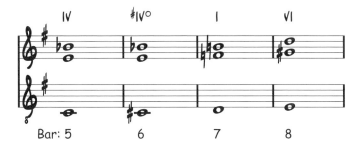

* Some recordings of this tune repeat the C in bar 6 instead of changing. This is an option for those who would like to play this tune, but don't have a C♯ to play in the bass.

Unlike *Centerpiece*, the II chord is now in its natural state as a minor 7ᵗʰ chord. Up until now, the students have been getting used to the tritone movement in which both notes move down or up a half step. When a minor 7ᵗʰ chord moves to a dominant, only *one* of the tones shifts, as shown:

Keeping in mind that material from Chapter 8 can be (and I suggest should be) taught alongside the blues, this progression will become familiar to students as well.

Comments

Our title tune was written by Charlie Parker and its primary riff stolen years later for the popular song *The Hucklebuck*. It begins as a simple riff blues, but expands the theme of the first four bars in the next four and contrasts it with a new theme in the last four. This kind of melody begins to step away from the riff blues format into a through-composed approach characteristic of much be-bop blues —*Billie's Bounce, Au Privave, Blues for Alice, Bloomdido*. Though these tunes are beyond the reach of our beginning student, *Now's the Time* is an excellent bridge to that form. The melody combines tones from both our blues scales, moving towards the more diatonic—and also chromatic—nature of the be-bop blues.

A THRILL FROM THE BLUES

51. A THRILL FROM THE BLUES: Milt Jackson

Focus

- AAB riff melody

- Expanded blues scale

- Extended chords

Extended chords

The tritone of the 3rd and ♭7th (with the root played by the bass) is the skeletal structure of the beginning chord voicing, getting the essential sound of blues harmony with the minimum of notes. The movement of these inner voices is clear, logical and playable by beginners. Now we're ready to expand from that base and add color to our chord by moving into the upper voices of the chord.

Extending to the upper voices is like adding blocks to a tower. From the triad built on 3rds, we added another minor third to make our ♭7th chord. Now we keep building with thirds:

The close voicing shown above is almost never used. The chords need to be pared down and opened up to give the notes room to breathe. Just as we removed the 5th in our 7th chord, so now we concentrate on just a few upper tones. We also want to keep in mind efficient movement between the voices. In the following voicings, we include the 5th and add the 9th and 13th to the tritones as follows:

Our five-note chord now will be split between three players in the Orff ensemble. The contra-bass will play the root, the bass, the tritone and the alto the remaining voices.

Below are the last four bars in their extended voices. Note the added color to the VI⁷ II⁷ V⁷ chords in the last two bars (for those curious, the VI⁷ and V⁷ extensions are ♯9 chords).

Additional Voicings

The reader new to jazz theory may be beginning to sweat profusely here and long for the simpler days of playing *Johnny Brown* or scat-singing the sounds of our name. Moving into the upper structures brings us away from the ground floor of beginning jazz to a place where some people get dizzy from the heights, overwhelmed by the expanding vista of harmonic possibilities. The ♭7th chord can handle a lot of tension and the number of available voicings is indeed daunting. This study is particularly the province of the piano and guitar players, though melody players must be familiar with these extensions as well. We will leave off here and refer those interested to the numerous books and recordings available (see Theory—bibliography). As enticement, some sample piano voicings are given that you may wish to practice (shown in their I-IV movement—find the V!) to accompany some of the blues exercises.

Comments

This is yet another winning blues by Milt Jackson, featuring a melody that contrasts the riff played twice in the first eight bars with an answering phrase in the last four (much like the earlier vocal blues). For a refreshing arrangement, begin the piece with the rhythm section playing their parts for one chorus and come in with the melody on the second chorus. Note that there is space at the end of each statement of the riff for the drums to add some fills.

BAG'S GROOVE

Milt Jackson
Arranged by Doug Goodkin

52. BAG'S GROOVE: Milt Jackson

Focus

• Key of E

• Vamp introduction

• Chordal melody

Key of E

I have chosen to begin this tune in the key of E for 3 reasons:

1. Our basic blues scale and bass vamp are both easily available on the Orff instruments. Though the students sang the ♭5th in the tune *Centerpiece* (in the key of G), this is an opportunity for them to play it as well.

2. This key works well for the beginning recorder player and is an excellent opportunity to integrate the recorder with the Orff ensemble, a common Orff practice.*

3. E is a great key for the beginning guitar student as well, both in terms of the chords and the improvising scale.

Bass, voicings, changes in E

The opening arrangement of *Bag's Groove* indicates it is a minor key blues. The whole tune, along with the improvisations, can be played as a one-chord version with a minor quality. However, it also works with the standard blues changes and this is a good opportunity for students to transfer what they know about the blues scale, tritones and walking basses and try to figure them out in the key of E. (You, the teacher, should try this also before looking at the answer below!)

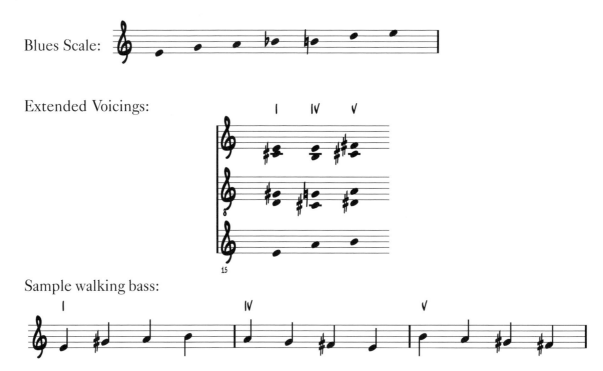

Blues Scale:

Extended Voicings:

Sample walking bass:

---

* The recorder isn't exactly a standard jazz instrument, though drummer Eddie Marshall has done some interesting things with it, and in a different context, Keith Jarrett as well. However, it is an excellent stepping-stone to the saxophone, clarinet and flute.

These exercises are essential to the success of all the material in this book—that the teacher, and ultimately, the students as well, don't simply play the given notes, but understand the theory behind them. Transposing melodies, bass patterns and chords to other keys is superb exercise for cultivating such understanding.

Note that this turnaround is similar to the one used in *Now's the Time*, that the upper extensions are similar to *Blues Legacy* and that the rhythm of these inner voicings is none other than our beloved *Soup, Soup*.

Melody

Bag's Groove features a new melodic device—simultaneous parallel melodies. Called paraphony in the Orff Schulwerk and found throughout Orff and Keetman's repertoire, a melody is given new color and character by a second (and here, third) voice playing a parallel melodic shape beginning on a different note. This is common practice in many musical styles, but has a special flavor in the pentatonic because the intervals are not constant—mostly 4ths, with one 3rd:

The student and teacher familiar with the device of paraphony found throughout the Orff literature will feel right at home here.

Like many of Milt's blues tunes, there is a skeleton structure that is ornamented by neighboring notes. If the students are ready for the authentic version, I include it here.

Comments

The practice of giving nicknames to blues musicians carried over into the jazz world and virtually every jazz musician has had a second christening as they earned their new name. "Bags" is the nickname of the vibraphone player whose tunes we have been enjoying, Milt Jackson. (He told me that it came from the bags under his eyes after staying up all night playing.) *Bag's Groove* is one of his most famous tunes, recorded by Miles Davis, Thelonious Monk, Gary Burton, The Modern Jazz Quartet, his own group, and others.

BAGS 'N' TRANE

MILT JACKSON
ARRANGED BY DOUG GOODKIN

Walking bass:

53. BAGS 'N' TRANE: Milt Jackson

Focus

- Key of D minor

- Minor blues

- Bass vamp & "So What" Chord

- Tritone substitution

Key of D minor

Just as the E blues scale is easily available on Orff instruments at the *la* pentatonic in the key of G, so is the D blues scale equally familiar—*la* pentatonic in the key of F.

Minor Blues

Bags 'n' Trane is a minor blues, expanding the expressive palette yet again. The absence of the tritone in the accompaniment of the first eight bars gives a different flavor to this blues style—instead of ♭7th chords, the I and the IV chords are minor 7th chords, spelled in root position follows:

　　Given our approach so far to chord voicings, it's clear that we will not simply play these chords as written above.

Bass vamp and "So What" chord

In this arrangement, the chords and the bass together create a harmonic ostinato known as a "vamp." Vamps are often performed over an unchanging pedal point, but in this case, the vamp changes with the IV chord. The chords played in the alto part are distinctly different from our tritones. They look like 6/4 triads, but the first chord is a suspension that "resolves" to the second, which, along with the root, is simply an inverted minor 7th:

The rhythm and voicing is borrowed from a famous Miles Davis tune, *So What*, and is my own choice of an arrangement—it is not used on the original recording. The full voicing, which could also be used here, is as follows:

Tritone Substitution

This is a good moment to reveal the concept of the tritone substitutions, yet another breathtaking example of mathematical order in the musical universe. The fundamental principle is this: **The notes of each tritone are shared by two different roots, which themselves are a tritone apart.**

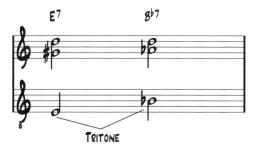

When E is the root, the G♯ is the 3rd and D is the 7th. When B♭ is the root, the G♯ (now A♭) is the 7th and the D is the 3rd. Sheer beauty to the mathematical mind!

Because they share the same tritone, either the E[7] or the B♭[7] chord can lead to the A[7] in the progression. Here we use the B♭[7] as a tritone substitution.

Comments

We now know who "Bags" is, but who is "Trane"? The initiated will certainly recognize him as that mighty engine who traveled into uncharted territory, the legendary saxophonist, John Coltrane. This tune headlines a recording of the same title featuring these two remarkable players.

The melody is a unique variation of the riff blues style. It states its opening motif in our familiar three-note blues scale pattern and completes the first riff mostly in its complementary three-note half. The first half then moves up a 4th and answers itself as before. This entire riff is then repeated. The macro-form is an unusual A B B, while the micro can be described a b c b c b.

For variety in the solos, the bass can walk, as given in the sample arrangement.

SUMMARY OF BASIC JAZZ BLUES PRINCIPLES

We have led the students—and ourselves as teachers—one step closer to our goal of independence. Because we have learned the basic functions of the different instruments and theoretical principles within the style, we no longer have to make each part explicit. Given a blues melody, the students now have sufficient information to fill in the accompanying parts, as well as room to make further choices. The following is a summary to date:

Drums

- The offbeat can be played on the hi-hat or snare drum (with brushes or sticks).

- The jazz ostinato can be played on the ride cymbal, top of hi-hat, or snare drum with brushes.

- The snare drum or bass drum can accent passages ("kicks") and /or fill in rests ("fills").

- The drum solo can use all the parts of the drum set.

Variations: Choose

- Which parts of the drum set will play the rhythms above.

- How to divide it up among students—one person, two? etc.

- Appropriate places in the particular piece to add kicks and fills.

- Places to change accompaniment in the form to give color and dynamics.

- Whether to include a drum solo or "trading eights."

Chord progression: Bass and tritones

- The chord progression will follow the basic 12-bar blues patterns.

- The root notes of the chords will be played in the bass (or contrabass if available) and the inner voices in the alto (or bass if contra bass is used).

- The inner voices will use chord tones 3rd and ♭7th, called tritones for short.

- The tritones will move by half-steps with the chord changes. (Whole step on V-IV).

Variations: Choose from the following options.

- Bass playing root notes "four to the bar."

- Walking bass.

- Tritones playing "four to a bar."

- Tritones playing a set rhythm.

- Tritone with ♭7th on the bottom; with 3rd on the bottom.

- Standard blues progression or variation (see summary, **Blues Variations).**

- Tritone extensions.

Improvisation

- The basic blues scales for improvisation is 1-♭3-4-5-♭7-8; its variant is1-2-♭3-5-6-8

- Soloists will be selected, improvising on the scale over the 12-bar structure.

- The soloist will play in swing rhythm, have a sense of home tone and create a conversational monologue drawing from rhythmic and melodic motifs.

Variations: Choose the following options

- The basic blues scale.

- The altered pentatonic blues scale.

- Combination of the above.

- Add the ♭5th to either scale.

- The 3rd on I chords, ♭3rd on IV and V chords.

Form

- The melody will be stated at the beginning and end of piece (generally twice each time).

- The middle section will be a combination of soloists and/or new riffs or themes.

Variations: Choose from the following options

- Begin with the rhythm section playing one chorus before melody enters.

- Begin with melody alone for one chorus before rhythm section enters.

- Begin with rhythm section and melody together.

- Decide the order of events and the specific orchestration.

With all of the above now understood, the teacher no longer needs to depend upon an arranger to publish the next jazz blues for the classroom.* The student no longer needs to have the specific rhythm on the ride cymbal taught or the bass pattern shown or the notes of the tritone named. We only need to teach the melody, clarify the tempo and set the form. From there, we can simply say: "It's a blues in G—choose your instrument and let's play!"

SELECT CHORD CHANGES IN THE BLUES

Having taken our driver-in-training course through the 12 bar blues, we're ready to hand over the wheel, along with a map of possible harmonic routes. This is still only a sketch of the possibilities, but enough to give a taste of the many variations possible. **Notice that the two unchanging landmarks in the blues progression are the I chord in bar 1 and the IV chord in bar 5.** Back in Chapter 4 *Hambone*, we promised more affirmation of the I-IV chords as being the fundamental progression of the emerging African-American style, and here is more evidence for the court. Most importantly, the beginning student

---

* This is not to suggest that there is no value in the work of talented arrangers. Such arrangements are an essential part of the band experience in particular. But for our beginning purposes, we are more concerned with the bare bones of the style that allows us to improvise in small groups, with creating our own beginning arrangements. From that foundation, we will also have an increased understanding of and appreciation for the worth of a great written arrangement.

must learn to hear these landmarks to help orient when lost. You'll note the increased density of the harmonic changes. In the first example, each chord plays for eight beats, with the first I chord continuing for sixteen! By the last example, chords change almost every two beats. This enlarged palette of harmonic color offers increased tonal shadings—beginning with *red pepper, yellow pepper, green pepper* and now adding *mauve pepper, fuchsia pepper, tope pepper*—and the increased harmonic complexity suggests new and more intricate routes in the melodic improvisation.

BAR	1	2	3	4	5	6	7	8	9	10	11	12
1	I7	I7	I7	I7	IV7	IV7	I7	I7	V7	V7	I7	I7
2	I7	IV7	I7	I7	IV7	IV7	I7	I7	V7	IV7	I7	I7
3	I7	IV7	I7	I7	IV7	IV7	I7	I7	V7	IV7	I7	V7
4	I7	IV7	I7	I7	IV7	IV7	I7	I7	II7	V7	I7	V7
5	I7	IV7	I7	I7	IV7	IV7	I7	VI7	II7	V7	I7	V7
6	I7	IV7	I7	I7	IV7	IV7	I7	VI7	II7	V7	I7 VI7	II7 V7
7	I7	IV7	I7	I7	IV7	IV7	I7	VI7	IIm7	V7	I7 VI7	IIm7 V7
8	I7	IV7	I7	I7	IV7	IV7	I7	bIII7	bVI7	bII7	I7 bIII7	bVI7 vII7
9	I7	IV7	I7	Vm7 I7	IV7	#IVo	I IIm7	IIIm7 bIIIm7	IIm7	V7	I7 bIII7	IIm7 bII7
10	IMAJ7	VIIm7b5 III7	VIm7 bVI7	Vm7 I7	AS ABOVE							

OTHER BLUES TUNES

This brings us to the end of our introduction to jazz blues. The journey from the *C-Jam Blues* to *Bags 'n' Trane* spans many years of jazz history and a wide range of theory. Following these tunes as they pass into new tempos, keys, scales, chord voicings, chord progressions and forms, we slowly build our understanding of the changing character of the blues. Each tune reinforces our previous knowledge and shows us something new.

Below is a list of other blues I've done with my students that are not included here. With a good ear, an understanding of the basics outlined here and the right recordings, ambitious teachers can now go on to arrange these tunes themselves.

SWING ERA

- *Happy Go Lucky Local* (Duke Ellington)—Riff blues in two sections with key change and breaks/walking bass (also a version called *Night Train*).

- *Things Ain't What They Used to Be* (Mercer Ellington)—Transposed riff, triplets melody.

BE-BOP

- *Sonnymoon for Two* (Sonny Rollins)—Call and response riff with descending melody.

- *Tenor Madness* (Sonny Rollins)—Chromatic be-bop melody.

- *Misterioso* (Thelonious Monk)—Chromatic melody, slow blues, a double-time section.

- *Birk's Works* (Dizzy Gillespie)—Minor blues with new changes.

- *Bluebird* (Charlie Parker)—Riff melody with shifting 3rds and a major 7th

- *The Blues Walk* (Clifford Brown)—Riff blues combining the two blues scales.

COOL/MODERN

- *All Blues* (Miles Davis)—Through- composed melody, V-$\sharp$V on turnaround, 6/8 meter.

- *Blues for DP* (Ron Carter)—Altered pentatonic scale with shifting 3rd.

- *Blues for Juanita* (Milt Jackson)—Riff blues.

- *Bright Blues* (Milt Jackson)—Another riff blues by the master.

- *Equinox* (John Coltrane)—Minor Blues with melody that shifts up at the IV chord

- *Freddie Freeloader* (Miles Davis)—Melody that shifts up at the IV chord, $\flat$VII chord in turnaround.

- *Gladys* (Lionel Hampton)—Advanced blues changes, with catchy through-composed melody.

- *Nostalgia in Times Square* (Charles Mingus)—Melody that shifts up at the IV chord, unique turnaround.

- *Splanky* (Neil Hefti)—Riff blues.

- *Stolen Moment* (Oliver Nelson)—Minor 16-bar blues, chromatic harmony.

FUNKY

- *No Blues (Pfrancin')* (Miles Davis)—$\flat$5th, VI-II-V-I turnaround.

- *Watermelon Man* (Herbie Hancock)—Extended 16-bar blues, rock beat.

THE MEANING OF THE BLUES: From the Heart to the Head

"When the higher flows into the lower it transforms the nature of the lower into that of the higher.

—MEISTER ECKHART

How strange that the words of a 13th century German mystic so aptly describes the evolution of the blues! If the blues began as a gut response to the soul in anguish, it sprouted its first wings the moment it crossed from mere feeling to song. From the first field holler, it continued to spiral upward until it crossed the threshold into jazz. There it animated the music with its raw power and in turn was transformed by the higher nature of jazz expression. Robert Johnson sang the pain of his life straight from the belly, but in the hands of Count Basie, the blues turned into a joyous affair. Between unmediated expression and cloaked repression lay transformation, the flowing of spirit into suffering. Compressed in the strong hands of the artist who had mastered technique and deeply studied the theoretical landscape, the coal of *Black Snake Moan* became the glittering diamond of *Misterioso*.

The reader may have noticed a change in tone as we enter more deeply into the theoretical aspect of jazz. Though it's occasionally amusing to dress up theory with fanciful language and sometimes helpful to animate it with imagery, we might as well face the reality head on—we are in a dryer world than the moist, soulful feeling of improvised expression. But it is a necessary and even a refreshing change—we all need some time to dry off and reflect. The important thing is that the theory flows from the tunes themselves and stays but a short time in the incubator of abstraction before it flows back into the music.

We have spent much time emphasizing the hands, hips and heart, but the brain is an organ also and the blood flows there just as fully as it does to the genitals and chest! We can feel the surge of pleasure and the warmth of emotion as the mind embraces each new concept. We take care not to linger too long in the initial rush of understanding, but to send the ideas back down to the hands to realize in technique, to the hips to keep them fertile, and to the heart, to remember their proper roles—to serve and widen expressive feeling. When the blood circulates freely in our jazz 4H club (hand-head-hips-heart), we win the blues ribbon.

Discography

Statements: Milt Jackson: Impulse GRD-130 (includes *A Thrill from the Blues*)

Bags Meets Wes!: Milt Jackson and Wes Montgomery: Riverside (includes *SKJ*)

Bags & Trane: Milt Jackson & John Coltrane: Atlantic Jazz 1368-2 (includes *Blues Legacy, Centerpiece, Bags 'n' Trane*)

MJQ & Friends: The Modern Jazz Quartet—A Celebration: Atlantic Jazz 82538 (includes *Bag's Groove*)

Gary Burton: For Hamp, Red, Bags and Cal: Concord Jazz-CCD 4941-2 (includes *Bag's Groove*)

Everybody's Boppin': Lambert Hendricks & Ross: Columbia CK45020 (includes a vocal version of *Centerpiece*)

Mood Indigo: Capitol Sings Duke Ellington: Capitol D 103056 (includes *Duke's Place [C Jam Blues]*)

The Original Recordings of Charlie Parker: Verve 837 176-2 (includes *Now's the Time*)

Prez Conferences: Lester Young: JassJ-CD-18 (includes *Jumpin' with Symphony Sid*)

CHAPTER 8: JAZZ STANDARDS

"Just a travelin' along, singin' our song, side by side."

Jazz began its journey travelin' "side by side" with a cast of colorful characters. When it hooked up with popular culture, it left its folk roots (though it never lost touch) and moved out into a wider world. 20th century America was destined to be defined by that culture and jazz was along for the ride. The vehicle was the emerging technology of media—radio, records and motion pictures.

America in the 1800's was a predominantly rural folk culture, grounded in the tradition of the local people and land, and loosely united through print and travel. The newspapers and magazines showcased the latest "fashion" and the growing rail system provided a swifter exchange of goods. Likewise, travelers passing through the village or town shared what they knew—be it a new product, a musical style or the latest political idea. By the turn of the century, the car was speeding up the urbanization process, but it was the radio that broke things wide open. Now the newest music, ideas and stories were instantaneously available to people around the country. No longer tied to the history, contour or climate of local culture, a city musician could be inspired to pick some country blues guitar and the country player inspired to play some urban licks. Equally important, the radio business became aware of an audience and music took on a new role—to speak to a mass market. Popular culture was born.

The record industry added fuel to the fire. The first jazz recording in 1917 was coincidental with the rise of its first great improvisers, whose contributions could not be captured in print (although there is much speculation about and lament for the unrecorded music of the legendary Buddy Bolden). Just as the study of European classical music history begins with the first notated compositions, so does jazz history begin with its "notational" medium, the recording. Now musicians and fans might hear their first call from jazz through a recording rather than a live performance. And the audience grew. Avid fans in Europe who may never have heard a live jazz performance would hungrily await the next shipment of records at the docks. A new riff recorded in New

York could now be practiced weeks later in San Francisco and become a part of the jazz vocabulary nationwide. The recording industry promoted jazz through preservation, distribution and occasionally, inspiration to create new works. It also continued to feed the hunger of popular culture, both striving to anticipate its preferred cuisine and determining its diet through the food it offered.

Finally, the movies made the myths of the culture visible to all, again both shaping and reflecting our collective imagination. While our ancestors looked to the heavens for divine inspiration, we also looked to the stars—Errol Flynn, Jean Harlow, Clark Gable, Mae West, Charlie Chaplin, and Greta Garbo. From the ragtime pianists accompanying silent movies to the Hollywood musicals, jazz was often the soundtrack of the American myth.

Today the arts suffer from the excess of media marketing. But in its youth, media culture was the artistic forum of the country. Recordings, movies and radio shows that were highly popular in their day became American classics. The songwriters were the poets of that culture, their songs, the anthems of our national psyche. In the hands of improvising musicians, they also became something else—the traveling companion of the blues singing the song of jazz.

Origins

The distant roots of the popular song go back to the minstrel shows, a traveling entertainment of dance, music and comic patter in which white performers in blackface parodied blacks. The motives behind such entertainment were a strange mixture of admiration for the black dance style, mockery of physical differences and sentimental justification for the barbaric practice of slavery by creating a mythology of blacks as childlike, carefree, content, happily singing and dancing under the care of their benevolent master. These traveling shows were a staple in the American entertainment world of the 1840's and 50's. After the war, black minstrel shows began to tour as well, taking the confused ignorance of racism to an absurd level—blacks wearing blackface to imitate whites imitating blacks! But these shows also brought a vibrant authenticity to the music and dance. The black minstrel show birthed a dance known as the cakewalk, a take-off on the high manners of the rich white folks. When whites began to do the cakewalk, the irony of blacks performing in blackface was joined by the strangeness of whites doing a dance created by blacks to parody whites! While minstrelsy created and perpetuated racial stereotypes that still resonate to this day and set in motion a national style of rational denial, it also was paradoxically the means by which the power and beauty of African-derived music-making began to leak into mainstream culture.

By the 1890's, the rural traveling minstrel show began to give way to the urban revue on a theater stage—vaudeville. Comic acts, magic tricks, gymnastic stunts, dances, dramatic sketches and songs were all part of the business called "show business." Many of the songs were sung by individuals rather than a whole troupe and as vaudeville gained in popularity, the forum for composing songs was established. "Song pluggers" were hired to advertise a song, some (like 14 year old George Gershwin) to play it on piano and others to sing it in restaurants, street corners, stores, anywhere a crowd was gathered. Some boys were planted in the audience to "spontaneously" join the singer on the stage, making the audience feel that the song was so catchy that it was bound to be a hit.

The primary technology for dissemination was sheet music for pianos, which were almost as ubiquitous in American homes as TV's are today. In 1900, Monroe Rosenfeld was sent by the New York Herald Tribune to do a story on the publishing industry, located in dozens of offices on West 28th St. between Broadway and 6th Avenue in New York City. As he approached the area, he heard the competing sounds of tinny pianos playing their songs through the open windows and dubbed the block Tin Pan Alley in his article. The name attached itself to the music that arose from it.

Vaudeville grew into the musical theater of Broadway and demand for the popular song form grew accordingly. Many of the songs were written specifically for a Broadway show (or later, a Hollywood movie), but took on a life of their own beyond their dramatic function. We're not likely to know the shows *Very Warm for May, Follow Thru* or *A Damsel in Distress,* but may be familiar with the tunes written for them—*All the Things You Are, Button Up Your Overcoat, A Foggy Day.* We probably know the tunes *Heart and Soul, Louise* and *I'm in the Mood for Love* without ever having seen the movies A *Song Is Born, Innocents of Paris* or *Every Night at Eight.*

Though some of the jazz artists were masters of the popular song form (particularly Duke Ellington, Billy Strayhorn and Fats Waller), the songwriting "culture" was predominantly white—Cole Porter, Harold Arlen, Irving Berlin, James Van Heusen, Hoagy Carmichael, Jerome Kern, the songwriting teams of George and Ira Gershwin, Rodgers and Hart, Lerner and Loewe. A large percentage of them were first-generation Jewish immigrants, and there is a further irony that two ethnic groups—blacks and Jews—who would never boast a president in the White House would define the American cultural landscape of the 20th century. (And yet more ironies—it was a Jewish man, Irving Berlin who wrote the hit song *White Christmas.)* These songwriters and the jazz singers that brought their creations to life were our 20th century troubadours, singing the same song as their medieval counterparts—the many faces of romantic love. Just listen to the titles of these songs:

> *If I Had You, It Had to Be You, I Didn't Know About You, I Don't Know Enough About You, I Wish I Knew, I Wish I Could Tell You, I Get a Kick Out of You, I Thought About You, The Very Thought of You, I'll Get By as Long as I Have You, I Get Along Without You Very Well, I Can't Face the Music Without You, I Will Wait for You, I've Got a Crush on You, I've Got You Under My Skin, I Only Have Eyes for You, I'm a Fool to Want You, Why Do I Love You?, I Don't Know Why I Love You So, I Wish You Love, I Can't Give You Anything but Love, Gee Baby, Ain't I Good to You? I Concentrate on You, I Remember You, I Cried for You, If Ever I Would Leave You, I'll Be With You in Apple Blossom Time, I Can't Believe That You're in Love with Me, Just You Just Me, You Won't Forget Me, If You Were Mine, You Go to My Head, I Mean You, I Loves You Porgy, I Love You Truly, I Love You*

Amidst the dullness of work in the Industrial Age, the pressures of the "rat race," the agonies of two World Wars and the Depression, love was the redeeming angel who touched our need for magic and mystery. When love struck, we were lifted from our mundane life to a transformed world, floating three feet off the ground or ascending to the heavens in company with angels:

> "Suddenly I saw polka dots and moonbeams..."
> "You're clear out of this world, When I'm looking at you, I hear, out of this world..."
> "Lately I seem to walk as though I had wings... like someone in love..."
> "Dearly beloved, how clearly I see, somewhere in heaven, you were fashioned for me"
> "Angel eyes knew you, angel voices led me to you..."
> "Darn your lips and darn your eyes, they lift me high above the moonlit skies..."
> "All at once am I several stories high, knowin' I'm on the street where you live..."
> "The night we met, there was magic aboard in the air, there were angels dining at the Ritz..."

While we spent our days struggling to achieve the American dream of material success, love stood ready each evening to penetrate our armor and leave us *"bewitched, bothered and bewildered."* *"Lost control and tumbled overboard,"* and amidst the heroic stance of the daily round, love provided the balancing act. These songs inspired us to search for true love, sang our feelings when we were touched and comforted us when love left us holding our hat—*"The memory of all that... the way you haunt my dreams... the way you've changed my life, no they can't take that away from me."*

Jazz Meets the Popular Song

Watered at its roots by the underground stream of the blues, jazz extended its branches towards the sunlight of the popular song. Where the blues sang of the forbidden elements of American culture—sex, pain, hardship and injustice—the popular song celebrated its sunny exterior—optimism, cheerfulness and romantic love. The cultural gap once again yawned wide. Where the African-American, by necessity and temperament, would go *through* the pain—*"Feel like holl'in, I feel like cryin', I feel so bad, baby, I just feel like dyin',"* mainstream American culture suggested stepping to the side:

> "Just put on a happy face..."
> "Just direct your feet, to the sunnyside of the street..."
> "You've got accentchuate the positive, elimynate the negative..."
> "Wrap your troubles in dreams and dream your troubles away..."

The clever lyrics, memorable melodies and beautifully crafted harmonies of the popular song repertoire were sufficient to capture the public's ear, but alone didn't have the authority to achieve the status of "art music." They needed interpretation from musicians who could ground their flighty sentiment in the depth of genuine emotion. They needed refreshment from the blues. The transmutation of the most mundane torch song into a moving soliloquy by Billie Holiday or an exquisitely crafted piano improvisation in the hands of Art Tatum is a legendary part of jazz history. Ira Gershwin once said, "I never knew how good my songs were until I heard Ella Fitzgerald sing them."

From the 1930's on, the blues and the popular song, later called the "jazz standard," formed an essential part of the jazz player's repertoire.

WEST MEETS WEST

We have already spoken of the distant roots of jazz as a meeting between West Europe and West Africa. Europe gave the language, some musical forms, instruments like guitars, pianos, double basses, trumpet, clarinets and saxophones and a system of harmonic/melodic theory that required study and practice. Africa gave musical impulses that integrated calls and responses, vibrant polyrhythms, percussive techniques, a dance aesthetic and community involvement. Nowhere is the marriage of West and West more evident than in the twin streams of the blues and jazz standards that informed (and inform) jazz. This is best illustrated in the following examples:

This old English folk song illustrates key features of the European aesthetic. Its legato tones and flowing phrases can be traced to the long lines of Gregorian Chant. Its accompanying chords are based on a system of tension and release that serve to evoke reflective emotion. It features a verse and chorus narrative form with parallels in the European literary tradition. It uses metaphor as a poetic device—the water that cannot be crossed is the wide gulf between the lovers themselves. Finally, the text about love comes straight from the troubadour tradition and concerns itself with personal feelings and an individual destiny, two strong strands in the European psyche.

By way of contrast, the African-American folk song *Soup, Soup* (see Chapters 2 and 5) features short, percussive phrases in a call and response form. There is no harmonic movement to speak of and its power comes from the groove of the rhythm (and later, the bass vamp). The text uses metaphor more as a survival strategy than for poetic effect and concerns itself more with affirming group identity than following one's personal drama.

By late 1800's, both strands were firmly established—an inherited British Isles folk tradition that led to Stephen Foster's songs and a newly created African-American folk tradition (already a blend of African sensibilities within European forms) that led to the blues. Now when you hear *C-Jam Blues*, it is easy to trace its short repeated phrases, percussive rhythms and small range of harmonic movement to its *Soup, Soup* ancestor. When you hear *Stardust*, you can recognize its long lines, romantic theme and chords begging to be resolved like two lovers leaning in for a kiss, as a descendant of *The Water Is Wide.*

The story of jazz is a shifting dialogue between these two traditions—the Afri-centric *folk* blues and Euro-centric *popular* composed songs that created a third tradition—the *classical* art form of jazz. To further thicken the mix, the blues and popular songs were themselves already mixtures of influences, the former having borrowed European elements of harmony, orchestration, and instruments and the latter having folded in snippets of African elements into its repertoire—syncopated rhythms, "blue" notes, call and response phrases. (It is little known that *Stardust* had originally been a faster piano rag before Mitchell Parish was called in to put words to it.)

When Louis Armstrong plays both *C-Jam Blues* and *Stardust*, it's as if all the feuding ancestors are finally sitting down at the banquet together and enjoying for one brief moment the soup served in the American melting pot.

IN THE CLASSROOM: Popular Songs in the Jazz Curriculum

"Orff teachers agree that the voice is the primary melody instrument."

—JANE FRAZEE [1]

"All you got to do is sing."

—DUKE ELLINGTON [2]

We sing every day at my school. In addition to the twice-weekly music and movement classes, the 1st through 5th grade gathers every day after lunch for 20 minutes of singing. Songs are generally arranged thematically—animal songs, motion songs, Appalachian songs, rounds, work songs, songs from around the world, and jazz songs.

Further pumped up and amplified by expanding medias and powerful business, the popular song tradition is larger and more pervasive than ever. Younger and younger children are listening to a pop music that both reflects and shapes their own time. In a culture that changes so rapidly, pop music represents a finger on the pulse that helps define each new generation. What is the value in having children learn the popular music from a radically different generation?

1. The popular songs of the 20's through 60's[*] represent a vital slice of American culture that, in combination with the shows and movies in which they were featured, reveal much of our 20th century cultural and mythological heritage. They help connect the children with a sense of past. This is revealed at my school most dramatically during our annual Grandparents' Day. Many of our grandparents were born between 1920 and 1940 (though lately, that is changing!), when jazz and popular music were just beginning. The look of pleasure and amazement on the grandparents' faces when their grandchildren sing along with them on *Has Anybody Seen My Gal?*, *Moonglow* and other hits from their youth is ample proof of the importance of keeping this heritage alive.

2. Knowing the standard repertoire is essential for every aspiring jazz student, both listeners and players. When we know a song, we can follow the improvisor's interpretation with increased understanding. Singing these songs gives us a concrete foundation for learning the abstractions of AABA forms, II-V-I chords, modulations at the bridge and other theoretical elements that we'll be exploring in this chapter.

3. The songs have intrinsic musical value, some wonderful lyrics and are fun to sing. Whenever I ask for requests at our daily singing time, many of these songs invariably are top on the list.

Despite these reasons, I find this material generally neglected amongst my Orff colleagues. What are the issues and how might we resolve them?

Pedagogical considerations: While our material to date has fit beautifully within the framework of Orff pedagogy, these songs take a leap in another direction. The

---

* Starting in the 1960's with songwriters like Stephen Sondheim, musical theater took a different stylistic turn away from the taste of jazz improvisers. Though a jazz musician today will still reinterpret the timeless gems of Porter, Gershwin and others, none will play music from *Jesus Christ Superstar, Les Miserables* or *The Lion King*.

pentatonic folk songs central to the lower elementary Orff program generally have a limited range with stepwise or small- skip motion, regular phrases, can be sung a cappella and require little or no harmonic accompaniment. This kind of material is vital to building improvisation skills and providing a base for future harmonic understanding.

By contrast, many of the jazz standards have a wide range, large leaps, chromatic notes, key changes, irregular phrasing and require a relatively sophisticated harmonic accompaniment to feel complete. How to reconcile these two worlds?

Though the pentatonic allows for musical hearing, understanding and skill to develop side by side, Orff never intended for any child's entire *musical* experience to be pentatonic. Working within the Southern German Bavarian culture, children were expected to continue *singing* music from that folk tradition, which was almost entirely I-IV-V based. This is true in the United States as well. Children in Orff classes continue to sing the classic two- or three-chord American folk songs, from *The Itsy Bitsy Spider* to *On Top of Old Smokey* to *John Henry*. Though these could be sung a cappella, most suggest a chordal accompaniment easily accessible to most teachers on guitar or autoharp.

The jazz songs have more sophisticated harmonies than American folk songs, which are essential to the song. *Bingo* sounds reasonably like *Bingo* without the guitar, but the melody of *The Sunnyside of the Street* sung alone is clearly begging for harmonic accompaniment. Some suggestions for teachers ready to dive into the repertoire:

- **Harmonic accompaniment:** The literate piano player can read from (and ultimately memorize) printed sheet music, as can guitar players (most sheet music usually includes guitar chords). The "ear" musician can follow the guidelines of root movement and chord voicing given in this chapter and figure out a basic accompaniment from this information.

- **Chromaticism and key changes:** Though pentatonic material is easier to understand, it isn't necessarily easier to *sing*. Children generally learn singing the way they learn speaking—by reflecting their aural environment. If these are the songs they are brought up with, these are the songs they can sing. On our school recording, *Bag's Groove*, you can hear a three-year-old singing a convincing version of *Somewhere Over the Rainbow*.

- **Range:** The range of the song *does* affect children's singing and songs with wide leaps do present difficult challenges. One solution is simply to choose songs with a workable range. Another possibility for the experienced jazz musician is to re-work the melody. The first phrase of *The Sunnyside of the Street* covers the range of a 12th, including a leap of a sixth, while Billie Holiday's version in her 1944 recording has the range of a 5th!

- **Vocal development:** It may be difficult for a vocal teacher working with the children on the precise diction of Western art music to feel comfortable with the breathy quality, deliberate slurs and "lazy" articulation of some jazz singers, but this can be an important part of the stylistic interpretation. Again, direct imitation is the best model for the children. It is important for them to hear a variety of jazz artists sing the same song to feel the range of vocal styles and attempt some imitation. Some excellent examples can be found on the many recorded joint ventures of Louis Armstrong and Ella Fitzgerald—their two markedly different approaches and timbres represent two ends of the expressive vocal spectrum.

- **Form:** Unlike many American folk songs with several verses, these songs tend to have a single verse. When it feels too short to simply sing it through once, play the song again on the piano or guitar and have the students:

  —Snap their fingers on the off-beat and clap when the bridge comes.

  —Scat-sing the melody , whistle the melody or vocalize instrumental sounds.

  —Improvise a "drum solo" or "hand tap dance" using body percussion.

  After one or more times through the song using one or several ideas above, all sing the song again. This approach helps prepare the jazz form of head-solo-head.

Teaching the Song

There are, of course, many ways to teach a song. Some standard practices include:

- Echo each phrase line by line and join them together.

- Sing the whole song several times and invite students to join any phrases they remember.

- As above, with words written on the board or large song sheet.

- Play the melody on the piano with words on the boards, inviting students to imagine how the words match the tones.

- Read the words and the melody from sheet music or fake-book notation (each with their own or shown via an overhead projector).

- Play recordings of the song and have the kids sing along.

It is pleasurable enough and challenging enough to simply sing the song and sing it well. But don't stop there! These songs, like all songs, deserve more discussion. Tell the children something about the person who wrote the song, when he or she lived, what he or she wrote it for (a Broadway play? a musical?). Play recordings of the song by different jazz artists and compare and contrast—what makes Ella Fitzgerald's version different from Billie Holiday's? (See some examples in Chapter 10.) Play instrumental versions of the same song and again discuss differences in interpretation—how is Art Tatum's approach different from Bill Evans's conception? Don't forget to talk about the lives of these artists as well!

So much of school is simply learning facts about people or things out of context. First singing the songs and enjoying them provides a context. The children's curiosity is now aroused and there's a foundation for appreciation. When Billie Holiday sings a different note in the melody than they just did, they're now prepared to notice it—and to ask why. When Ella starts to sing, they're primed to listen—will she sing that note like Billie or like them? When she sings it her own way, they're delighted by the surprise. And what are those notes Art Tatum is playing between the phrases? From a single song, the entire history of jazz can be taught!

- **Selecting material:** As always, the most important criteria for selecting material is your own relationship to the song. Songs that you already know and love will be communicated in your teaching most effectively. The appropriateness of lyrics, attention to level of complexity, a cross-section from different decades, and possibilities of later ensemble play are other considerations. The following list represents some of the songs I've done with children over the years.

SHOW TUNES TO SING WITH CHILDREN
The "happy" songs:

Side by Side—A great song about sticking together.

The Sunnyside of the Street—The optimists' anthem.

High Hopes—The importance of determination and a positive attitude to achieve one's dreams is highlighted here in this song sung by Frank Sinatra in the film "A Hole in the Head."

Pick Yourself Up—Companion to *High Hopes* in terms of persevering in the face of adversity.

Ac-cent-tchu-ate the Positive—Another variation on the optimist theme, with good vocabulary-building words.

Songs of the 20's:

Mares Eat Oats—Great nonsense lyrics that make sense.

Five Foot Two—Similar chords as the Charleston and a good entry into the Roaring 20's—flappers, diamond rings, furs, etc.

Ja Da—Good introduction to scat, and later ensemble piece.

Charleston—The James P. Johnson classic to accompany the dance.

Button Up Your Overcoat—Great lyrics; the words "bootleg hootch" invite a discussion of Prohibition.

Skinnamarink—A great love song for all ages, complete with hand motions.

Songs of the 30's:

Ain't Misbehavin'—The Fats Waller classic—an American must.

Summertime—The classic Gershwin tune.

I Got Rhythm—Essential to later introduction to be-bop.

Chattanooga Choo-Choo:—One of my students' all-time favorites.

Somewhere Over the Rainbow—The classic from "The Wizard of Oz," good for teaching the interval of an octave.

Let's Call the Whole Thing Off—Fun lyrics, great contrasting recordings by Ella Fitzgerald, Billie Holiday, Harry Connick and others.

Let's Do It—A primer in sex education for the older kids.

Sentimental Journey—A nice opportunity for simple harmony.

Don't Fence Me In—Cowboy meets show tune in this Cole Porter classic.

Blue Moon—A show tune later reincarnated in 50's rock.

Moonglow—An addition to the "moon medley" and great ensemble piece.

Songs of the 50's and 60's:

Girl From Ipanema—The bossa-nova classic. Be sure to do it from both sexes point of view, which makes for a good language exercise in changing pronouns.

My Favorite Things—Wonderful extension possibilities with kids making their own list of favorite things. Also a good lead-in to John Coltrane and his classic recording of the tune.

Que Sera—From the Hitchcock film "The Man Who Knew Too Much" with Doris Day, these lovely lyrics have served us well in various school ceremonial occasions, especially saying goodbye to departing students.

Centerpiece—A blues already played in ensemble (see Chapter 7).

PLAYING JAZZ STANDARDS

Having sung the songs, the sense of the phrasing, the sounds of the chords and chord progressions should be in our ears. Now we need to bring them into our hands and minds. Following the by-now familiar route of moving from the concrete (singing the songs) to the abstract (analyzing the theory) and back to the concrete (playing the songs), we not only learn specific tunes, but begin to connect the threads between the tunes and understand the guidelines for successful improvisation within each tune.

Rhythmic Elements: The rhythmic qualities already familiar in our work with the blues will stay essentially the same. Like the blues, the jazz standard repertoire began as a sung form. As a result, most tempos range from slow (called *ballads)* to medium, with occasional up-tempo tunes. Though there tends to be general agreement on tempo set by the original tune, interpretations by different artists of the same tune can vary the tempo widely. For example, the Gershwin tune *Summertime* is sung by Ella Fitzgerald and Louis Armstrong at metronome marking 66, played by Miles Davis at 112, by John Coltrane at 160 and Bruce Forman at 184 (virtually three times the speed of the first!).

The rhythms that accompany jazz standards follow the same guidelines as the blues— hi-hat on 2 and 4, ride cymbal ostinati, snare drum filler and bass drum accent. Most are in 4/4 or 2/4 meter, though after Fats Waller wrote *Jitterbug Waltz* and proved that jazz could swing in 3/4 time, other jazz standards were written in 3/4 time—*Someday My Prince Will Come, Hi-Lili, Lover,* among them. (Interestingly enough, virtually all jazz songs written about children are in 3/4 time: *A Child Is Born, Waltz for Debby, Little B's Poem, Little Niles.)* The swing feel inherent in the blues carries over into the playing of jazz standards.

Phrasing: Why did the early jazz improvisers love playing these songs? The prominent element of the new American popular song genre that separated it from turn of the century popular music like *The Man on the Flying Trapeze* was not only its infectious ragtime-influenced rhythm, but its short two bar phrases with space for instrumental response. This next incarnation of African call and response, already once reborn in the blues, made these songs familiar ground for the jazz improviser. Compare the phrasing of these Anglo-American folk songs with the Anglo-Afro-Judeo show tune:

> "This old man * he played one * he played knick knack / on my thumb"
> "Old MacDonald had a farm * ee-i-ee-i-/o * *"
> "Go tell Aunt Rhody * go tell Aunt Rhody *"
> "There was a farmer had a dog and Bingo was his name-o"

In these examples, there is barely a beat to pause in between phrases. In the following examples, there are pauses of three to six beats between phrases.

George and Ira Gershwin

> 1. "Let the drums roll out! * * * * Let the trumpet call! **** While the people shout!***
> Strike up/ the band! / "
> 2. "It's very clear * * * * / Our love is here to stay * * * * Not for a year * * * * But ever and
> a day * * * * "
> 3. "'S wonderful! *** 'S marvelous! * * * * You should care *** for me!"
> 4. "A foggy day * * * * in London town * * * * * Had me low * * * and had me down"
> 5. "The way you wear your hat * * * * The way you sip your tea * * * * The memory of all
> that * * * * No, no, they / can't take that away from / me."

Cole Porter

1. "I've got you * * * Under my skin * * * * * * I've got you * * * deep in the heart of me."
2. "Night and day * * * * * you're the one * * * * * * only you beneath the moon and under the sun."
3. "You'd * * * be ** so easy to love * * So easy to idolize all others a-bove."

Duke Ellington and Bob Russell

1. "Do nothin' till you hear from me * * * * Pay no attention to what's said."
2. "Missed the Saturday dance * * * * Heard they crowded the / floor."

Lyrics

Though we are more concerned here with the purely musical considerations, we would miss a great deal of the beauty and intelligence of these songs if we neglected the lyrics—subject, syntax, rhyming and other linguistic acrobatics. In the marriage between poetry and music, the music clearly wears the proverbial pants in the family. As philosopher Susanne Langer puts it, "In a well-wrought song, the text is swallowed hide and hair." [3] But in the spirit of a more equitable relationship and one that Orff's love affair with speech strongly suggests, a short survey of the popular song lyric is in order.

Earlier I proposed that popular music was born with the advent of recordings and radios, but the printing press had already helped promote a type of popular song genre disseminated through sheet music. In the 1890's, these songs came from the European forms of verse and chorus. Inspired by the imported Vienesse waltz craze, many of the popular songs were in 3/4 time—*After the Ball, Daisy Daisy, A Bicycle Built for Two, In the Good Old Summertime,* and others.

By 1899, the same year that Scott Joplin published his best-selling ragtime piece, *The Maple Leaf Rag,* ragtime had already come to Tin Pan Alley with a song like *Hello My Baby*. When George Cohan penned *Give My Regards to Broadway* in 1904, he not only helped establish the new American ragtime style over Viennese operettas, French opera bouffe and the British operettas of Gilbert and Sullivan, but prophesized the connection between songs and a musical theater that grew from minstrelsy to vaudeville to the Broadway show, and later, the Hollywood musical.

Ragtime demanded not only a different form and phrasing from a song like *After the Ball*, but a different type of lyric as well. The mawkish sentiment of the older style, expressed outright with lyrics like *"Break the news to Mother, She knows how dear I love her;"* and *"Oh promise me that you will take my hand, the most unworthy in this lonely land… Hearing God's message while the organ rolls, its mighty music to our very souls, no love less perfect than a life with thee,"* was replaced by bluesier reactions to lost love *("I know why I've waited, know why I've been blue…")* and more exuberant proclamation (*"Send me a kiss by wire, Baby, my heart's on fire").* The vernacular of the minstrel songs crept in (*"member dat rainy eve dat I drove you out…")*—and the humor *("Oh, Mister Johnson, turn me loose! Don't take me to the calaboose!").*

As ragtime's influence on popular songs gave way to a new emerging style and the urban life of the roaring twenties transposed the key of popular culture, a new kind of lyric emerged. Influenced by the anti-sentimental, witty, sophisticated, urbane society verse of Dorothy Parker, Ogden Nash, P.G. Wodehouse (each of which, incidentally, tried their hand at lyric songwriting), lyricists like Lorenz Hart, Ira Gershwin, Cole Porter and even Irving Berlin were writing a new kind of verse distinct from both *After the Ball* and *Hello My Baby*. As described by Carolyn Wells, "Society verse is sophisticated, but its language is terse, idiomatic, and in the conversational key, not formal and elevated. It must not be ponderous or sentimental—enthusiasms are modified, emotions restrained, its tone playfully malicious, tenderly ironic or satirically facetious." [4] Dorothy Parker's terse gem sums it up: "*I will stay the way I am, because I do not give a damn.*"

Elsewhere in the poetic world, free verse was coming into its own, breaking out of what was feeling like the oppressively regular meters and symmetrical iambs of classical poetic forms. The poet Mary Oliver describes it thus:

> "Free verse was a product of the times. Perhaps it resulted from a desire on the part of writers at the beginning of this century to alter the tone of the poem. Perhaps it had something to do with the increasing idea of a democratic and therefore classless society in America. In order for the tone of the poem to change, the line had to change. Now a line was needed that would sound and feel not like formal speech, but like conversation. The poem was no longer a lecture, it was time spent with a friend." [5]

While the jazz improvisations of Louis Armstrong were proclaiming a conversational art, songwriters and lyricists were on a similar track, poeticizing in short phrases that broke up lines in unexpected ways. Listen to the poetic acrobatics of lyricists as they set out on the high wire of the new vernacular phrasing, with special attention to the wit of rhyme and assonance:

> **Berlin:** "Come let's <u>mix</u>, where Rock-e-fell,-ers walk with <u>sticks</u>, or um-ber-el. as in their <u>mitts</u>, puttin' on the <u>ritz</u>."

> **Gershwin:** "We may never, never meet again, on the bumpy road to <u>love</u>, Still I'll always, always, keep the mem'ry <u>of</u>—"

> "He may not be the kind of <u>man some</u>, girls think of as <u>handsome</u>."

> "You <u>jazz it</u>, <u>as it</u>, makes you hum."

> "Sure, dey did dat <u>deed in</u>, De Garden of <u>Eden</u>."

> **Hart:** "Sometimes I think I've found my <u>hero</u>, But it's a <u>queer ro</u>—, mance."

> **Fields:** "A fine romance, with no <u>kisses</u>, a fine romance, my friend, <u>this is</u>."

> "I'm under your <u>spell, but</u>, how can I <u>help it</u>?"

> "For heaven <u>rest us</u>, I'm not <u>asbestos</u>."

> **Porter:** "<u>Do do</u>, that <u>voodoo</u>, that <u>you do</u>, so well."

> "You're a <u>rose</u>, you're Inferno's <u>Dante</u>, you're the <u>nose</u>, on the great <u>Durante</u>."

It is time well spent with the children (in collaboration with the language arts teacher?) to tune their ear to this artful poetry. The music of the speech, the cleverness of the rhyme, the humor, the imagery, are a delight to be heard. In an age when the bar of poetic language has been significantly lowered, an analysis of these lyrics can help students develop a taste for nuance, metaphor and subtlety.

Form

Tailor-made for a specific kind of entertainment, the popular song's form borders on a formula—generally a forgettable (and rarely played by jazz musicians) verse of 16 bars, followed by the main body of the song, often called the chorus or refrain. The refrain is typically 32 bars long—an A section of 8 bars, a repeat of that A section, often with a slight variation near the end (A[1]), a B section of 8 bars called the bridge or the release and a final A section. The bridge is characterized by a brief change of key, change of melody and change of text. Here are some examples of famous popular songs that follow the AABA model above:

Ain't Misbehaving (Fats Waller)
Birds Do It (Cole Porter)
Blue Moon (Rodgers and Hart)
Blue Skies (Irving Berlin)
Can't Help Loving That Man (Jerome Kern)
Heart and Soul (Hoagy Carmichael)
I Got Rhythm (George & Ira Gershwin)
My Favorite Things (Rodgers and Hammerstein)
Over the Rainbow (Harold Arlen)
Satin Doll (Duke Ellington)

Though the AABA form was the most common, many songs used an ABAC form, with the C section often beginning like the B, but ending quite differently. Some examples:

All of Me (Simons and Marks)
A Foggy Day (George & Ira Gershwin)
Blame It on My Youth (Levant and Heyman)
But Beautiful (Burke and Van Heusen)
Dearly Beloved (Kern and Mercer)
Easy to Love (Cole Porter)
Embraceable You (George & Ira Gershwin)
Gone With the Wind (Magidson & Wrubel)
Here's That Rainy Day (Burke and Van Heusen)
I Should Care (Cahn, Stardahl, and Weston)
My Romance (Rodgers and Hart)
Someday My Prince Will Come (Churchill and Morey)
Tenderly (Gross and Lawrence)
Yesterdays (Kern and Harbach)

Orchestration

These tunes were—and are—played in combos ranging from solo piano to big bands. In keeping with their more European roots, strings are often used as well (a choice rarely found in the blues). Though, as we have noted, the Orff instrument ensemble is a bit too light for the blues, I have found the sound a charming choice for the jazz standard. The orchestrations that follow give the skeleton structure of standard harmony that leads to a basic understanding and an authentic sound. With these principles in mind, we are ready to begin.

Young jazz singers singing "Ain't Misbehavin'."

PERDIDO

Harry Lenk and Ervin Drake

Juan Tizol
Arranged by Doug Goodkin

54. PERDIDO: Juan Tizol, words by Harry Lenk and Ervin Drake

Focus

- II-V-I progression

- Circle of 5[ths]s

- AABA 32-bar form

II-V-I Chord Progression: Learning how to play the II-V-I progression is the first step into the jazz standard repertoire and *Perdido* is a great starting tune for our purposes. As we have noted, jazz theory is essentially the same as Western European classical theory, but with some different points of emphasis and some modifications. The V I cadence at the center of tonal classical music is present in the popular song, but extended to a II-V-I cadence.* As in the blues, we begin with the root progression. Have the students:

- Sing the root progression of the A section using numbers:

  (II II V V / II II V V / I I I I / I I I I)

- Find the corresponding notes on their instrument in the key of C (D D G G etc.).

Chord spelling: Whereas the triad is at the center of beginning classical theory, the fundamental jazz chord is a four-note chord. The three fundamental variations, shown here with their shorthand notation, are as follows:

Have the students:

- Sing the individual tones of the major chord in arpeggio form using solfege (do -mi-sol-ti), numbers (1-3-5-7) and/or letter names (C-E-G-B).

- Divide group in fours and sing the arpeggio, with each group stopping on pre-assigned note to sound the full chord.

- Repeat as above with dominant chord—(do-mi-sol-te, 1-3-5-♭7, C-E-G-B♭)

- Repeat as above with minor chord—(do-me-sol-te, 1-♭3-5-♭7, C-E♭-G-B♭)

- Create three shapes, one for each chord. Play chords on piano or guitar while students identify the correct chord spelling through their shapes.

These chords are derived from what is called the scale-tone chords. A simple way to think of this is to form chords starting with each note in the scale using only notes in the scale. In the key of C, all chords will use the "white" notes only. In the key of F, all white notes except for B♭:

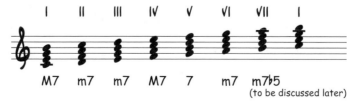

---

* This progession is used in Western art music as well—see the first four measures of Bach's Prelude No. 1.

You might notice some furrowed brows as your students struggle with this lesson in music theory—some genuinely fascinated and others genuinely frustrated. Don't push it longer than you need to—the more important and practical application is the actual inner voices they will play. However, for your own understanding as a teacher, it is a good practice to play the scale-tone chords in every key.

Voicing: The II-V-I progression contains each of the three major chord types in their natural states—minor, dominant and major. Once the students are familiar with the root motion, add the inner voices. As in the blues, the order of importance is the root, then the 3rd and 7th, and eventually the 5th. The inner voices of the 3^{rds} and 7^{ths} should move as little as possible. Instead of playing the full 7th chords in their original position,

we study the movement of the 3^{rds} and 7^{ths}. Have the students:

• Identify the 3rd of the II chord in the key of C (F).

• Identify the 7th of the V chord (F). Verbalize the movement. (It stays the same.)

• Identify the 3rd of the I chord (E). Verbalize the movement. (It goes down a half-step.)

• Sing the movement of the 3^{rds} and 7^{ths} above, with others singing or playing the root motion.

• Repeat above process, beginning with the 7th of II chord (C) moving down a half-step to the 3rd of the V chord (B) and staying in place for the 7th of the I chord (B).

• Sing and play the voicings of the II V I progression using roots, 3^{rds} and 7^{ths}.

Students can now understand, hear and play the harmonic accompaniment in the above arrangement of the A section of *Perdido*. Moving from the 7th to the 6th on the I chord is not functionally necessary, but keeps some harmonic movement and interest alive.

The Circle of Fifths

The bridge of *Perdido* introduces the next vital piece of harmonic theory—the circle of fifths. This concept is the cornerstone of Western harmonic theory, central to modulation through different keys. The tempered scale was created in Bach's time to maintain consistent tuning in this harmonic journey. The logic of the twelve keys with their ♭ and ♯ signatures is made clear in the following diagram. Beginning at C with no sharps or flats, traveling a 5th down (or 4th up) brings us to the key of F with one ♭, another 5th down to B♭ with two ♭'s and continuing in this manner adding one flat to each key until the halfway point of the circle G♭ or F♯. We continue back towards C through the sharp keys, subtracting one ♯ for each new key.

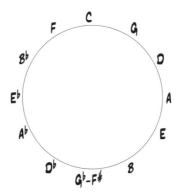

No tunes travel through the full circle of fifths, but many, from Bach to Duke, move through parts of it. *Perdido* moves from E to A to D to G, as does this excerpt from Bach's *English Suite II* (note that the chords in both examples are *altered* chords, that is, all except the V chord have their natural spelling altered to dominant chords. That means the 3rds and 7ths again form tritones and the students familiar with the tritones from the blues will once again feel at home):

Circle of fifth progressions tend to suggest **melodic sequence,** repeating a melodic pattern a step up or down. Melodic sequence is found throughout music of different eras, cultures and styles. Vivaldi was quite fond of them, as was the pianist Bill Evans and as are various Middle Eastern melodists. Many of the tunes given here (*Blue Moon*,

I Got Rhythm, Stompin' at Savoy, Opus One, Dizzy Atmosphere, Little Suede Shoes) use melodic sequence in the bridge, though not always in the circle of fifth pattern.

For your own growth and development, look through a songbook of tunes from the 20's through 50's and note the use of sequences in the bridge. Share it with the children, who are hungry to know how songs are put together and will be delighted to learn yet another "trick of the trade."

The Break

This arrangement of *Perdido* follows the classic AABA form, but adds an additional section at the end, called the **break.** This etude-like figure moves from the IV chord stepwise down to the I and then back up again, playing each chord as an arpeggio with some passing notes to give color. This is both a challenging and satisfying pattern for the mallet player and both kids and adults get excited about mastering it.

Improvisation

At this point, the students have sung and played the melody, sung, played and examined the harmonic structure, reviewed the rhythmic accompaniment and clarified the form. After putting all these elements together and playing the tune, they're now ready to improvise.

We discovered a basic scale in the blues that would work over all the chords while improvising. Is there a comparable scale for the II-V-I progression that would allow students to continue improvising without the extensive theoretical knowledge required for the mature jazz solo? The answer is a resounding... almost. In this tune and the ones that follow, the major pentatonic scale (Orff teachers rejoice!) will generally work fine. A brief analysis reveals that this scale contains three of the four chord tones in the I chord (C-E-G) and II chord (D-A-C) and two in the V chord (G-D). Though no improvisation of a master jazz player will use the pentatonic scale exclusively, analysis of Swing Era improvisations of jazz standards reveals some pentatonic-based riffs and sensibilities. This example from a Teddy Wilson solo illustrates this point, as he answers the opening pentatonic phrase of *My Blue Heaven* with an improvised pentatonic response:

I have found that some kids can also improvise successfully using the full diatonic scale, using their ears to tell them when a note suggests resolution or repetition. With the shifting chords, there is neither a note that will be dissonant throughout (for example, the tense F over the C chord works well with the II or V chord) nor a note that will be consonant throughout (the C works with the I and II, but is tense with the V). In the spirit of experimentation, by all means, have the students try diatonic improvisation.

When we come to the bridge in this and other tunes, we reach the moment when we can no longer improvise with one scale over all the chords. Some possible solutions:

1. Play a drum solo.

2. Play the melody and return to the improvisation on the next A.

3. Embellish the melody by changing the rhythm and using neighboring tones.

4. Play arpeggios with rhythmic variations on the chord tones.

5. Select an interested advanced student to work out an improvisation.

The next step in improvising on II-V-I is beyond the introductory scope of this book. For those interested, an excellent starting point is to isolate some melodic II-V-I fragments from be-bop tunes (*Donna Lee, Groovin' High, Confirmation, Move, Yardbird Suite, Ornithology,* etc.) and practice playing them in all keys. These are the etudes of the jazz player, helping to build a vocabulary from stylistically tried-and-true examples. There are also a number of jazz method books with II-V-I exercises for the motivated student.

Comments

This marvelous tune was written by Juan Tizol, the Puerto Rican valve-trombonist who helped bring a Latin jazz style into Duke Ellington's band. It is a versatile tune, equally playable as an up-tempo Swing dance number, a medium tempo ballad or a Latin style number (some suggestions for the swing/Latin conversion follow later).

Having played, heard and analyzed the essential rhythms, phrasing, form, chord structure and improvising scale of *Perdido*, the student is not only ready to play this particular tune, but has the beginning tools to play other similar tunes as well. As in the blues, each new tune builds from this base to reveal another piece of jazz theory and practice.

Student improvising in the C pentatonic scale.

BLUE MOON

Lorenz Hart

Richard Rodgers
Arranged by Doug Goodkin

Blue_ moon   you saw me stand-ing a - lone___
moon   you knew just what I was there for
moon   now I'm no long - er a - lone___

with-out a dream in my heart___   with-out a love of my own
you heard me say-ing a prayer for   some-one I real-ly could care
with-out a dream in my heart___   with-out a love of my own.

Blue_ for   and then there

sud-den-ly ap-peared be- fore_ me   The on - ly one my arms could ev - er hold

DA CAPO AL FINE

55. BLUE MOON: Richard Rodgers and Lorenz Hart

- I-VI-II-V chord progression

- Modulation at the bridge

I-VI-II-V Chord Progression

The idea of a harmonic progression that yields endless riches of melodic variation is as old as "Greensleeves" and Pachelbel's "Canon." Common in the Renaissance under such names as chaconne, ground bass and La Folia, it fell out of favor by Bach's time, though there are some isolated examples in the literature (as in Bach's own *Passacaglia and Fugue in C Minor* and Chopin's *Berceuse*). We've noted the reincarnation of the "Greensleeves" descending pattern in *Hit the Road Jack* and my *Cookie Jar* arrangement and the chord changes in the blues certainly fit in this category.

Now we introduce another archetypal pattern that will be familiar to your students' ears. Anyone who teaches children knows how enthusiastic they become when they recognize something familiar—"Hey, I heard that song on a TV ad!"—and that makes it all the more exciting when they can not only learn to play it, but come to understand how it works.

Perhaps the most familiar entry point is that classic piano piece of children's culture (and also an old jazz standard), *Heart and Soul.* Ask different students to demonstrate the bass part. Some may play it like this:

while others like this:

The second is more relevant for our purposes here and can be reinforced by the following well-known camp song:

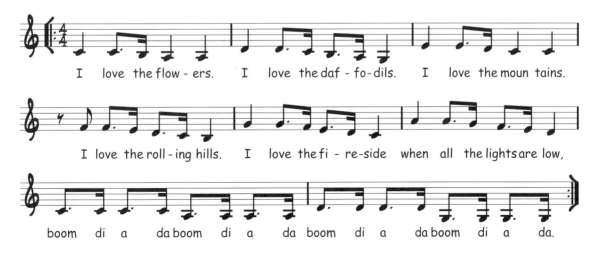

The students will hear the bass pattern in the "boom dee ya da's" and it should be a simple task to find it on the Orff instruments. Note that if you play it in the key of C, you need to either start on the high C or play the A above the C.

To demonstrate the potency of this progression, ask the students—and here they could use help from their teachers or parents—to brainstorm other songs that use this progression. From both the jazz standard and early rock (sometimes with minor adjustments) comes:

> *Blue Moon, Heart and Soul, The Way You Look Tonight, Can't Help Lovin' That Man, Stormy Weather, Sh-boom Sh'boom, Dream Dream Dream (Everly Brothers), Sherry, Stay (The Four Seasons), Silhouettes on the Shade (Herman's Hermits), I Love the Flowers*

• Sing one verse of each of the above and then have each student choose one of them. With some playing the bass pattern on xylophones or piano, enjoy a giant quodlibet (two or more songs that fit together) fest, stacking melodies over the unchanging bass.

You will note how the arrangement follows the 3rds and 7ths voice movement introduced in *Perdido* instead of the classic *Heart and Soul* piano model, with the addition of learning how to move from the VI chord to the II. You may also note the inversion of the progression—while *Perdido* is essentially a II-V / I-(VI) progression, this is I-VI / II-V.

The Bridge

The bridge begins with the archetypal II-V / I pattern and then repeats it in a new key—E♭. This is a fantastic opportunity for the children to see if they can figure out the voicings in the new key. For those without chromatic Orff instruments, I suggest playing the bridge on a piano or keyboard. Once again, improvisation over changing keys will present some challenges for beginning students—consider the suggestions for the bridge in *Perdido*.

Comments

Many people are surprised to learn that Rodgers and Hart wrote *Blue Moon*, being more familiar with the 60's doo-wop version by the Marcels. It is a winning song with the children, not only a member of the I-VI-II-V *Heart and Soul* club, but also a standard in the "Moon Medley" series (*Shine On Harvest Moon, Moon River, Moon Over Miami, Moonglow*). This year, I had two separate groups of 8th grade students and taught it to one group in the key of C in swing rhythm and another group in the key of F in Latin rhythm.

I GOT RHYTHM

Ira Gershwin

George Gershwin
Arranged by Doug Goodkin

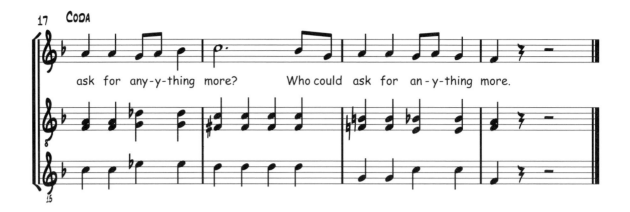

ask for any-y-thing more?   Who could ask for an-y-thing more.

56. I GOT RHYTHM: George and Ira Gershwin

Focus

• Vocal rendition of instrumental parts

• Extending the I-VI-II-V progression

• Key of F

Activity

• Sing song without accompaniment, snapping on offbeat. (Save ending variation for later).

• Sing bass progression with chord numbers, still snapping on offbeat:

> I VI / II V / I VI / II V / I III / IV♯ / V V / I (bom bom bom)

> III III III III / VI VI VI VI / II II II II / V V V (bom bom bom)

• Repeat full bass progression with vocal sound imitating bass—*"Doom"* or *"Bom."*

• Sing melody with vocal trumpet sound (no words).

• Divide group in half—one sings bass, other melody: Practice ending.

• Practice whispered vocal equivalent of:
    hi-hat: "* chick * chick"
    ride cymbal: "tsss tsi-tsi tsss tsi-tsi tsss..."
    bass drum (filling in the spaces of melody): " * * * * boom boom!"

• Assign vocal drummers, bass players, trumpet players and soloists: perform!

• Discuss the theory, reviewing the known (swing, offbeat, etc.) and introducing the new.

"Rhythm Changes"

I Got Rhythm begins with the I-VI-II-V chord movement, but caps it off with an ascending progression (you may recognize it as a major version of the opening bass used in *Bag's Groove* in Chapter 7 or the first phrase of the melody in the children's game *Down by the Banks of the Hanky Panky)*. This extended pattern gives increased harmonic movement and tension, further fertilizing the possibilities of melodic variation. In the be-bop era, so many tunes based on this pattern were composed (see list at the end of the chapter) that the term "rhythm changes" (from the song title) was coined to describe this chord progression. Two jazz musicians meeting for the first time can jam on these commonly understood chord changes without having to know a common melody. Now when they hear two musicians say, "Do you want to play a blues in B♭ or rhythm changes in F?," the children are initiated into the secret language of jazz.

Note that the bridge follows both the circle of fifths and melodic sequence. Also note that the original tune has an additional melodic tag at the end that extends the form by two bars. I often leave this for the very last time through the melody.

Comments

Rhythm, music, love, nature—who could ask for anything more? Ira Gershwin's lyrics are a hymn praising the musician's joy (though that same musician might add, "A little money to pay the rent?"). As we have noted, brother George's choice of chord progression went on to become an improviser's delight in the be-bop era, almost as fertile as the blues for spinning out melodic variations. Used to be-bop versions, I've always conceived of this as a tune to play fast, but my 8th grade student Will Gaines sang it to me one time in a slow, languid tempo and showed me a whole new facet to this song. He later shared his interpretation in a performance for 1,500 music teachers at the 2002 American Orff Schulwerk Conference in Las Vegas—and brought down the house with both his fabulous singing and his closing lyric: *"I got Carl Orff, I got Keetman, I got Gershwin, who could ask for anything more!"*

STOMPIN' AT THE SAVOY

57. STOMPIN' AT THE SAVOY: Benny Goodman, Chick Webb, Edgar Sampson, Andy Razaff

Focus

• Chromatic movement

• Orchestration of call and response riffs

• ♭9 chords

Activity

• Teach the following dialogue:

> 1) Hello 2) How are you? 1) Hello 2) How are you?
>
> 1) Ho-la 2) ¿Como estás? 1) I'm fine. 2) So am I.

• Repeat as above (A section). Create an eight measure B section of free conversation between 1 and 2. Return to A section.

• As above, both playing and singing the following arrangement.

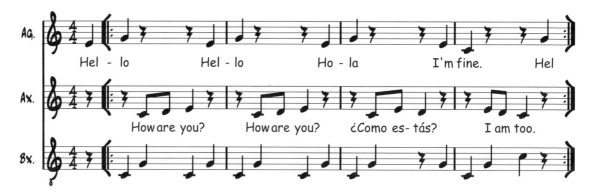

B section: Improvisation in C pentatonic in AX and AG over this drone.

D.C. AL FINE

• Changing the rhythm of the melody to *Soup, Soup,* accompany students on piano or guitar with the chords and response to *Stompin' at the Savoy.* During the B section, all stop playing and talk to each other for eight measures.

• As above, with students improvising in C pentatonic over piano accompaniment on A sections.

The Orff-Jazz Connection

The above sequence demonstrates how one can learn the essentials of the piece—the melody, the call and response structure, the AABA form—by treating it as a beginning Orff arrangement and then take a surprising and exhilirating left turn into jazz! Any beginning student can quickly learn the melody, improvise in the pentatonic scale and sound great—that is, with the teacher playing the chords on piano. This approach also makes transparently clear the difference between the pentatonic scale over a drone and over changing chords. Three other pieces included here can be developed as above—*Jumpin' at the Woodside, Dizzy Atmosphere* (both major pentatonic) and *C-Jam Blues* (minor pentatonic).

Comments

This classic from the big band repertoire was not written for a Broadway show or Hollywood musical. It is clearly a dance piece and the shared authorship of the four composers suggest that it may have evolved from a jam session, with each contributing a little piece of it.

Pedagogically, this tune is a summary of much that we have experienced. The *Savoy* rhythm is *Soup, Soup* displaced in another part of the measure and the tune's clear call-and-response format hearkens back to early games like *Soup, Soup*. If we did our Lindy Hop homework, we will have discovered that the Savoy was the Harlem ballroom where much of the exciting dancing and music of the '30's happened—and we most certainly will choose to review our dancing with this piece! *Stompin' at the Savoy* shares the same key signature as *I Got Rhythm*, uses the basic I-VI-II-V progression in the A section and a circle of 5ᵗʰs progression in the bridge. The familiar A section progression has a couple of interesting twists here—a distinct harmonic rhythm that leaves space for the call and response of the melody and the V7♭9 and VI7♭9 chords that create more harmonic color and tension. When improvising, the harmonic rhythm can upgrade to four to a bar, as follows:

I I I I / V V V V / I I I I / VI VI VI VI / II II II II / V V V V / I I I I / V V V V

Another new addition to our expanding vocabulary is the chromatic movement in the bridge, increasing the energy of the harmonic rhythm and the color of the chords by shifting back and forth to a neighboring chord a half step up: IV7 ♯IV7/ IV7 / ♭VII VII/ ♭VII etc. Also worth noting is how the bridge of *I Got Rhythm* takes a III VI II V route to get back to I, whereas *Savoy* goes from IV to ♭VII to ♭III to ♭VI to return home. Why does this work? Because of the tritone substitution (introduced in *Bags 'n' Trane)*—the tritone of ♭VI7 is the same as II7, thus easily leading to the V7 that turns it all back to the I.

Earlier, the students practiced Lindy Hop to recordings. Now is the moment to recreate that magical mix of dance and live music that animated the Savoy in your classroom. Once the students learn the piece, have half play and half dance—and then switch!

MOONGLOW

WILL HUDSON, EDDIE DE LANGE, AND IRVING MILLS
ARRANGED BY DOUG GOODKIN

It must have been Moon-glow.
I still hear you say - ing.

Way up in the blue.
Dear one hold me fast.

It must have been Moon-glow
And I start in pray - ing

that led me straight to you.
Oh Lord please let this last.

We_____ seemed to float right through the air_____

58. MOONGLOW: Will Hudson, Eddie De Lange and Irving Mills

Focus

- Diminished chords

- Expanded chord progression

Comments

This companion moon song to *Blue Moon* has a catchy melody and sounds great on the Orff instruments. The repetition of the first three melodic phrases over changing chords follows the principle we examined in the blues—a single "noun" defined anew by three different "adjectives." The first phrase is underpinned by a IV-♭VII7, the second by a I-II7 and the third, our familiar II-V, giving the illusion of a new melody each time. The last phrase is a single note, again re-defined by each changing chord. What are these changing chords? The last in our series of basic spellings—diminished chords.

The Diminished Chord

Earlier we named three common chord spellings—major, dominant, minor. Assuming the major as the given, the dominant is formed by flatting the 7th. If we keep the flatted 7th and flat the 3rd, we get the minor. Continuing in this progression, we flat the 5th to get the half-diminished chord. If we flat the 7th yet again, we get the diminished chord, the last in the series of basic chord spellings.

Another, perhaps simpler way to think about the diminished chord is to begin on any note and build a chord from minor 3^{rd}s.

If we look at the fourth chord, we notice that it is simply an inversion of the first one. If we formed a diminished chord starting on each scale tone, we would discover the following startling fact: *There are only three diminished chords!* Starting on any note of each chord, there are four possible "inversions."

All this is satisfying to our delight in mathematical order, but doesn't help us understand the greater question: *What is the function of the diminished chord in jazz?*

One answer is, "To serve as a passing chord." The diminished chord carries a lot of tension (note that it consists of *two* tritones) and invites resolution.* (You may recognize

---

* In modern jazz of the 60's and beyond, the diminished chord and scale was elevated from mere passing and color status to a statement in its own right. Herbie Hancock's piano work on *Freedom Jazz Dance* (from the Miles Davis album *Miles Smiles*) is a good example of "sitting on" the diminished chord without resolving. For our purposes now, we'll keep it confined to its traditional role.

the silent movie cliché of playing ascending tremolo diminished chords when the hero is in trouble.) We first met this chord in the blues *Now's the Time* in the progression from IV7 to I7.

Another function is to provide harmonic color. That is how it works in *Moonglow*, as two diminished chords change the character of the melody note G.

Moonglow is unusual in that it starts on a IV chord rather than the customary I or II. The four previous tunes were in the keys of C or F—this arrangement introduces II-V-I progression in the key of G. Once again, the bridge follows a short circle, but starting on a different chord than any of our previous songs. This is an excellent opportunity to integrate the school choir and/or a talented vocal soloist with the instrumental ensemble. The major pentatonic will serve for improvisation in the A sections, with the usual options during the bridge (restate the melody, ornament the melody, chords alone, drum solo, etc.).

PENNSYLVANIA 6-5000

Jerry Gray and Carl Sigman
Arranged by Doug Goodkin

59. PENNSYLVANIA 6-5000: Jerry Gray, Carl Sigman

Focus

• Relative minor

• Diminished chords

Comments

This novelty piece was featured in the Hollywood movie about the bandleader who made it famous—"The Glenn Miller Story." The melody begins with an arpeggio of an inverted 6th chord reminiscent of *Jumpin' with Symphony Sid*. On the third repeat, the upper B shifts to C. Why? To accent the arrival of the II chord underneath. There's a break at the fourth beat of bar six, filled in by—a phone ringing (you can simulate by playing the inside of a cowbell) and a spoken telephone number—"Pennsylvania 6–5000!"

Glenn Miller used to play at the Pennsylvania Hotel near Penn Station in Manhattan and Pennsylvania 6-500 was its phone number. This piece uses a clever advertising strategy—people listening to the tune on the radio could call the hotel to find out when Miller was playing. The "Pennsylvania 6" part of the phone number may need a little explanation for the modern generation. You can tell them about the old days when words were used as a memory device—the first two letters of the word (PE above) then needed to be converted to numbers (736–5000).

There are several interesting musical connections here. The rhythm of the phone number is played on the note G, similar to the one-note ending of *Moonglow*. *Moonglow* also used diminished chords to add harmonic color and here we find it again in bars 4, 5 and 6 are I ♭III°/ II / V. This progression is an alternative to the familiar I-VI-II-V used in *I Got Rhythm* (and can also be used as a substitute progression in *I Got Rhythm)*. Like *Blue Moon*, there's a change to a new II-V-I progression in the bridge and a short sequence in the melody.

And there's more to come. After we play the tune, there's a new section (composed by this author) with a boogie bass and a I-I-I-I-II-V-I-I progression very similar to a tune coming up in the next chapter—*Jumpin' at the Woodside*. It has call and response riffs, blue notes, outlined triads, a veritable treasure trove of revisited concepts that increases our jazz vocabulary. As we play tune after tune from the same stylistic genre, we get the constant reinforcement that leads to an in-depth understanding.

The Relative Minor

The relative minor of any key is a minor third down (the la below the do) and shares the same notes as the parent scale.

The bridge in this tune shifts to the relative minor and then returns to the V through another II-V-I progression. This is good news for the soloists, as they can continue to improvise in the G scale, but shift the home tone to E in the first part of the bridge and to D in the second. (As before, I recommend starting with G pentatonic scale.)

Fake Books

Following this sequence of chord progressions, root movements, chord spellings and voicings, the student might be prepared to figure out his or her own arrangement from a shorthand notation like Gm7 C7 / FM7. In the jazz world, "fake books," an underground compilation of tunes that just gave the melody and chords, were the working musician's constant companion. The trained jazz musician could "read between the lines" and create his own chord voicings. This circumvented the sheet music approach and allowed for a convenient storage and transmission of a greater number of tunes— what took four pages of sheet music might take one page in a fake book.

However, what was convenient for the jazz musician was unfair to the songwriter or jazz composer. Fake books were (and are) illegal because the songwriters never received the royalties that sheet music earned them. I'm using past tense because, though fake books undoubtedly still exist, they have largely been replaced by "real books" (see bibliography)—similar compilations written in jazz shorthand, but with legal permission granted by the composers. The added advantages of the "real books" are that composers can check and correct the given version, whereas fake books were subject to the interpretative whims of the transcriber.

For the "final exam" of this chapter, orchestrate your own arrangement of the next tune.

The Pennsylvania Hotel today.

LET'S CALL THE WHOLE THING OFF: George and Ira Gershwin

60. LET'S CALL THE WHOLE THING OFF
Focus • Arranging from chord symbols

Comments

It seems fitting that this chapter on jazz standards concludes with a Gershwin piece. Mythologically speaking, Gershwin symbolizes a significant piece of the American cultural landscape of his time. Born in New York to Russian-Jewish immigrants, somewhat of a truant in school, begins taking piano lessons at 12, drops out of high school at age 15 to work as a song plugger in Tin Pan Alley, writes his first popular song *When You Want 'Em, You Can't Get 'Em; When You've Got 'Em, You Don't Want 'Em* and earns $5 in royalties, accompanies singers in vaudeville, shows his interest in black musical culture with his tune *The Real American Folk Song Is a Rag*, writes *Swanee* for a Broadway show and begins to get recognition when Al Jolson's version turns it into a hit. Meets the great classical composer Maurice Ravel and bridges the world of European classical composition (rhapsody) and an evolving American jazz vernacular (blues) with the debut of *Rhapsody in Blue* in 1924. Goes on to write immortal tunes for various forgettable shows, often with his lyricist brother, Ira, and eventually goes to Hollywood, moving from Broadway to movies. Also continues to write other classically inspired works (Concerto in F, Preludes for Piano, etc.) and pens the first jazz opera, *Porgy and Bess*.

In a uniquely American mythos of success, the ragged Jewish truant from the streets of New York is rubbing shoulders with Hollywood stars and when he dies tragically young from a tumor at age 39, thousands of mourners attend simultaneous funerals in both Los Angeles and New York. Gershwin once said that "jazz is the result of the energy stored up in America" and his genius was to tap into that energy, to drink from both the European and African founts and help create a distinctly American music.

This tune is one of his many gems and its humor appeals greatly to children. New verses can be added by the students. Make sure to play the ebullient recording by Louis Armstrong and Ella Fitzgerald—their humor, connection and overall musicianship make this piece come alive beyond the composer's expectations.

I can't resist suggesting that you and your students try another version titled: "Let's Carl the Whole Thing Orff."

FURTHER DEVELOPMENT OF THE JAZZ STANDARD

Jazz and popular music were *"a travelin' along, singin' their song, side by side"* in the '20's and '30's—the hey-day of the popular song as written for Broadway and Hollywood musicals. Jazz musicians like Fats Waller were writing Broadway revues and playing in the pit bands, popular songwriters like George Gershwin were drawing heavily from the jazz idiom. Though rooted in different parts of the garden, they encouraged each other's blossoming. The fruit they bore in those early years proved the most tasty—in 1930 alone, over 25 tunes were penned that are still played today by jazz musicians![*]

The musical continued its journey in the mid-40's and 50's—but with the rise of be-bop, the popular song in the jazz world took a turn in the path. Players began composing new tunes based on the chord changes and structure of old songs. We have already mentioned *I Got Rhythm*, whose prolific chord progression fathered such be-bop classics as *Anthropology, Moose the Moocher, Shaw 'Nuff, Salt Peanuts, Oleo* and *Rhythmnin'*. Charlie Parker based his tune *Ornithology* on the song *How High the Moon, Scrapple from the Apple* on *Honeysuckle Rose*, Thelonious Monk's *Evidence* on *Just you, Just Me*. This practice allowed musicians to showcase their advanced melodic ideas within familiar structures and also let them sidestep copyright issues.

At the same time, major artists continued to push out the borders of the tunes themselves with altered chords, phrasing and rhythmic interpretation. Thelonious Monk's rendition of *I Should Care*, Charlie Parker's *Embraceable You*, Dizzy Gillespie's *I Can't Get Started*, Miles Davis's *Summertime*, Sonny Rollins's *Surrey with the Fringe on Top*, and John Coltrane's *My Favorite Things* became classic re-interpretations. The popular song, alias jazz standard, was proving to be as durable as the blues, inviting each generation anew to mine its riches.

But the 60's were another story. After four decades of the Broadway gold rush, the gold standard suddenly changed. While the jazz artists of the 20's through the 50's were often improvising on *contemporary* popular songs, the repertoire of musical theater of the next 40 years took off in a different direction—and jazz didn't follow. The new generation of songwriters—Jerry Herman, Henry Mancini, Stephen Sondheim—inherited much from their ancestors, but mostly lost their vital connection with jazz.

By the 70's, the rock revolution had hitched across the country from Haight Ashbury and taken the Laker flight from London to arrive on Broadway. But *Hair* and *Jesus Christ Superstar* had no more to offer the jazz musicians than *The Best Little Whorehouse in Texas*. The Broadway musical forged on to the 90's, but as *Annie, A Chorus Line, Cats, Les Miserables* and other hit shows make clear, the link with jazz was broken forever. The *stories* of the shows themselves sometimes proved more sophisticated than the corny plots of the 30's, but the magic of the singable tune that the audience leaves whistling was gone.

Culturally, something else happened in the 60's—America lost its innocence. With Selma, Alabama, three assassinations and a shameful war televised for all to see, the romance was over. The tender love songs gave way to the growing rage of Black Nationalism and the searing, fiery probings of Cecil Taylor, John Coltrane, Eric Dolphy, Miles Davis and Ornette Coleman echoed the social climate of unrest. Though Bill Evans kept the torch of jazz standards lit throughout the 60's with his timeless reinterpretations, most jazz musicians moved into the realm of extended compositions/ improvisations that pushed out the limitations of song form into broader areas. This direction

---

[*] See *Jazz: America's Classical Music*, Chap. 5, p. 220, for a listing of these tunes.

continued into the 70's, with the additional fuel of the rock revolution and subsequent jazz/rock fusion.

As the social climate swung back to a conservative footing in the 80's and 90's, jazz likewise re-grouped and unearthed the old treasures that had lain somewhat dormant for two decades. The proliferation of recordings titled *Standards* was almost eerie. From the avant-garde to the jazz mainstream, virtually every noteworthy jazz musician took a pass at redefining this repertoire—Keith Jarrett, Chick Corea, Anthony Braxton, McCoy Tyner, Herbie Hancock, Wynton and Branford Marsalis, Sonny Rollins, Pat Metheny and more all revisited the standard repertoire in the light of new harmonic voicings, rhythmic approaches and group textures. Though it may have reflected marketing pressure from record producers to cash in on the cult of nostalgia, this look backwards was not nostalgia on the *artist's* part. It was a time of watering the roots before (or more accurately, while) branching out into new musical territory.

Jazz had grown from its association with musical theater, widened its expressive range and touched a larger audience. Whereas the blues as an honest expression seemed to belong to black jazz musicians, white musicians like Stan Getz, Bill Evans, Lee Konitz and Jim Hall could bring something valuable to the music via the "Standard" route. Now its folk roots of blues and pop roots of standards joined to create a classical form—the jazz composition.

THE MEETING OF LIGHT AND SHADOW

When I was young, my family used to take the Staten Island ferry to visit my grandparents. I loved the taste of the freshly baked soft pretzels, can still remember the smell of the sea air and the enchantment of the twinkling lights of the Manhattan skyline as we glided across the waters. This feast of the senses was completed by the lush orchestrations of Jerome Kern songs on the car radio. I was in an American dreamtime, a mythological landscape whose contours and secret places were revealed by singing strings and lone saxophones. I knew nothing of Jerome Kern nor the jazz musicians who improvised on *All the Things You Are*, *The Way You Look Tonight* or *Smoke Gets in Your Eyes*, but those songs became vivid landmarks in a terrain that was forever my home.

I heard them again played by my father on the organ, accompanying the nighttime song of crickets or wafting upstairs to tuck me in at night. *"The evening breeze, caressed the trees, tenderly…"* They were there with me as I lay spread out on the couch watching old movies on TV, initiated into the intricacies of romantic love, American style. I learned that when love struck, those sweet chords would start ringing and the poetry of the lyrics would rise to my lips. When I later experienced first-hand the joy and pain of love, these songs sang my feelings, from *My Shining Hour* to *My Foolish Heart*. They let me know that someone somewhere understood my elation, confusion, enchantment and despair when it came to "the story of, the glory of, love."

In the years that followed, my musical journey took me far afield towards new songs I needed to hear. But no matter how entranced I was by a moonlit gamelan performance in Bali or moved by a powerful drum ensemble at a South Indian festival or calmed by the gongs and bells of a Japanese zen center, a few notes of Ella Fitzgerald singing *Stardust* transported me home like no other music. Amidst my hope to become a "world citizen," I realized that I was also a person from a specific time and place—America in the 20th century. Especially *urban* America—the swirling mass of crowds, cabs and chaos brought into focus by a piano punctuating intimate conversation in a dimly lit corner of a nightclub.

Now the Verrazano Bridge spans the waters of the Staten Island ferry and the wide-eyed country that believed it was the light of the world is gone. Between 1929 and 1932, the country was in the throes of a Great Depression—but over 60 glorious tunes were penned that still thrive today. We didn't have money, but we had music—and who could ask for anything more? Today, in the midst of economic prosperity, little that we hear on the radio is likely to last longer than Andy Warhol's "15 minutes of fame." We have money, but we have lost our vision. Beginning in the 60's, the dark shadows leaked through the cracks in our carefully constructed optimism. Vietnam and Watergate opened them wider and even Reagan's empty cheerfulness couldn't repair the damage. Another Great Depression stole over the land and has us by the throat today. We grasp desperately at the straws of "family values," forgetting about all of those—jazz musicians, for example—who we refused to welcome into the family. We try to drive the dark away with the bright lights of TV and computer screens, but the statistics of teen crime, drug abuse and suicide keep rising.

We have passed directly from innocent naiveté to despairing cynicism and missed the route to healing. Our sunny optimism was hiding our dark shadows, but it also sustained us collectively, gave meaning and hope to our lives, a hope we now must rebuild on the cornerstone of grief. We cannot afford nostalgia, but as we pass into the shadows, we need to remember the light. These songs hold a great beauty that is uniquely ours—when we hear them, we can remember the taste of salt-pretzels, the smell of the sea air, the dazzle of twinkling lights of the New York skyline—and fall in love all over again.

Endnotes

1. Frazee, Jane: *Discovering Orff*: Schott: p. 20

2. Ellington, Duke: Lyric from *It Don't Mean a Thing if It Ain't Got That Swing*

3. Langer, Susanne K.; *Problems of Art*: Charles Scribner's Sons: p. 84

4. Wells, Carolyn: *A Vers de Societé Anthology*: Charles Scribner's Sons

5. Oliver, Mary: *A Poetry Handbook*: Harcourt, Brace & Co., p.69

Bibliography (songbooks and real books)

Encyclopedia of Jazz Standards: Warner Brothers

The Decade Series: Song's of the 20's/30's/40's/50's: Hal Leonard

Reader's Digest Treasury of Beloved Songs

The New Real Book: Chuck Sher Co.

The Real Little Ultimate Jazz Fake Book: Hal Leonard

Jazz Theory

The Jazz Piano Book: Mark Levine; Chuck Sher Co.

Other

The Poets of Tin Pan Alley: A History of America's Great Lyricists: Philip Furia: Oxford University Press

Easy to Remember: The Great American Songwriters and Their Songs: William Zinsser: David Godine Publisher

Other Suggested Jazz Standards Playable by Children

Don't Get Around Much Anymore (Duke Ellington)

Honeysuckle Rose / I Got Music (Fats Waller/Frank Loesser-Burton Lane)

I'm Beginning to See the Light (Duke Ellington)

Jeepers Creepers (Harry Warren/ Johnny Mercer)

Jersey Bounce (Wright/Plater/ Bradshaw/ Johnson)

Just a Gigolo (Leo Casucci)

Puttin' on the Ritz (Irving Berlin)

Santa Claus Is Comin' to Town (Haven Gillespie/J. Fred Coots)

Sweet Georgia Brown (Bernie, Pinkard and Casey)

Sweet Sue (Harris/Young)

Eighth graders perform with Stefon Harris.

CHAPTER 9: JAZZ COMPOSITIONS

Imagine jazz as a flowing river, fed from one direction by the underground spring of the blues and from another, by the main stream of popular culture. As the two tributaries join, they create a third branch—the jazz composition. Though it may have elements of both, the jazz composition often moves beyond the strict forms of the 12-bar blues and the 32-bar AABA song form. Of the 86 tunes represented in The Smithsonian Collection of Classic Jazz, approximately one quarter are blues, one third are jazz standards and the remaining, jazz compositions.

We have seen how each new style of jazz redefined the blues and jazz standards. It's a long way from Bessie Smith's *Empty Bed Blues* to Ornette Coleman's *Blues Connotation*, from George Gershwin's *I Got Rhythm* to Charlie Parker's *Shawnuff*, but with some careful listening, we can understand that they're different points on the same river. The rhythmic flow might change to white-water conditions, the melodic twists and turns and sudden drops might call for greater alertness as we paddle, the rocks in the river may demand an expanded repertoire of harmonic paddle strokes, but the river is still contained within the banks of the blues or jazz standard structure. When it comes to original compositions, we may find ourselves in a lagoon or lake or estuary or the ocean itself. We have entered some new territory.

From the very beginning of jazz, tunes written by the great improvisers themselves have formed a part of the repertoire—Louis Armstrong's *Weatherbird*, Fats Waller's *Jitterbug Waltz*, Duke Ellington's *East St. Louis Toodle-Oo* were significant parts of the early jazz soundscape. The dance compositions of Bennie Moten and Count Basie shared the stage with blues and jazz standards at the Savoy Ballroom while Duke Ellington took the emerging improviser's art into the country of composition without losing its citizenship. From 32-bar songs to massive extended suites, Ellington captured the essence of jazz expression in set pieces while still leaving room for improvisation. His Beethovenesque massive work was balanced by the Chopinesque jeweled miniatures of Thelonious Monk, the genius of short compositions. Monk mostly kept to the basic forms of blues and jazz standards, but the rhythmic, melodic and harmonic conceptions in tunes like *Misterioso, Straight No Chaser, Evidence, Criss-cross, Trinkle-Tinkle* and others were so distinct as to feel like new forms of jazz composition. Changes in improvisation inspired new compositions, which in turn invited new twists to the improviser's art. Miles Davis's *So What* and *Blue in Green*, Bill Evans's *Peace Piece* and *Time Remembered*, John Coltrane's *Giant Steps* and *Central Park West*, Ornette Coleman's *Lonely Woman* and *Ramblin'* catapulted jazz conception beyond the 12-bar blues and 32-bar standards.

By the 1960's, jazz's immigration laws loosened considerably and the passport office was flooded with applications. The lost cousins of the African diaspora were finding each other again and jazz was hosting the reunion. The resulting music at the party rang out with African polyrhythms, Latin riffs, Calypso beats, Brazilian syncopations and even rock grooves. John Coltrane took a transatlantic voyage in his imagination to *Africa*, Dizzy Gillespie spent *A Night in Tunisia* and then *A Night in Havana* on the forbidden isle of Cuba (documented in a film by the same title), Sonny Rollins visited his Caribbean grandparents in *St. Thomas*, Stan Getz had a magical blind date with *The Girl From Ipanema* on the beaches of Rio and Miles Davis moved in with his wayward children and cooked up some *Bitches' Brew*.

Word got around and in the 70's and 80's, people came drifting through from all over the globe. The house was filling with electric pianos, synthesizers, electric guitars, sitars, tablas, violins, steel drums, talking drums. Jazz was being spoken with Indian accents, African dialects, Japanese inflections and even bluegrass twang! While the McCluhanesque global village shrank, jazz's borders expanded. Not only were its native speakers venturing out—Randy Weston moving to Morocco, Yusef Lateef to Nigeria, Sonny Rollins to India, Don Cherry studying in countries the world over—but "foreigners" were learning the language via the Parker-Berlitz method, listening, imitating and absorbing the vocabulary and grammar of the American native speakers via records (and occasional live contact). Their native accents inevitably flavored the jazz language. As early as 1960, jazz pianist John Lewis said:

> "The originals in jazz, the strong new creators, are no longer to be of exclusively American origin. There's no telling now where the shaping forces will come from" *

By the 90's, the one-room shack of jazz had grown to an elaborate palace. Could that tiny four-letter word support all that weight? The 1996 San Francisco Jazz Festival answers with a resounding "Yeah!," hosting the following acts under the roof of jazz (groupings mine):

---

* A sampling of active recording jazz artists today would reveal over fifteen different nationalities represented.

CLASSIC JAZZ REPERTOIRE (Modern interpretations of jazz standards, blues and original compositions):

- *Sonny Rollins*: The master saxophonist who spans five decades.

- *George Shearing*: The British pianist who forged his distinctive sound in the 50's.

- *Max Roach*: The master drummer and one of the founders of be-bop.

THE LATIN CONNECTION:

Chico O'Farrill: Afro-Cuban jazz composer.

THE WORLD MUSIC INTERFACE:

- *Guitar Trio: Paco De Lucia, John McLaughlin, Al Di Meola:* Flamenco meets India meets jazz/rock.

- *Silk Road: Asian Concepts in Jazz:* Includes *Zakir Hussain , Mark Izu, Miya Masaoka, Francis Wong and Hafez Modirzadeh.*

- *A Tribute to Don Cherry: Charlie Haden, Dewey Redman, Nana Vasconcelos and Peter Apfelbaum,* all artists who collaborated with Cherry in his world music fusion.

RETURN TO ROOTS (Recreating earlier styles):

- *Roots and Blues: John Lee Hooker, Ruth Brown and Charlie Musselwhite*—Mississippi Delta meets R & B.

- *Stride Piano Summit: The Legacy of Fats Waller*: Seven jazz pianists interpret Waller's repertoire in company with 80 year old trumpeter, Doc Cheatam.

- *History of Jazz Piano: From Ragtime to Avant-Garde*: Dick Hyman demonstrates the evolution of jazz piano styles.

JAZZ/ROCK FUSION:

- *B-3 Organ Salute:* Bop, blues and R & B meet on the Hammond B-3 organ.

- *David Sanborn Group:* An eclectic blend of historical jazz and rock styles.

- *Backyard Alchemy: The Bay Area Jazz Scene*: Jazz infused with pop, funk, reggae, hiphop, avant-garde, world beat, acid jazz-contemporary fusion.

IN THE CLASSROOM

In this chapter, we'll discover that just as we are beginning to grow comfortable with a coherent definition of jazz, the rules are going to change. We'll find that some contemporary compositions may attract the kids' ears as the music comes closer to the pop music of today. We'll hear how today's mandate for multicultural education can be beautifully fulfilled through a study of jazz. We'll be relieved to feel the tension of our increasing theoretical demands relaxed as we return to some simpler harmonies easily accessible to the beginning student. We'll cover some old ground—"pre-jazz" pieces and swing dance tunes, and enter some new territory, ranging from Latin to rock to rap. We'll create our own version of the multi-faceted San Francisco Jazz Festival in the schools. No ticket needed—just an open mind, an attentive ear and the welcoming gestures of jazz hospitality.

JUMPIN' AT THE WOODSIDE

Count Basie
Arranged by Doug Goodkin

61. JUMPIN' AT THE WOODSIDE: Count Basie

Focus

- Riff melody/ key of C
- Blues connections
- Boogie bass
- New Bridge
- Fast tempo

Activities

- Here is one way I introduce this piece.

  "A man dies and arrive at the Pearly Gates. St. Peter says, 'You know, your did some good things in your life and some bad things. So I'm going to give you the choice of Heaven or Hell.' 'Can I get a sneak preview?' asks the man. 'Okay,' says Peter, 'but I can only show you 10 seconds of each.' So the man steps into Heaven and there he sees people in white robes gently walking in beautiful flowering fields while they sing:

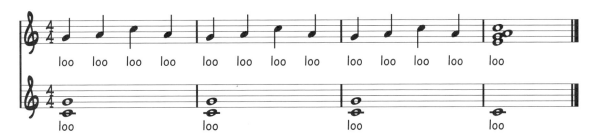

  "Ten seconds later he steps into Hell and enters a dark, smoky jazz club with a band playing:

  "When the ten seconds are up, he rushes back to St. Peter and says, 'No contest. Reserve me a table at that jazz club.' An instant later, he's seated at the table, settling in for an eternity of great jazz. Out comes the band and they start playing":

  (Repeat above ten or twenty times until the students get the punch line.)

- Review all vocal parts and teach the change in measures 5 and 6. Discuss how a simple little change is sufficient to change Hell into Heaven.

- Analyze form—aaba= A. AABA for the whole song. Teach the bridge vocally.

- Sing the whole song miming instruments—basses pluck bass, melody plays saxophone, response plays trumpets and trombones hands on the bells to make the "waa-waa" sound.

- Transfer to xylos with suggestions from students as to how to divide up.

- Decide with the group how to orchestrate the call and response riffs (wood-metal? alto-soprano? voice-instrument? combinations of the above?).

Extensions

- Play excerpts from *Sing a Song of Basie* by Lambert, Hendricks & Ross (Impulse—GRD 112) and follow how they create text for instrumental parts. Play a tune from the CD (like *One O'Clock Jump* back to back with Basie's original).

- Have a small group create text in a similar way for *Jumpin' at the Woodside.*

Comments

This live enactment of an old joke (often used with the tune *Perdido* or Monk's *Straight, No Chaser)* helps make another Orff- jazz connection as we hear the contrast between a drone-based pentatonic ostinato and a jazz counterpart. It also provides an interesting way to learn the form and understand the power of variation within repetition. Following good Orff practice, it prepares all the parts in the body and voice before moving to the instruments.

Having stomped at the Savoy in the last chapter, it only makes sense to jump at the Woodside in this one. In contrast to the popular songs penned for Broadway or Hollywood that later were adapted by jazz musicians, this Count Basie classic came directly out of the jazz culture. It represents a mix of jazz standard style—a 32-bar AABA form, II-V-I changes and circle of 5ths progression—and blues style—call and response, short riffs and walking boogie bass.

Bass and Chords

The boogie style bass should feel familiar from some of the walking bass patterns of the blues. The I / I / I / I / II / V / I / I implied harmonies are simpler than our previous pieces and allow us to concentrate on mastering the faster tempo. Now instead of tritones, the close voicing of a M6th chord is used in the opening measures, shifting effortlessly to a chord that can both function as a IIm7 chord and an extended V7 chord. Note that when divided between two players, the top player doesn't have to change notes during the A section.

Note also the inverted *Soup, Soup* rhythm simplified here from the original.

The chordal response split in two parts can also be played by one player with four mallets.

Bridge

This bridge introduces yet another new progression, characterized further by three 7th chords (which can be voiced with the familiar tritones) and one 6th chord. Most recordings feature a short improvised solo on the bridge. Here you can play the chords alone or make up a little melody.

Improvisation

This tune shares more with *Jumpin' with Symphony Sid* than its opening verb—it is also a good chance for kids to make up their own riffs on the pentatonic scale and begin to stack them. In the arrangement above, I give a model of a second melody paraphrasing the tune from *Lester Leaps In*.

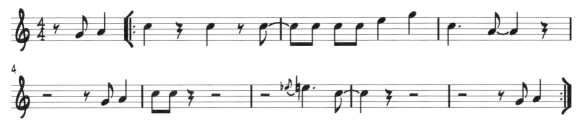

In addition to, or over and above, the riffs, students can try improvising in the C pentatonic scale, even continuing throughout the bridge. The bridge of this tune is also a good moment to consider a short drum solo.

Like *Stompin' at the Savoy*, this is a great opportunity to have one group play and one group dance. Experiment with the comfort level of tempo—this is meant to be played fast!

Oh, yeaaahh!

SING, SING, SING

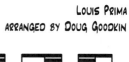

RETURN TO A. PLAY ONCE THROUGH.
THEN GO TO C

4-BAR DRUM INTERLUDE
THEN PLAY AABA WITH RECORDER MELODY.
DRUM INTERLUDE TO D
CONTINUE DRUMS TO CODA

62. SING, SING, SING: Louis Prima

Focus

• Drum solo

• ABCD

• Modulation

Comments

It was Benny Goodman that made this tune famous, featuring an opening drum solo by Gene Krupa that pre-dated *Wipe-Out* by 30 years! The tune moves beyond the AABA song form to what boils down to a long string of riffs and solos. The form, though simplified from the original, is more ambitious than our previous pieces. The melodies and riffs in the six sections offer a different kind of challenge than the head-solo-head format (though solos could be integrated here as well). My students were delighted to discover that they could memorize the following sequence:

Drum Interlude; Intro.; A A B A C C Drum; Intro; A A B A Drum, D D D D Coda

The melody here is simplified from the original and the B section melody borrows from Jimmy Lunceford's *Organ Grinder Swing* and substitutes the tune *"I Love Coffee, I Love Tea"* (a tune similar to the original B section). The C section modulates to A minor. The drum figure underneath the tune is a refreshing change from the usual ride cymbal.

Is there anything familiar here? The shift from major to relative minor in *Pennsylvania 6-5000* is reversed here, with an A section in minor and the B section in its relative major. The bass pattern in the C section is basically the same as the first section of *The Cookie Jar*, while almost all melodies and riffs are major or minor pentatonic (including the b5th). The order of our sequence is yet again confirmed!

DIZZY ATMOSPHERE

Dizzy Gillespie
Arranged by Doug Goodkin

Da capo

Ornamented Melody:

63. DIZZY ATMOSPHERE: Dizzy Gillespie

Focus

• Chromatic Bridge

Comments

Music teachers are busy people. Much of this book is designed to make your work easier by offering simple arrangements of fantastic tunes playable by kids, with suggestions about how to teach them, where they came from and where they might lead. Yet in my own experience, the further the search for material, the deeper the experience of teaching it. There's a story behind every tune chosen in this book, an 'a-ha" moment in which the tune I needed in the moment seemed to appear.

Of course, this is not an entirely passive experience—I'm not just sitting around waiting for miracles to occur. My antennae are up and alert, open and receptive to whatever is passing by. And what precisely am I looking for? In general, a tune that is playable and provides enough immediate satisfaction that the kids are motivated to buckle down and learn the hard parts. *Dizzy Atmosphere* is a perfect example of the above—a repetitive four-note melody that sounds great accompanied on piano with the *I Got Rhythm* changes (much the same way *C-Jam Blues* is a good starter for the blues progression). I've taught this tune to adults who are "non-musicians" and the joy and excitement on their faces when they play the simple melody accompanied by piano and drums is a wonder to behold!

My 8th grade class that learned this piece had already played *I Got Rhythm*, so it was easy for them to "plug in" the "rhythm changes" at a faster tempo. When we came to the bridge, they stopped and listened to me on the piano and then continued to play the final A section. Asked to describe the bridge, they were both able to perceive that it was a melodic sequence and that the chords were different than the original Gershwin changes. The inner voices shifting down by half steps on the chromatic instruments were no problem, but the melody—especially the first two phrases—was an exciting challenge. One of the students took it on as her project and mastered it. A year later, she came to visit the school and the moment she entered the music room, she went over to her instrument and played—guess what?—the bridge to *Dizzy Atmosphere!* She was proud that she remembered it.

As you search for your own tunes, this mixture of instant success and long-term challenge will be a key factor in how it all works with your students. And naturally, your own excitement and enthusiasm about the tune will be an important factor as well.

MY LITTLE SUEDE SHOES

Charlie Parker
Arranged by Doug Goodkin

64. MY LITTLE SUEDE SHOES: Charlie Parker

Focus

- Swing/Latin

- Arpeggios

- Conga Drum

Comments

This lovely little piece by Charlie Parker fits perfectly into the genre of jazz standard—32 bars long, AABA form, and mostly II-V-I progressions—with the notable exception that it is an instrumental piece and not a song. The melody is refreshingly simple in comparison to the acrobatics of most be-bop tunes, easily playable and supremely logical. Ask the children to verbally describe the structure of the melody to exercise their analytical musical minds. (An opening figure that is the same for the first three phrases, going up at the end on the first and third, down on the second, etc.) The arpeggios on the bridge introduce this important musical concept—playing the notes of a chord in a single note sequence. Practice other variations of these arpeggios, changing both rhythm and direction, which can later be incorporated in the solos.

The Latin Conversion

This tune, along with *Perdido* and *Blue Moon* in the previous chapter, works well played both in swing rhythm and Latin style. Sometimes such tunes are played in swing for the A sections and Latin in the bridge—or reversed. We'll take a longer look at Latin jazz in our next piece, but for now a simple "Latin conversion chart" will do.

- Change from swing rhythm to even 8th notes.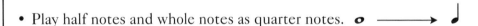

- Play half notes and whole notes as quarter notes.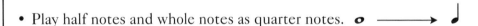

- Change ride cymbal pattern to straight 8th pattern on the hi-hat.

- Play clave rhythm——with stick on the edge of the snare drum.

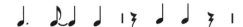

- Play conga drum as follows:

- End with "cha-cha-cha!"

LISTEN HERE

Eddie Harris
Arranged by Doug Goodkin

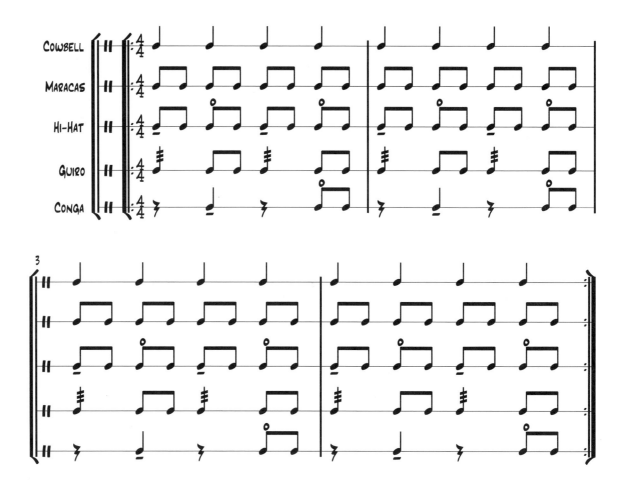

65. LISTEN HERE: Eddie Harris

Focus

• Latin rhythms

Activity

Though we have arrived at the place where a step-by-step description of the teaching process is no longer necessary, our new subject of Latin style bears some special attention.

　　Below is a possible sequence towards realizing this piece:

Dance

• Dance to the original recording of *Listen Here* (LP: The Best of Eddie Harris: Atlantic SD 1545), starting from a basic cha-cha-cha step.

Rhythm parts

- Demonstrate each percussion instrument. All play each rhythm vocally, miming technique, and vocalize the sound of the instrument.[*]

- Transfer to the actual instruments and layer-in rhythms one at a time. When all parts have entered, play the bass to prepare for the next step.

Bass

- Break the bass pattern down into two halves, practicing the first half and leaving the second 4 beats silent, then reversing, and finally putting them together. (Don't forget our rule of teaching all parts to everyone, regardless of instrument. If there aren't enough instruments—and even if there are—sing!)

- Clarify the sticking pattern on xylophones—alternating hands in the first half, then moving the left hand up to begin the second half, alternating hands again.

r l r l r l / l r l r l r l / r

Melody

- Sing the melody. All join.

- Clarify the entrance of each phrase (the first phrase on beat 4, the next three on *2 and).*

- Clarify the relationship of the first phrase and bass (the same figure displaced).

- Have all sing the melody while keeping beat with the cowbell. Altos/soprano play melody.

Chords

- All speak the rhythm of the piano part. Sing tritones.

Whole Piece

- Practice solos in the basic blues scale (G B♭ C D F G) over bass and chords. During the solos, the ensemble riffs the first phrase of the melody every 8 beats:

ETC.

---

* For a great model of vocal percussion, see "Una Forma Mas" © 1995 Sire Records by the Cuban a capella group Vocal Sampling (the first cut, "Montuno Sampling," is a good example).

- Set order of entrances and order of solos. Include a percussion solo where all melodic/harmonic parts drop out and percussion section continues, with or without a lead soloist on congas or timbales.

- Have one or several groups choreograph a cha-cha sequence.

- Perform and enjoy!

Comments

This tune has special meaning for me, as I used to listen to it as a teenager driving the streets of Newark, New Jersey, on the edge of this strange new world called jazz. When I came across it at a record store years later, I realized it was the perfect tune for my students, with its driving bass vamp, I-IV chord structure (similar to *Hambone* in Chapter 5), simple melody and exciting Latin rhythms. It was also great fun to teach this at a course in Spain, completing a loop from Spain to West Africa to Cuba to New York and back to Spain again!

Keeping our historical thread moving, let's take a brief look at the Latin influence in jazz.

Young student playing bongos.

LATIN JAZZ

Jazz's beginnings in New Orleans made a "Latin connection" inevitable. This Caribbean port invited the flow of music from the Spanish Caribbean, and from Central and South America and such influences made themselves heard in jazz from the beginning. At the turn of the century, Scott Joplin wrote *Solace: A Mexican Serenade* while W.C. Handy visited Cuba in 1900 and folded in a Habanera rhythm in the B section of his *St. Louis Blues*. In the 1920's, Jelly Roll Morton added "Spanish seasonings" to his band, The Red Hot Peppers, with compositions such as *The Crave* and *New Orleans Joys*. By the 1930's, Duke Ellington collaborated with Puerto Rican trombonist Juan Tizol to write *Perdido* and the North African flavored *Caravan*. A decade later, Cuban drummer Chano Pozo and Dizzy Gillespie added fuel to the Latin infusion with *Manteca* and Dizzy revisited North Africa, be-bop style, with *A Night in Tunisia*. In the 50's, Sonny Rollins introduced jazz calypso with *St. Thomas* and Miles Davis collaborated with Gil Evans on *Sketches in Spain*. Antonio Carlos Jobim and Stan Getz brought Brazil into the widening Latin influence with the bossa nova hits *The Girl from Ipanema* and *Desafinado*. Today, jazz continues to share the kitchen with its Latin neighbors, with musicians like Jerry Gonzales cooking up some Thelonious Monk tunes with hot sauce and Cuban pianist Gonzalo Rubalcaba re-visiting some of Dizzy Gillespie's favorite recipes.

What is the nature of the Latin-jazz connection? The historical answer is a subject for a 10-volume book or PBS Series!* The journey might begin in the Middle East traveling west via *Caravan* to spend a *Night in Tunisia* before settling in Morocco, where the first fusion music between Arabs and black Africans took place. This fusion in turn traveled north to the Iberian Peninsula and Spain, where Arabic influences abound.

When Spain colonized the New World and imported African slaves, its music, already influenced by black Africa, Arab Middle East and Christian Southern Europe, met again with African influences and a new style of fusion emerged, markedly different from its North American counterpart. Rather than the rebuilding of Africanisms traced in our study of jazz, music in the Spanish slave colonies maintained much of its African foundation while absorbing influences from Spain, for the following reasons:

1. Some slave owners—in Cuba, in particular—choose to keep the tribes together because they felt they worked better. This helped keep the culture—and music—intact.

2. Many allowed the slaves to continue drumming, feeling that it helped diffuse tension and kept them focused on their work.

3. In the conversion to Catholicism , many Africans secretly maintained their religious—and thus, music and dance—practice by "folding" African deities into the worship of Catholic saints.

The result was that the music of Cuba, the Dominican Republic and Puerto Rico (as well as Brazil and Haiti, where Portuguese and French ran similar slave colonies) retained much of its African rhythmic soul. The meeting of these cultures with jazz first made itself felt in those *rhythms*, and that (along with the added color of conga drums, bongos, claves, timbales and maracas) remains its decisive contribution.

---

* And sadly neglected in Ken Burns's jazz series.

How do Latin rhythms differ from the jazz triad of offbeat, syncopation and swing? Where the ride cymbal serves as the point of reference in jazz, the clave pattern is the fundamental glue of the rhythmic ensemble.

(REVERSE CLAVE)

Syncopation continues to abound, but swing rhythm is firmly replaced by "straight" rhythm. Now eighth notes written ♫ ♫ are really played as written!

Naturally, these are but the smallest beginning steps. Latin music is a field as vast and complex as jazz itself. The reader is referred to a few choice sources in the bibliography for a more thorough account.

JAZZ FUSION

If the Latin influence on jazz represented a family reunion of long-lost African cousins, jazz/rock was the re-uniting of an African-American young adult with his long-lost grandfather. Fathered by black rhythm and blues musicians like Louis Jordan (himself a child of the Chick Webb Big Band), rock and roll grew up in the 50's and started its own family tree. By the late 60's and 70's, jazz met its wayward grandchild and they began jamming at the Fillmore East with the Miles Davis band, Chick Corea's Return to Forever and Weather Report—and the jazz/rock fusion was born.

Meanwhile, rock itself was also connected to its Latin relatives. From Chuck Berry's *Havana Moon* to the hit tunes *Spanish Harlem* and *La Bamba* to the clave rhythm transposed to guitar on *Bo Diddley* and the Rolling Stones' *Not Fade Away*, to the hit group Santana, the Latin influence made its presence known.

Many jazz/rock pieces share a few characteristics with their Latin cousins. Rock rhythm, like Latin rhythm, is played straight. Jazz/rock drumming uses more of the drum set, with the bass drum finally moving to a more prominent role. *Tequila*, with its Latin A section, jazz boogie B section and overall rock feel has been played by Latin bands, big bands and rock groups. *Watermelon Man*, Herbie Hancock's jazz/rock blues, was made famous by the Cuban drummer Mongo Santamaria.

As rock and Latin music flows into mainstream jazz, the definitions are getting pushed further out. Now 8th notes are played evenly instead of swung. The ride cymbal and hi-hat give way to the bass drum and snare drum. The electric bass may replace the acoustic upright and the keyboard the piano. Shall we plug in the glockenspiel?

Our next piece is my own attempt to move in this direction.

EARTH DAY RAP

DOUG GOODKIN

INSTRUMENTS CONTINUE THROUGHOUT
EACH GROUP DELIVERS EARTH DAY INFORMATION "RAP" STYLE.
BODY PERCUSSION FOLLOWS (2×S)
CONTINUE IN "RONDO" FORM (RAP. BODY PERCUSSION. RAP. ETC.)

The sky is high_ and the o-cean is deep, but we can't treat the plan-et like a

gar-bage heap. Don't wreck it, pro-tect it, keep part of it wild,_ and

think a bout the fu-ture of your great grand child. Re - cy- cle, bi-cy-cle, don't you

drive by your- self,__ don't buy those plas - tic prod-ucts on the

sup er-mar-ket shelf. Boy-cott, pe-ti-tion, let the big bus-iness know, that if we

mess it up here there's no-where else we can go. Don't shrug your should-ers, say

"what can I do?" On-ly one per-son can do it and that per-son is you!

66. EARTH DAY RAP

Focus

• 8-beat rhythm

• Rap text

Comments

This is one of the few pieces of my own that has traveled beyond the walls of my class-room—there's even a version in an Australian songbook! Written for a school Earth Day celebration, it returns to the style of the pieces in Chapter 5, with its one chord accompaniment, color chords similar to *Green Sally Up* and *Hambone*, and *la* pentatonic scale. Its point of departure is the rap style and rhythm.

"Rap" rhythm

Now's the time to bring the evolution of the offbeat out of the footnote in Chapter 2 and into the music. The expansion of offbeat feel in the 2/4 meter of ragtime and dixieland (1 *and* 2 *and)* to its incarnation in the swing and be-bop era in 4/4 (1 <u>2</u> 3 <u>4</u>) to yet another augmentation in the funk, jazz-rock and rap of the past 30 years in an 8-beat feel (1 2 <u>3</u> 4 / 5 6 <u>7</u> 8) is a fascinating study of augmentation. This arrangement simplifies that feeling to a beginner's level, dividing the drum set between various instruments. Now the snare drum takes on a new function. Instead of the subtle brushwork duplicating the ride cymbal pattern or the kicks and fills giving rhythmic drive, the drumstick sounds squarely on the 3 and the 7. Keep the bass going throughout and answer each two-line rap with the drums (an augmented call and response!). This insures the balance—the drums are generally too loud for the unamplified voices.

The phrases of this rap are generally more square than street rap, but the vocal inflection should try to match the rap style—have the kids show you.

The author celebrates the *Earth Day Rap* with Bobby McFerrin at a school celebration.

WORLD MUSIC FUSION

Now we arrive at the most recent chapter in the story of jazz—the expansion of the mother tongue through contact with new instruments, new rhythms, new scales and new forms that come from virtually every corner of the globe. For lack of a better term, "world music" is the label that describes both indigenous music in its traditional form and the new forms emerging from the confluence of distinct cultures. Every style of music is being redefined through the instant connections of the global village—from Irish folk groups using didgeridoos to classical composers using African rhythms. Jazz, already a hybrid music, is right there on the front lines of intercultural exchange.

From the very beginning, jazz was one of America's most welcome exports. During World War I, Europe went to Europe when the U.S. military sponsored a tour of James Reese Europe's band, to great acclaim. When Sidney Bechet went to France to play in 1919, a Swiss conductor was so impressed that he predicted "His own way is perhaps the highway the whole world will swing along tomorrow." Armstrong and Ellington, sponsored by the U. S. State Department, toured the world as America's "ambassadors of jazz."

Not only was jazz brought to distant shores to enlarge other cultures' definition of music, but the visiting jazz musicians were also treated to the music of the host cultures, both informally on the streets and formally in concerts. When the likes of Duke Ellington and Dave Brubeck, both compositional thinkers, heard these new sounds and rhythms, it was only natural that these musics would influence their compositions as well. Inspired by his 1964 Asian tour, Duke Ellington wrote *The Far East Suite*, putting Indian, Japanese and other "exotic" spices into his native jazz idiom. He also would write *The Virgin Islands Suite* and *La Plus Belle Africaine.* Dave Brubeck, similarly influenced by his travels, wrote *Blue Rondo a la Turk, Maori Blues, Castilian Drums* and *Koto Song.*

By the 70s, the European-based recording company ECM featured European, American and Brazilian jazz artists, as well as collaborations between them. Pianist Randy Weston moved to North Africa, trumpeter Don Cherry studied various musics worldwide, Colin Walcott played the Indian sitar and tabla, Andy Narell brought the steel drum into jazz. Influences were pouring in from all corners of the globe, connected by the loose thread of familiarity with an existing jazz repertoire and a passion for experimentation, exploration and improvisation. This next piece presented here, one of the early examples of "world music fusion," offers a tiny window into an enormous and growing soundscape.

67. BLUE RONDO A LA TURK: Dave Brubeck

Note: Because of copyright restrictions, the score of this piece is not included here. However, it is readily available in many publications of Dave Brubeck's music (*Dave Brubeck Anthology*: *Volume Two*: Hansen House: ISBN Q 8494 0351 0).

Focus

• Rondo Form

• 9/8 meter

• trichords

Rhythmic Preparation

• Practice the Keith Terry 9 pattern introduced in Chapter 3. While performing, speak each of the following versions:

> Numbers: 1 2 1 2 1 2 1 2 3 (3x) 1 2 3 1 2 3 1 2 3
> India: Taka taka taka takita (3x) takita takita takita
> Bali: Tjak tjak tjak tjak-tjak-tjak (3x) tjak-tjak-tjak tjak-tjak-tjak tjak-tjak-tjak
> Fruit: Apple apple apple pineapple (3x) pineapple pineapple pineapple

• Practice a pat-clap version as follows:

• Play either or both versions above along with the recording (*The Dave Brubeck Quartet: Time Out*: Columbia CK40585). (Either or both together can also be an introduction in the actual performance, followed immediately by the drums.)

Melodic Preparation

• Introduce the idea of the trichord—three succesive notes going up or down.

• With xylophones set in the key of F (B♭ instead of B), explore some trichord patterns as follows:

• Play the first phrase of the melody with the bass.

• On chromatic instruments, have students figure out a minor version beginning with C and A following the same shape (use G♯ instead of G). Show that they have "discovered" part of the B section of the piece.

• Proceed to teach each section of the piece.

Comments

This piece is the perfect summary of the specialized approach to jazz via Orff Schulwerk, as shown by the following:

- It plays well and sounds good on the Orff instruments, offering just enough challenge to make it exciting to try and a pleasure to master.

- The odd meters and mixed meters found throughout the Orff repertoire are reinforced.

- Its reference to Turkish rhythms parallels the Orff practice of multicultural sources.

- The rondo form, use of trichords and shifting major/minor tonalities are also common in Orff literature and connect directly with the European classical music study.

- It is a meeting point of three distinct genres—jazz (**Blue**=Blues), European art music (**Rondo**= Mozart's *Turkish Rondo*) and world music (**a la Turk**= Turkish rhythm.)

Odd Meters

Though Fats Waller's *Jitterbug Waltz* broke new ground as a 3/4 jazz tune back in 1942, jazz has lived most of its life within the 4/4 border. In the late 1940's, Dave Brubeck, a classically trained pianist studying with French composer Darius Milhaud, was encouraged by his teacher to apply his compositional studies to jazz. In 1951, he formed a quartet that was so popular on the college circuit that he became the second jazz musician (after Louis Armstrong) to make the cover of Time magazine. Throughout its sixteen-year tenure, its role in the development of jazz was a debatable point among aficionados, but one contribution is indisputable—the exploration of odd meters. Compositions by Brubeck and his alto player Paul Desmond probed the possibilities of jazz in 7/4 *(Unsquare Dance)*, 10/8 *(Countdown)*, 11/4 (Eleven Four), 5/4 *(Take Five*—the most famous of them all and a million-seller record in the early 60s), and our piece here, in 9/8. Though modern jazz still leans towards the 4/4 groove, it has learned to swing in all meters and we can thank Brubeck for opening that door.

Trichords

The number of melodies constructed with the three-note cells called trichords is impressive. I have found examples from medieval times through contemporary compositions in the Western classical tradition and many more in the folk tradition. Though less common in the jazz tradition, some jazz standard melodies use them as well:

Autumn Leaves

My Heart Stood Still

The Way You Look Tonight

Blue Moon

Once the students understand the main concept, this melody based so heavily on trichords becomes much easier to play and remember.

Form

The A section can be played on the standard Orff instruments, but chromatics are needed for the B & C sections. I have had my advanced piano players play all parts with the ensemble. Because some of the later sections were too challenging for my beginning students, I have simplified the form here.

All of the above qualities and more make this piece a wonderful choice with an advanced ensemble. The combination of the odd meters, high level of technique, fast tempos, complex forms and review of the blues with opportunities for improvisation is a fabulous summary of our study. However, there is another personal connection that makes this piece especially meaningful for me.

Dave Brubeck

Dave Brubeck's album *Time Out* was my first introduction to jazz. I was 13 years old. When my daughter Talia turned 13 and began studying the alto saxophone, I decided to give her the same album as a gift. Sure enough, some of the music really captured her ear and she immediately had me teach her *Blue Rondo a la Turk* on the piano and later tried it on the saxophone. The experience also brought *me* back to this music that I hadn't listened to for over 30 years. I had heard so much jazz in that interval and learned so much about what makes good jazz and mediocre jazz. How did this music hold up?

In a word, "Great!" The music had—and has—its own charm and unique style, its own integrity and its own *sound*. Like Lee Konitz, Gerry Mulligan, Bill Evans, Stan Getz and other notable white jazz players of the 50s, 60s and beyond, Brubeck and his band had come to the music with respect and integrity and added the gifts of their own experience and background. It might not be a sound to everyone's taste, but it was an unmistakably personal voice and that, after all, is the point every jazz player strives to reach.

Each year, I make a goal to try something new, and this last year, my two goals were to do some pieces in odd meters and other keys. *Take Five* leaped out as a possible starting point and when I saw the 8th grade's excitement in trying to master it, I quickly added another Brubeck piece in 3/4—*Theme from Mr. Broadway*. When I began working with 7th grade on trichords, *Blue Rondo a la Turk* was the obvious extension. Within the first month of school, I had three Brubeck pieces going.

Imagine my delight when I discovered that Dave Brubeck was coming to perform at The San Francisco Jazz Festival. We quickly arranged for the whole 8th grade class to go. For many students, this was their first jazz concert. We waited around afterwards and convinced Dave Brubeck himself to come out and have his picture taken with the kids. He was friendly, warm and generous with his time and the kids were thrilled. The next day, the kids wrote letters, and a sample one is printed below:

> It's hard to describe the feeling I felt when I walked downstairs in the morning and learned that we had 25 tickets to the Dave Brubeck concert. I could immediately picture Mr. Brubeck and his quartet playing *Take Five* and everyone cheering.

When Dave started to play his first tune, accompanied by the amazing bass player and drummer, and then the saxophone and flute, I was impressed by how beautifully the instruments complemented each other. The concert was great—I was in awe when Dave Brubeck played *Take Five*; it was absolutely fabulous.

When I am old and have lived for many, many years, I will remember the night when Dave Brubeck's quartet and my 8th grade class met. In thirteen years of living, I have never been so lucky as to meet one so famous as Mr. Brubeck. The night of November 2nd will be in my mind till my soul calls it quits.   —NICK MAKANNA

It was a perfect evening—all the stars were aligned. I finally got to meet the man who introduced me to jazz when I was in 8th grade and had the opportunity to see him open the door to that world to my 8th grade students.

Throughout this book and in my teaching, there is strong emphasis on the African-American spirit at the core of jazz and an attempt to both honor and thank the creators of the art form. But it is also important to acknowledge that jazz is larger than any one group, that it was a mixture of black and white from the beginning. We should note the contributions of all musicians, black, white and hispanic, who keep the music going and growing and give children of all ethnicities and genders a chance to see and hear models of "people like them" who have something important to say. Dave Brubeck brought me through the door that led me to Earl Hines, Art Tatum, Thelonious Monk—and also to Bill Evans, Chick Corea and Keith Jarrett—and for that I am eternally grateful. How ironic that it was an Anglo-American man who introduced me to jazz and an African-American man (Avon Gillespie) who introduced me to Orff Schulwerk!

Dave Brubeck with students/faculty of The San Francisco School.

68. FREE JAZZ

New Experiences

• No preconceived structure

Activity:

• Have students in groups of two to four choose instruments.

• With remaining students as audience, each group freely improvises a piece without any prior discussion. One begins with a sound or a phrase, the other responds and they continue in conversation until the piece feels like it is over.

• Both listeners and performers comment on what happened; what worked, what didn't.

• Next group performs.

• If possible, record each piece.

Comments

This type of activity is common fare in Orff Schulwerk. We've already experienced similar pieces in Chapter 3 while exploring the sounds of our names—now it is transposed to melodic instruments. The beauty of such experiments is that they require the most important skill of musicianship—listening. Let's take a brief look at the parallels with the historical development of such improvisation in jazz, which, for lack of a better term, became known as "free jazz."

FREE JAZZ

Jazz began as a *folk* music, organically grown from the needs of a particular cultural group. It grew into a *popular* music, serving to entertain large populations of people of mixed backgrounds. It blossomed into a *classical* music, meeting the artist's need for self-expression and touching those who took the time to *listen* and recognize themselves in the music. As a classical music, each new generation absorbed the lessons of the form and, following in the wake of a few original creators, expanded the boundaries of that expression, mostly by increased abstraction of rhythm, melody and harmony.*

By 1960, three such creators felt limited by the steady beat of the rhythm section and confined by the harmonic box of melodic improvisation over chords. Just as the be-bop originators broke out of the swing dance box, so did Ornette Coleman, John Coltrane and Cecil Taylor revolutionize their be-bop inheritance, each in markedly different ways. Ornette Coleman kept a sense of the rhythmic flow, but searched for melody free from chords and rhythm free from meter. Working without piano, his groundbreaking album *Free Jazz* gave both a title and a tone to the movement in 1960. Coltrane turned back towards a more African polyrhythmic sense (realized in drummer Elvin Jones) and a polymodal melodic approach sometimes referred to as "sheets of sound." Listeners could neither easily snap their fingers nor whistle his improvisational licks. Cecil Taylor went the furthest out, abandoning all sense of metronomic rhythmic beat, recognizable melody and functional harmony in his churning, dance-like and trance-like primal expression.

---

* This progression in jazz mirrored the development of Western art music. Wagner's opening to *Tristan und Isolde* pushed the upper limits of the harmonic system inherited from Bach, Debussy further stretched the definition of melody and harmony, Stravinsky broke open the rhythms and Schoenberg finally threw the whole tonal structure out and replaced it with his 12-tone system.

The free jazz movement ranged between sheer indulgence and moments of brilliance, as the quality of listening was raised to the highest degree, entering each sound without preconception and following it to its intuitive conclusion. Requiring the same intense listening from the audience, its commercial success was necessarily limited. It continued to develop in such groups as The Chicago Art Ensemble and took a different turn in the piano solos of Keith Jarrett.

Without recognizable objective criteria distinguishing "good" free jazz from "bad" beyond the subjective response, free jazz could only go so far. Though no entire schools followed in their trails, Coleman, Coltrane and Taylor left their mark. After the increased reflective distance of cool jazz and technical complexities of be-bop, it returned jazz to a more primary heart-based and body-based expression. It upped the ante for listening in both individual solos and collective improvisation. By discovering what was possible without a predetermined structure, artists brought a new intensity and freedom to their improvisations within more structured tunes.

The work of the Keith Jarrett Trio—bassist Gary Peacock, drummer Jack De Johnette and pianist Keith Jarrett—is a good case in point. Performing mostly jazz standards for the last fifteen years, they recently performed a concert of "free jazz." In the liner notes to the recording (*Inside Out*, ECM records), Keith Jarrett comments:

> "Sometimes we have to turn things inside out to see what they're made of....People who don't understand free playing are not free to see it as an amazingly important part of the true jazz history. Where's the form? Don't ask. Don't think. Don't anticipate. Just participate. It's all there somewhere inside. And then suddenly it forms itself.

> "We need to be even more in tune with each other to play this way, without material, and even more attentive. Every possibility is available if you take away the tunes, but only some are valid under the circumstances. It is only our sensitivity to the flux that determines whether the music succeeds or fails."

Just participate. Be sensitive to the flux. Be attentive to each other. This not only defines the basic credo of Orff Schulwerk, but also reveals the basic fact of jazz itself. Without the structure of the tune or the expectation of a given vocabulary, the task is more difficult because the possibilities are wider, but in essence, the sensibility is the same whether the trio is playing the same tune for the 100th time or an entirely free improvisation. As you will read in the student comments on attending jazz performances in the next chapter, what strikes them is the *communication* between performers, the way that they're alive to the moment and alert to the next possibility.

99% of what passes for music education is about learning the specifics of a language, repeating and attempting to rise to what already exists in terms of scales, phrases, techniques, expressive devices, pieces and so on. This, of course, is absolutely fundamental to help us gain control of sound so that we can play what we hear and hear what we play. Yet jazz is also about the sound that does not yet exist until we bring it out in the air and that requires *relinquishing* control and letting the music speak for itself, allowing it to find its own way into form.

The three year olds I teach are marvels of free improvisation, unhampered by any notions of correct techniques and musical rules. They embody the raw musical impulse we all share, and some fascinating music evolves from their encounter with voice, drum and glockenspiel. They are firmly in the stage that Alfred North Whitehead calls "Romance," that first magical encounter of possibility. By the time they are in elementary school, they enter the developmental stage of "Precision," in which they are hungry to know specific techniques and classified ideas and eager to gain more precise control over their creative impulses. This stage continues through college, with the techniques getting more specific and refined and the ideas getting larger and more complex. In music, this means drones moving toward three-chord accompaniments to extended voicings and elaborate progressions, pentatonic scales moving to diatonic to chromatic, simple canons moving towards fugues, and so on. "Precision" is where most music education begins and ends. But jazz insists that there's one more stop—what Whitehead calls "Generalization," a return to Romance armed with the tools of control, but open to letting go of control. Jazz simply calls it "finding your own voice."

Orff's contribution to this dynamic tension between control and flow is a thorough understanding of the value of Romance *at each stage of musical development*! It is naive to think that children can be brought up on a steady diet of Romance and that jazz musicians can simply play freely without studying their scales or Lester Young solos, but it is equally damaging to imagine that students can spend their lives in the right and wrong world of Precision and suddenly be free at the end of it all. My experience in Orff Schulwerk convinces me that a healthy dose of Romance is necessary *every step of the way.* This is not mere conjecture—it is backed by thirty-two years of releasing the joy of Romance with preschool, elementary, middle school students, conservatory students, teachers, parents, Zen monks, computer corporate managers and more.

This book is very much concerned with teaching a stylistically correct vocabulary of jazz that mirrors its growth and development, but each activity opens the window to some degree of exploration and improvisation. Each rule given appears absolutely true—and it *is* for the particular style of the moment. But as we move through the sequence, we begin to understand that the rules are only *provisionally* true, that they change across time and across styles. And, that some of the most glorious moments come from breaking the rules!

SILENCE

CHARLIE HADEN

Chord Progression

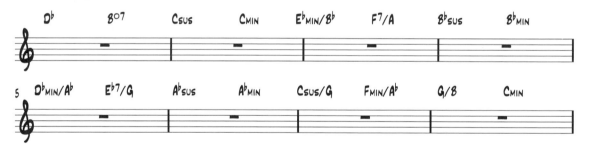

69. SILENCE

Focus

• Chorale style

Activity

• Teach all parts vocally to all.

• Divide into soprano and alto (tenor optional).

• Change vowel sounds each time through.

• Take turns reading from jazz quotes during singing.

Comments

This beautiful piece by bass player Charlie Haden stretches our notion of what jazz is. There is no offbeat feel, no syncopation, no swing rhythm, no blues chords or bent notes, no riffs or jazz melody. Indeed, there's barely a melody at all, just a chorale-like chord progression that seems to come more from Bach than Bird. In this version, it is sung with a pure head tone intonation and there is no improvisation. Why is it jazz?

Simply put, because it was composed by a jazz musician and played by jazz musicians. Charlie Haden was part of the revolutionary Ornette Coleman ensemble in the late 50s and 60s and has continued to play in a wide variety of settings. He has recorded this piece with various players from all walks of jazz. The distance we have traveled from *Head and Shoulders* to *Silence* is considerable, but if we—and the children—can feel the connection, we will have come to understand and appreciate the breadth and depth of this American art form we call jazz.

This is a perfect ending piece to our study and the one I use to close my jazz class. The double entendre of the title further qualifies it, as I always say music must begin and end in silence. I usually teach it by ear, but sometimes have the parts notated. The top two voices accompanied by the piano are sufficient for the effect of the piece, but if there are tenors or contraltos available, the bottom voice can be sung as well. Different vowel sounds for each time through add color and direction, moving from the closed sounds of humming to "oooh" to "oh" to "ahh" and back again. While singing, soloists take turns reading the jazz quotes in the pages to follow. We bring the voices of the jazz musicians into the circle and let them sing out over silence.

THE AFRICAN-AMERICAN EXPERIENCE IN JAZZ

"After emancipation...all those people... needed the music more than ever... trying to find out from the music what they were supposed to do...They learned it wasn't just white people the music had to reach to, nor even their own people, but straight out to life..."

—Sidney Bechet

"It was tough traveling through the South in those days. We had two white guys with us—the bus driver and Joe Glaser, Louis Armstrong's manager. If you had a colored bus driver back then, they'd lock you up in every little country town for 'speeding' . It was very rough finding a place to sleep in the South. You couldn't get into the hotel for the whites, and coloreds didn't have any hotels. You rented places in private homes, boardinghouses and whorehouses. The food was awful and we tried to find places where we could cook. We carried a bunch of pots and pans around with us."

—Pops Foster speaking of traveling with the Louis Armstrong band in the 30's

"I listened to the anguish in her voice and the lyrics seemed to be about my own problems. I started to cry."

—Sam Rivers commenting on a Billie Holiday performance

"He wasn't strong enough to last long. It's hard out there for a black man in this society. If you let all those pressures get to you and then start to slide all the way along with them, they will do you in."

—Dizzy Gillespie speaking of Charlie Parker

"You know what annoys the hell out of me? It's when people come up and ask if I ever recorded any serious music."

—Jimmy Garrison

"People have died for this music. You can't get more serious than that."

—Dizzy Gillespie's response to the question of jazz and "serious" music

SELF-EXPRESSION IN JAZZ

"A note doesn't care who plays it-whether you're black, white, green, brown or opaque!"

—Clark Terry

"When I came up, I got my own vibrato. You could tell me anywhere you heard me. Any of the cats that had any kind of name, you could tell them by the sound they got."

—Roy Eldridge

"The thing that makes jazz so interesting is that each man is his own academy...If he's really going to be persuasive, he learns about other academies, but the idea is that he must have that special thing. And sometimes you don't even know what it is."

—Cecil Taylor

"I say play your own way. Don't play what the public wants—you play what you want and let the public pick up what you are doing, even if it does take them fifteen, twenty years."

—THELONIOUS MONK

"Music is your own thoughts, your experience, your wisdom. If you don't live it, it won't come out in your horn. They teach you there's a boundary line to music. But, man, there's no boundary line to art."

—CHARLIE PARKER

"Playing jazz is like talking from your heart. You don't lie."

—BUNK JOHNSON

"I just try to play with feeling and heart. All worry gets you is more worry. I just don't worry. I'll tell you one thing: my playing seems to work."

—THELONIOUS MONK

JAZZ AND SPIRIT

"If you don't have the whole spiritual thing, I don't think jazz is complete. To me, a musician is just a transformer. It's like I receive the music from somewhere else...If I can't communicate, I don't care how hip the music is supposed to be, how avant-garde, how square or whatever, I don't think it's worth producing."

—JIMMY HEATH

"Coltrane took it out of being a hip musician and into being a musician of value, of worth to the community. A musician to relate to, a musician to raise kids by."

—FRANK LOWE

"Once you become aware of this force for unity in life, you can't ever forget it. It becomes part of everything you do. My goal on meditating on this through music remains the same. And that is to uplift people, as much as I can. To inspire them to realize more and more of their capacities for living meaningful lives."

—JOHN COLTRANE

"I must play music that is beyond this world. That's all I'm asking for in life and I don't think you can ask for more than just to be alone to create from what God gives you."

—ALBERT AYLER

"Jazz is the symbol of the triumph of the human spirit, not of its degradation. It is a lily in spite of the swamp."

—ARCHIE SHEPP

Other Suggested Jazz Compositions Playable by Children

SWING:
Opus One—Tommy Dorsey

Happy go Lucky Local—Duke Ellington

In the Mood—Glenn Miller

Jitterbug Waltz—Fats Waller

Topsy—Edgar Battle/Eddie Durham

BE-BOP:
Good Bait—Tadd Dameron

I Mean You—Thelonious Monk

Midnight Sun—Lionel Hampton

Oop Bop Sh Bam—Dizzy Gillespie

Pent-up House—Sonny Rollins

Well You Needn't—Thelonious Monk

JAZZ ROCK:
All My Life—Leon Parker

Canteloupe Island—Herbie Hancock

Chameleon—Herbie Hancock

The Cure—Keith Jarrett

Memphis Underground—Herbie Mann

Spooky—Classics IV

Watermelon Man—Herbie Hancock

LATIN JAZZ AND BOSSA NOVA:
Mambo Diablo—Tito Puente

One Note Samba—Antonio Carlos Jobim

Oye Como Va—Tito Puente

Morning—Clare Fischer

Ponciana—Bernier/ Simon

Soul Sauce—Dizzy Gillespie/Chano Pozo

Summer Samba—Marcos and Paulo Valle

Tico Tico—Abreu

CHAPTER 10:
JAZZ IN THE SCHOOL CURRICULUM:
PUTTING IT ALL TOGETHER

"When kids don't learn about their own heritage in school, they just don't care about school…I think the schools should teach kids about jazz."

—MILES DAVIS

In The San Francisco School curriculum, it is the 8th grade year that is devoted specifically to an intensive jazz study.* Most of the students entering that program have been making music in school for eleven years. They have sung virtually every day of their school life, danced, moved, recited rhymes and poetry, played an impressive variety of percussion instruments, recorder and Orff instruments, and improvised in all those mediums. Jazz has not been the center of their school music program—it has shared the stage with the full range of styles that speak of our diverse American heritage. These students have sung songs in Spanish, performed the English North Skeleton Sword Dance, danced the Chinese Lion Dance, played Brazilian samba and learned West African xylophone pieces. All these experiences have allowed them to celebrate the heritages on the left side of the hyphenated Americans we all are.

Yet though the students sincerely come to appreciate *all* the music they have done, they seem most at home with jazz. Playing a Balinese gamelan piece is like trying out an intriguing new cuisine, but jazz is home cooking—learning how to make those dishes they've been served their whole lives. More than any other musical experiences—and perhaps because its history is a blend of these diverse heritages—jazz speaks to the "American" side of the hyphen.

---

* This curriculum can be found on the school website: www.sfschool.org

Though the intensive study outlined in this book is primarily in 8th grade, the jazz thread runs throughout the children's school experience. As young as three years old, they're singing simple call and response songs like *Soup, Soup* and can already identify the style of music called jazz. At six years old, they're working on their jazzwalk and hearing about their first jazz musicians. (One of my first graders astounded her grandfather when she heard some music and asked him, *"Is that Louis Armstrong with his Hot Five or his Hot Seven?"*) At eight years old, they're clapping on the offbeat and playing spirited versions of games like *Johnny Brown*. They're also singing songs like *Chattanooga Choo-Choo* and *Side By Side*. By ten, they're playing pieces like *Who Stole the Cookies From the Cookie Jar?* and trying out their first jazz solos. By the time they reach 8th grade, they're ripe for the intensive jazz study, with a solid repertoire of skills, an openness to self-expression, a basic theory background and a lot of music in their ears. They've traveled a long arc beginning at three years old singing *Shoo Turkey* and ending eleven years later swinging *Stompin' at the Savoy*.

In this chapter, we will revisit the ideas and material presented in the context of an actual curriculum—in this case, an 8th grade Orff program meeting three times a week for forty-five minute periods. The model offered here gives the tune and basic chords—in the spirit of jazz, you are invited to take it out to the woodshed and "make it your own."

CLASS STRUCTURE

Throughout this book, we have tried to keep the threads of jazz tied together—history, aesthetics, theory, listening and practice. How does this actually work in the classroom?

Two of the three classes weekly are spent learning and playing the pieces. As suggested in the lessons given in this book, kids learn all the parts before deciding on one for a particular piece—and then try a different one for the next piece. All pieces are taught by ear and by hand, with some melodies, chords or forms put on the board for the visually inclined. We generally work on two or three pieces at a time and then perform them informally for anyone walking down the hall, and formally in concert.

The third class is devoted to learning about the musicians and listening to their music (listening program to follow). Homework is given out and collected here.

HOMEWORK

In the first editions of this book, the description of my homework assignments was as follows: "The homework generally consists of a short biography (average one-page typed) about a given jazz musician. They must list two sources and write the description in their own words—no printouts from the Internet! We discuss the possible sources at the beginning of the year—encyclopedias, jazz history books, recording liner notes, the Internet, etc.—and talk about their relative advantages and limitations. Students keep their assignments in the music section of their school binder. At the end of the year, they collate them into a book that represents their own personal history of jazz.

"The last assignment is a more in-depth study of a jazz musician of their choice. They also choose a recording from the artist and lead a listening class with the rest of the group. In this class, they must prepare a process that will involve the listeners. This has ranged from making questionnaires to telling stories to inviting their classmates to dance to the music.

"For years, I resisted choosing a jazz history textbook on the grounds that textbooks felt antithetical to jazz. They reduce the wide range of colorful information to a monotext, change all the flowing verbs of jazz discovery to solid nouns of jazz facts. When students find their own resources, they hear a multiplicity of voices. During the sharing time, they teach each other in ways not possible when all read from the same text.

"I since have made a compromise of sorts. Since I've yet to find a jazz history textbook that does justice to the roots of jazz in the way explored here, I have not only written such a book for my students, but made a compilation of key recordings as well.* When we get to the biographies of musicians, I continue to emphasize a multiplicity of sources.

"Below are the year's homework assignments, divided into three trimesters, with eleven classes per trimester. (You will note the missing "fourth trimester"—the last 40 years in jazz! This is the class I've yet to teach—but it gives me something to look forward to!)

"At the beginning of each class, students share their information and then we listen to selections from the artist. By moving between learning *about* the musicians, listening to their music and playing pieces by select artists, the students get a more complete view of the subject. As the order below shows, they also get a feeling for the history of jazz and how it developed and grew."

---

* I hope for both to be available to the public in the near future.

YEAR'S HOMEWORK ASSIGNMENTS

First Trimester—Jazz origins, Blues, Ragtime, Dixieland

1. What do you know about jazz?

2. African-American Folk music

3. The blues; Write two blues verses

4. Bessie Smith

5. Scott Joplin

6. Jelly Roll Morton: Take-home test

7. Louis Armstrong

8. The "Roarin' 20's": Listen to Louis Armstrong

9. Review homework; create study sheet

10. Study for test

Second Trimester—The Swing Period

1. Count Basie

2. Duke Ellington

3. Social dance interview—grandparents' generation

4. George Gershwin/Cole Porter

5. Ella Fitzgerald/ Billie Holiday

6. Fats Waller/Art Tatum

7. Coleman Hawkins/Lester Young

8. Bix Beiderbecke/Benny Goodman

9. Women in Jazz—Lil Hardin, Mary Lou Williams and more

10. Create study sheet/study for text

Third Trimester—Be-bop and Beyond

1. Charlie Parker

2. Dizzy Gillespie

3. Thelonious Monk

4. Miles Davis

5. Milt Jackson

6. Bill Evans

7. John Coltrane

8. Final project: create book from homework assignments; study for test

HOMEWORK REVISITED

In light of increased homework loads in all subjects and sensitive to the students' over-busy lives, I have revised my homework policies, giving one assignment per month rather than one each week. Instead of researching each musician on their own, I present each musician in the listening class. They fill out a sheet during the lecture and keep this in a notebook as a jazz musician textbook of sorts (and study sheet for future tests). Below is a sample sheet:

8th Grade Listening Class—Lionel Hampton

Name _____

1.   Where and when was Lionel Hampton born? _____

2.   What was his nickname? _____

3.   What three instruments did he play? _____

4.   What was unusual about his piano style?

5.   What else was he known for in the music world? _____

6.   Name two of his most famous tunes _____

7.   What historic moment happened in 1930 in a studio with Louis Armstrong?

      _____

8.   What historic moment happened in 1936 with Benny Goodman?

      _____

9.   What was his wife and manager's name? _____

10.   What song does he quote while improvising on Stardust? _____

11.   Why does Marian McPartland call him a humanitarian? _____

      _____

12.   When did he die and how old was he? _____

13.   What does he do on the tune Sweet Georgia Brown? Why is this song famous?

      _____

In the monthly assignment, my intention is to make assignments both more family-friendly and creative. For example, the first assignment is to listen to the selections from a collection I compiled titled *Roots of Jazz, with* one's family and choose one to discuss. Students then share their reflections back in the listening class. Parents have reported that they've been delighted to share a listening experience with their child, a rare event for many young teens and their parents made possible by a mandatory school assignment!

Another example of the more personalized assignment was inspired by reading various biographies of jazz musicians written for young children (see Jazz History Resources at the end of the chapter). Students read about Louis Armstrong's life and take *one* event to write in a story form. My hope is to eventually compile the best of these stories and "publish" our own jazz biography for the younger students in the school. Here are two examples of such stories:

Everyone in the recording studio was close to fainting from the extreme heat. They were all wondering how long it would take their "special guest" to arrive. They all wanted to get the broadcast over so they could go home and sit in front of their fans drinking lemonade. Everything had to be perfect on this show: the special guest was an African American and he was going to be nationally broadcast.

Everyone was nervously checking their watches—five minutes until showtime! Just then, a stocky man in a crisp suit strode into the studio. He carried a black case with the imprint of a trumpet on the side. It seemed like the heat had not affected this man—his suit looked like it had been newly ironed and there was not a trace of sweat on it. The producer jumped to his feet, welcomed the man and brought him straight into the soundproof recording studio.

The man smiled at the small crowd of people in front of him. He knew that it was important for the show to succeed, but did not show any signs of nervousness. As the first African-American to broadcast a radio show, he hoped that new opportunities might open up for African-Americans when he showed the world what he could do.

A small man behind the glass divider gave the countdown: "Ready to roll- 5, 4, 3, 2, 1-you're on!" The man smiled and turned to face the window, as if he were giving a live performance. "Hello, ladies and gentlemen, and welcome to the show," he said. "My name is Louis Armstrong." He then picked up his trumpet and began to play. People all over the country listened to his beautiful music. And they are listening still.

-SOPHIE HERIOT

It was one of those days that seemed hot enough to dry up the Mississippi River. I was still a young'un and livin' in the Waif Home. It'd be a half year until I finally got out. On that steaming day, all us kids in the House band got taken out with our instruments and starting marchin' up and down those New Orleans roads. As we walked, we played and played and played. We played any song that came to mind and then a few more after that. I was on the tambourine and I played to the beat of my feet. "Fwump-fwump-fwump-fwump."

None of us had shoes, so our feet were soon sore from walking on the hot roads and stones were caught between our toes. Sometimes we'd hop on one foot to cool off the other. After two hours of playing, we passed some high-falootin' folks having a picnic. They called out to us "Hey kids! Play us a song!" So we struck up *When the Saints* and played our hearts out. We finished with a flourish and I went up to them and held out my tambourine. They dropped a few bucks into it. I brought the money over to Mr. Davis, our band leader and he smiled. We all went back to the Home, tired, but happy. A few days later, one of the boys in the band got a shiny new cornet. After listenin' to that boy play that cornet, I decided I wanted to play too. After that boy left, I started up on the cornet and I was pretty good, too. By the time I got out, I was ready to go show my idol, King Oliver, what I could do. But that's another story.

-KATIE ARBONA

TESTS

I have spoken fancifully throughout about a new form of "final exam"—a performance in which students contribute to every step of the process and the final grade is a measure of the community feeling and quality of emotion aroused. At the same time that this foretells a new style of education, its purpose being to *balance* the traditional approach, not entirely *replace* it. When it comes to accountability for solid information, a good old-fashioned written test still serves our purposes well. If nothing else, for students trained in our system, it brings the importance of this information up to par with quadratic equations, verb conjugations, and the Louisianna Purchase.

These tests also help the students feel accountable for the information and help assess each student's individual understanding. The test grade accounts for a small portion of the overall music grade, which is balanced between history, theory, ensemble skills, singing skills, participation and responsibility. As you can see from the following example, the test itself is a balance of listening, jazz facts, theory and personal reactions.

We often prepare for the tests in class with a cooperative group game of "Jazz Jeopardy." Modeled on the TV game show, students form teams and answer questions (or more properly, find the questions to the answers!) from the various categories on the test. The students themselves write many of the questions (answers) on file cards put on a homemade Jeopardy board. This team study returns us to our group-based learning style and game-like approach while helping everyone review the vital information.

Following is a sample of a final exam covering the entire year's study.

8TH GRADE MUSIC FINAL EXAM

SECTION 1—THE MUSICIANS

Identify the following musicians as either songwriters, composers, bandleaders, singers, instrumentalists (name instrument) or a combination of the above. (Ex. Duke Ellington was a songwriter, composer, bandleader, and piano player.) Name one memorable characteristic of their music or personality. (Ex.: Charlie Christian was one of the first jazz players to use electric guitar.) Extra credit if you include his or her nickname.

1. SCOTT JOPLIN: _____

2. JELLY ROLL MORTON: _____

3. LOUIS ARMSTRONG: _____

4. COUNT BASIE: _____

5. DUKE ELLINGTON: _____

6. BILLIE HOLIDAY: _____

7. ELLA FITZGERALD: _____

8. FATS WALLER: _____

9. ART TATUM: _____

10. GEORGE GERSHWIN: _____

11. CHARLIE PARKER: _____

12. DIZZY GILLESPIE: _____

13. THELONIOUS MONK: _____

14. MILES DAVIS: _____

15: JOHN COLTRANE: _____

16. Name a jazz bass player: _____

17. Name a jazz drummer: _____

18. Name a jazz guitar player: _____

19. Name a jazz musician alive today: _____

20. Name your favorite jazz musician: _____

SECTION II—JAZZ TUNES: LISTENING

Match the styles of the following tunes. Extra-credit if you can name the tune and musician.

1.   a. Ragtime

2.   b. Dixieland

3.   c. Swing

4.   d. Be-bop

5.   e. Latin

SECTION III—JAZZ FACTS

Answer any 10 of the following 15 questions (no extra-credit for any above 10)

1. Ragtime was a style for A) solo piano B) marching band C) jazz quartet___

2. Dixieland began in the A) 1940's B) 1960's C) 1920's _____

3. What style of jazz did the big bands play? A) Be-bop B) Swing C) Dixieland

    _____

4. Whose musical career started in reform school? _____

5. Who sang THE EMPTY BED BLUES? _____

6. What jazz composer won the Presidential Medal of Freedom? _____

7. Who wrote AIN'T MISBEHAVIN'? _____

8. What singer often wore a white gardenia in her hair? _____

9. What was the name of the new style of jazz in the 40's that Charlie Parker helped create? _____

10. What pianist had a controversial style and wrote 'ROUND MIDNIGHT?

    _____

11. Name the 3 instruments in the jazz rhythm section_____

12. What is the form of the jazz standard? _____

13. Name 3 parts of the trap set _____

14. What is the B section of a jazz standard called?_____

15. How many measures (bars) in a typical blues? _____

SECTION IV—JAZZ CULTURE AND DEVELOPMENT

Write a short essay (two paragraphs), in your own words, on one of the following topics:

• **The Blues**—Origins, form, feelings, key musicians, etc.

• **How Jazz Changed**—Changes in style, instruments, ensembles, relation to dance, etc.

• **Social Conditions**—Poverty, racism, acceptance or rejection in mainstream culture, etc.

SECTION V—EVALUATION (ungraded)

Name the thing or things you'll most remember from this year's music study, what you appreciated learning and suggestions for me to improve the course or my teaching style.

LISTENING

> "A cold winter afternoon in Boston and I, sixteen, am passing the Savoy Cafe in the black part of town. A slow blues curls out in the sunlight and pulls me indoors. Count Basie, hat on, with a half smile, is floating the beat with Jo Jones's brushes whispering behind him.

> "...the blues goes on and on as the players turn it 'round and 'round and inside out and back again, showing more of its faces than I had ever thought existed. I stand, just inside the door, careful not to move and break the priceless sound. In a way, I am still standing there."

> —Nat Hentoff

Each jazz fan and player has his or her own story about the "first time." A wistful smile comes over the face, recalling that magical moment when something inside was stirred by the cry of a horn or the brush of a cymbal, when a whole world suddenly opened, new and alluring, yet strangely familiar. The music seemed to be speaking to you alone, saying exactly what you needed to hear. You didn't study in a school to learn about the music. The music chose you.

Many jazz lovers have had that experience of being chosen by the music. People who were not stirred by European classical music or country music or rock and roll felt their dormant musical selves kissed awake by the prince (or rather, the Count, the Duke, the King, the Prez or the Lady!). They found their musical mate. These people might question the wisdom of "teaching jazz." After all, jazz musicians don't come to their profession through career counseling—they respond to a calling. Jazz aficionados don't listen to jazz from social duty—they feed their soul-hunger. From this point of view, there is no need for jazz in music education. Those who need it will find it—or rather, it will find them.

They are right. Without love, no meaningful learning takes place. Analysis of the separate components of jazz typical of the schoolroom approach goes no further towards awakening love than computer-dating printouts do. There must be a chemistry that is more than the sum of the parts. If there's no chemistry, there's no love. If there's no love, there's no appreciation.

Yet they are not wholly right. If we stay locked up in one room, we may never meet our potential mate. And even if we get out, we may not recognize him or her. Music, like personal relationships, is not always love at first sight (or hearing). Many people begin deep relationships indifferent or even hostile to a person (or a music) that they grow to know and learn to love. My own case is a good example of a slowly cultivated appreciation for jazz that blossomed into love. My experiences with my students, both young and old, confirm this truth: **there is a direct link between appreciation and understanding.** Thus, teaching jazz can move along the process of awakening love. Anya, one of my 8ᵗʰ grade students, affirms this:

> "Studying and learning jazz was very enjoyable because my mom always listens to jazz and I didn't enjoy it before. But now since we studied jazz this year, I've appreciated it more."

Ginger echoes this sentiment:

> "I never thought jazz was my thing. I stuck to pop and classical. Studying jazz this year opened the door—it's awesome!"

More affirmation came from teaching my adult jazz course. Like many jazz fans, I had taken it for granted that people understood the relationship between the statement of the song and the subsequent improvisation. Yet I discovered that many had not been prepared to follow jazz through the "road map" of the chord progression and form, and therefore, they felt the musical journey as random and meaningless, wandering with no sense of direction. Without the key to understanding, the deeper meaning of the music was on the other side of a door. That door was dramatically unlocked for one student in a teaching moment I will never forget.

I had played a recording of an improvisation on the jazz standard *Embraceable You* by the great Charlie Parker. This version is unusual inasmuch as it begins without first stating the melody. The task of the class was to try to guess the song by following the chord progression and the occasional allusions to the melody in the improvisation. Only two out of the 25 people were able to guess correctly. We then named the piece, listened to the improvisation again and quietly sang the melody underneath. The aforementioned student, with a look of amazement on his face, confessed in awed tones that this was the first time he understood how to *listen* to jazz. He described how Charlie Parker's improvisation seemed wild and directionless in the first listening and didn't make any "sense," but when we sang along, the exact same phrases seemed tame by comparison, beautifully embellishing, circling around and coming back to and through the melody we were singing. It was hard to believe that they were the same notes being played. Nothing had changed, of course, except the most important element—his perception and understanding of the musical thinking!

Jazz may grab us or we may court jazz, but in either case, we need understanding to progress, which means education. If we're fortunate enough to hear the music, we still might miss the message because no one had prepared us to *listen*. Students must have a sense of what to listen *for*. They also need an *invitation* to listen—time and space to move the music to the foreground.

The following are some strategies to help our student awaken their innate listening potential. These exercises can be used in either the playing or listening class.

Moving to music

Moving *to* music helps us learn how to be moved *by* music. Structures for this activity are given in Chapter 4.

Guess the tune

How many teachers have played Mozart's *Eine Kleine Nachtmusic* or Beethoven's *5th Symphony* and have had their students shout out joyously—"I know that! I heard that on TV!" However much we might despair about sound bytes of great classics being associated with crass commercial products, the child's delight in recognizing something is irrefutable.* Choosing pieces that they may already know helps them move from the known—the piece itself—to the unknown—the particular interpretation of the piece. They are more likely to understand and appreciate the subtleties of elaboration if they are familiar with the model.

---

* And the adult's delight as well! Listen to Keith Jarrett's improvised introduction to *Someday My Prince Will Come* on his *Still Live* recording (ECM 1360/61) and note the audience's wild applause when he finally plays the recognizable melody!

It is clear that knowing the song is the key first step—hence, the importance of teaching the songs in their original form. In my case, I take advantage of the foundation of tunes I lay down in the elementary singing time by choosing versions of those pieces by the jazz musicians they study later. For the beginner, simply recognizing an instrumental version of a song is a first step. For an intermediate level, choose a more obscure opening statement of that song—Oscar Peterson's *Ja Da** is a good example. At a more advanced level, students can begin to recognize songs by their chord changes and more obscure melodic inferences—as in the Charlie Parker *Embraceable You* example noted.**

Try other tunes by turning the volume on during the solo after the statement of the melody.

Cued response

Here's a mistake I have often made: "Listen to the form of this song," I tell my students, and at the end ask what it was. One student raises her hand and answers "AABA" and I say, "Right!" satisfied that the whole class has thoroughly understood when in fact, only one student has understood and perhaps even she simply guessed the answer because she noticed it on the board where I had scrawled it during the previous class!

Many current assessment techniques suggest that there must be a way for *all* the students to show what they know. In listening, the cued response is one way to get a sense of what they hear. I like to begin it in a group for the same reasons we do much group work—it gives a safe space to make some mistakes while simultaneously helping students learn through the response of their classmates.

Simply put, the cued response means: *When you hear this, do that.* "This" is the concept you are focusing on at the moment, "that" is any kind of active physical response, as in:

• Clap once when the improviser reaches the bridge.

• Slump in your chair, then sit up straight when the tune modulates to a higher key.

• When you hear the bass solo, you can go to your next class.

The real test is to do the above with their eyes closed so there are no visual cues from other students. Closing the eyes also helps some students focus their listening.

Imaginative response

This approach is best prepared by teaching the students a relaxation posture. Lying flat on the back, feet slightly apart, palms facing the ceiling, eyes closed—talk them through a tightening and loosening of each part of the body (one arm at a time, one leg, etc.) following the breath, tightening on the inhale, letting go on the exhale. On each out breath, the body should feel heavier and sink deeper into the floor. Now the attention is drawn inward and the body and mind are prepared to give full attention to the music.

This technique is a wonderful way to listen for long periods of time to music and is especially conducive to imaginative response, i.e., letting pictures and stories emerge from the music. After preparing them as described above, I play a selected piece of music—and usually join them on the floor. Their job is simply to let the music suggest images, scenes or story lines, following it through its many changes. At the end, we (or those who are still awake!) reconvene in a circle and share the images and stories that

---

* *Tracks: Oscar Peterson piano solo*: BASF MC 20879

** *Smithsonian Collection of Classic Jazz*:

emerged. The more programmatic pieces of the Duke Ellington Band (*The Happy-Go-Lucky Local, Overture to a Jam Session, Harlem Air Shaft, Liberian Suite,* etc.) and the extended works of John Coltrane (*Africa, Om, Meditation, Ascension, Kulu Se Mama,* etc.) are fantastic for this.

Descriptive response

In this exercise, students have the freedom to choose their own modality of listening. The direction is simply "Listen and write down something about this music." I have found this to be a remarkable affirmation of Howard Gardner's Theory of Multiple Intelligences. By leaving them free to write about what they hear, students will naturally gravitate to certain preferred modalities—some write about musical patterns, some about images, some about stories, some about qualities of sound, some about movements and gestures, some about emotions and most with some mixture of the above. Listen to the variety of reactions to a section of John Coltrane's *A Love Supreme* (8th graders from 1999):

> "Feeling: This is coming from the heart."
>
> —ERICH STAHLKOF

> "Sad, lots of feeling in every note. City in pain, cars honking and people screaming, pain, fast sob."
>
> —SIANNON GALL

> "Physical response: It doesn't make me want to get up and dance, but it makes me want to tap my foot."
>
> —LILY RACHLES

> "Image: This song reminds me of a turtle in striped pajamas dancing on a coffee table in his living room. I don't know why, but that's what's in my head—a turtle in striped PJ's dancing on a coffee table in the living room. Go turtle!"
>
> —MORIAH ORTIZ

> "Pattern: Sax sounds random, but it really does have a set path."
>
> —MAX NEWMAN

> "Sax reaches up and down, flutters some, drawn out, then goes spilling out notes, seems to go in an organized way, but wherever it wants to go."
>
> —GINGER JACKSON-GLEICH

> "Confusing, chaotic, changing constantly, but also repetitive."
>
> —MARLEY SHEPARD-OHTA

There is a school of thought that says the child is the teacher and all we have to do is listen. Taken literally, this produces a confusing and ultimately abusive style of schooling and parenting. This book is testimony to how much responsibility a teacher must take in sharing his or her knowledge and experience with the students. But there is a level of intelligence, musical and otherwise, in every one of my students that I can take no credit for and this kind of listening exercise is a perfect example of it. I am constantly in awe of how much these kids can directly hear separate from the whole vocabulary of jazz sensibility and understanding we're striving to develop. Their comments often go right to the core of artistic purpose and beautifully express the ambivalence of authentic art. They seem to understand that Coltrane's improvisation is at once "changing and repetitive," "random and traveling a set path," "organized and going wherever it wants to go." When Lily says that *"John is really into his music and I admire that he could be so involved…maybe he is trying to say that he is free and alive, full of energy,"* and Ryan says, *"I can feel the vibe. The rhythm feels like it's running through my blood,"* they are as articulate as any writer of liner notes. I believe Coltrane would be pleased to hear their response—and as intrigued as I am by that "turtle in striped pajamas!"

The same class listened to Thelonious Monk's rendition of *'Round Midnight* and again, following their own intuitive genius, came up with the same ambiguities that the most articulate jazz writers use to define the genius of Monk:

> "Childish, yet complex."—ERICH STAHLKOF
>
> "Relaxing, off-key notes."—HOLLY SMITH
>
> " Beautiful, spaced-out."—LILY RACHLES
>
> "Sounds like a lot of mistakes; pretty."—TRULISE CRAYTON (an unconscious paraphrase of Monk's title for one his tunes—*Ugly Beauty.)*

Yet in celebrating the intuitive responses above, I don't want to overshadow the importance of developing a vocabulary for descriptive listening. Recently I had my 8th graders listen to two challenging performances by Thelonious Monk—his solo on *Bag's Groove* and his solo piano rendition of *I Should Care* (both are on disc 4 in The Smithsonian Collection of Classic Jazz). In the following descriptions, you can hear the native intelligence of the children come forth, but also the fruits of their experience in playing jazz, in learning its theory and structure, and in listening to many examples. When someone says "it sounds like the wrong chords," it means she has learned what sounds like the right chords. When another says "its changes are unexpected," it shows he has come to learn what to expect. When another compares his use of space and silence with Art Tatum, it means she has a larger vocabulary that enables her to compare and contrast. Without the whole fabric of this approach—playing, knowing, listening—behind them, I'm convinced that the students would not be as articulate as they are. Listen to these pieces yourself and compare your reactions to those of these 8th graders.

> "(Bag's Groove): How Monk travels through the blues. He's thinking and you can tell, choosing the notes systematically. It sounds like he's playing the wrong chords, but it works. He's thinking, remembering and thinking. It's odd, but I like it."
>
> —CLAIRE TURNER

> "(I Should Care): How he plays a jazz standard: The suspense is hard to take. You want to hear it, but he's thinking and he knows you want it so he doesn't give it to you right away. He draws you deeper in, then surprises you with odd chords and fast scales. It's romantic with a twist, his thoughts coming at you through the notes."
>
> —CLAIRE TURNER

> "(Bag's Groove): Sounds kind of off-key, but also like he planned his solo out before he did it. He knew what sounded good together, even if we don't think so."
>
> —EMILY HERMAN

> "(I Should Care): Chunks of notes. Sharp notes that he lets float. Lots of flourishes. Unexpected. Didn't follow the rules."
>
> —JACKSON ANDERSON

"(Bag's Groove): Cheerful, bright piano sound in contrast with the clunky bass. As it climbs higher, it becomes more daring. The sound is still vibrant, but his chords sometimes sound like someone stepping on glass. His changes are often unexpected. He seems to find an improvisational theme almost by mistake and then running with the feeling. Very intelligent—gives you a chance to breathe."

—Will Gaines

"(Bag's Groove): Starts simple, repeats same thing, but embellishes it the next time. Uses silence with bass and drums to his advantage. Unlike Art Tatum, he doesn't have to fill up every moment with sound. He uses the silence to make you want to hear more! It's better to do something really cool, then let the listener soak up the bass and drums and then do something cool again. Whereas Art Tatum played really fast and amazing things constantly, Monk made his ideas stand out, letting you really hear them and appreciate them. He chooses his notes carefully, making each one stand out it tell its own story."

—Micaela Linder

Focused descriptive response

This exercise uses a scientific method of observation. Separate from any emotional or imaginative account (turtles in striped pajamas), the student simply describes exactly what he or she hears. Of course, "simply" rarely is—it takes a great deal of precise attention and, as quickly becomes apparent, precise language and previous knowledge as well; i.e., instead of "some low, thunky sound comes in", it helps to know that "the bass enters." This exercise also makes clear that music exists in time, and trying to describe it as it's playing is a bit like sketching a running rabbit—in the act of recounting what just has happened, the next thing has already happened!

Thanks to the miracle of recording technology, we have the luxury of repeated listening—and this exercise demands it. It is best to start with a short excerpt and play it many times. On each repeat playing, students can check their previous observations and, ultimately, anticipate them. Once the ear knows more or less what's coming, it's free to notice the next level of detail. After the students' initial try, a few leading questions are helpful:

"Name all the instruments you hear and the order they enter in."

" What register is the piano in?"

"This time, focus your ear on the drums. Next time, notice the bass."

This last question is a fantastic way to reveal the hidden treasures of the bass and drums. Because these instruments often play background roles, they get lost in the mesh of the music—everybody watches the quarterback in the football game and rarely think to focus on the linemen. Becoming conscious of the *whole* texture is part of our musical development. This is easier in live music, where our eye may be caught by the character of the players or the dance of their technique, but is equally important in recordings.

Student-led listening

Preparing students for listening takes a great deal of work on the part of the teacher. He must do his homework—come to know the music inside out, decide which points to highlight, how long an excerpt to play, adapt the lesson to the knowledge and capacities of his students, and more. One night I was working in this manner, contrasting two versions of Gershwin's *You Can't Take That Away From Me*, one by Ella Fitzgerald and another by Billie Holiday. I spent nearly two hours wrestling with the essential question—"How can I help the students hear what I hear?" I prepared various questions for cued response, both satisfied that I was ready to guide them in listening and frustrated that there was so much I hoped for them to hear.

As they walked into class the next day, another idea came to me. I had been reading Jane Healy's excellent book *Endangered Minds* at the time and a phrase of hers rose up—"*Whose brain is growing today?*" Mine certainly did for two hours the night before as I worked to make the connections between the two versions and what we had studied in class. If I simply came in and told the students what I heard—an unfortunately all-too-common technique in teaching—they would use only a tiny sliver of their brain power. If I asked leading questions while they were listening, as I planned to, they would be more engaged, but still aimed towards my answer.

That morning, I decided to try something different. I described to them the process that I went through the previous night and asked them to imagine that they were the music teacher preparing for the class the way that I did. Their job was to come up with the questions that they would ask their students to evoke a full listening experience. The energy in the room shifted noticeably—the lights lit up in their brain and they listened to the music with different ears. Here are some of the questions they came up with, from the sublime to the ridiculous:

- Which instruments play the "response" phrase?

- What is the song about? Can't take what away from me?

- Did people dance to this?

- Does the singer always stay with the melody? Why, maybe?

- Are the instruments the same in both songs?

- How does the singer's voice interact with the instruments and vice versa?

- Do the singers smoke?

- How is it that the singer influences the piano player's riffs?

- What do you notice about the tempo of the two versions?

- How does the beat difference affect the feeling of the song?

- How is the phrasing different in each version?

- What is the relationship between the singer and her subject?

The clever teacher may be excited about this idea, thinking that she can give this assignment to the students and skip her own two-hour preparation! Before all us poor, overworked teachers get too excited about the prospect, let's ask Jane Healy's question again: "*Whose brain is growing today?*" If it's only the teacher's, it's a problem. If it's only the student's, it's also a problem! *Both* need to grow together. The activity just described was partially successful *because* of the work that I put in. I'm not suggesting that this activity replace the teacher's guided responses, but supplement them. One helps raise the students towards the teacher's understanding, the other draws out the fresh pereptions of the student.

Repeated listening assignment

My definition of music with depth is that in which you can always discover something new. As much as I enjoy 50's and 60's rock 'n' roll for dancing, driving, and soothing nostalgia baths, I can anticipate each note after a few listenings. By contrast, the "Kyrie" of Bach's *Mass in B Minor* and the "Psalm" of Coltrane's *A Love Supreme* still yield surprises after countless listenings.

The "final exam" of the listening side of our jazz development is given near the end of the 8th grade year. Students select a piece of jazz of any length and over the course of a week, must listen to it six times, writing about what they hear each time. What they choose to write about is left open. The following example from a student is a fantastic summary of the various techniques we've explored, moving from simple observation to greater nuances and specific musical terms and organically flowering into imagery and story. Had the assignment been limited to one or two listenings, the piece would not have opened for her as it did. (Her work is all the more commendable for the length of the piece she chose—10 minutes and 28 seconds!)

Basin Street Blues—Miles Davis: Seven Steps to Heaven by Ariel Dekovic

DAY 1: First part slow. Conversation between Davis and piano. Bass strumming in the background settles into snare drum with whispering sound. Piano just chording in the background. Smooth. I like it. Davis alone, then ensemble comes in. Trumpet has a voice-like quality. Tempo picks up a little. Bass easier to hear. Drum coming in more strongly. Volume over-all picks up. Sounds like drummer drops his stick some. Piano solo. Sounds a little empty without Davis. Pianist uses the whole piano. Drops back. Good dynamics. Drums go out. Davis comes back in soft, subdued. Piano staccatos a couple of notes. Contrast with trumpet's long ones. Ends with long trumpet and piano playing a chord.

DAY 2: Trumpet has vibrating sound. Piano doesn't connect the notes. Piano lets trumpet take over. Fills in unused space. Trumpet has a vibrating sound when it hits the high notes (repeat). Piano comes in more. Drum taking independence. Piano connecting notes more; interspersed with staccato. Piano chords fuller when trumpet isn't playing. Piano scales up keys, likes to tremolo on the piano. Walking bass stronger now. Using pedal, more dynamics. Drums a steady 1-2. Piano alone, chording down and trumpet comes in subdued. Long notes, piano long notes alone. Climbing up keys. Trumpet almost like a slide whistle. Trumpet's low notes contrast with piano high notes. Mellow ending.

DAY 3: Piano slow chords. First two measures the trumpet plays a pattern, then the piano answers almost the same pattern and notes with just a touch of improvisation. Piano improvises, then trumpet answers almost the same. Piano touches in chords that fit trumpet's notes. Trumpet is suspended and piano resolves the notes. Walking bass louder, trumpet spurts like water. Trumpet has the lead, piano, bass and drums watch and follow, but are seasoned to be also independent. Trumpet has three loud toots and piano echoes. Trumpet walks up and so does bass. It almost seems as the bass walks down the trumpet goes up. Picks up speed. Volume increases. Trumpet suspended in high notes, returned down, but constantly takes a little visit to the high keys. Then it scadoodles down to the lower area. Bursts out. Piano solo=staccato. Does a pattern, once, twice, brings it down to another key and then reverses it and goes up. Bass walks down. Drum doesn't improvise. Switches to cymbal and hi-hat. Only piano—trumpet comes in. Piano long notes, short notes on trumpet—short on piano. Piano echoes trumpet. Bass walks down.

DAY 4: Trumpet waverly sounds. You can hear the air going through. Pattern goes-down-up-down-up-up-up, steady, slow. Long notes, can't hear the breath as much. Trumpet echoes and repeats itself. Repeat (above pattern). Three toots, softer, more connected. Like a trickle of water with just a few rocks to make ripples in the liquid. A couple of waterfalls dropping down. River getting louder, more rapids. More volume—water coming from other sources. Starting to meander, curve, then it drops off, picks up speed. Going downhill, rushing water. Hits rocks and banks along the way. Water is deep, trumpet is low, getting shallower. Water ends in a lake—no trumpet. Piano—fish jumping, swimmers, frogs, water skinners. Variety; life, full, lively, never still. Swimmer just jumped off raft—frog caught a fly. Fish goes deep and music follows fish. Wiggles around. Swims around stuff; hands sing whole keyboard. Fish caught in undertow. Pulled into new river. Trumpet backs in, slow, meandering, old river. Fish relaxes, lets current take him, no rapids, trickles off into small lake—end.

DAY 5: Bird trying to take off (baby) takes flight. Soars, dips down, comes back up, glides along, catches some turbulence. smooth ride. Higher. Evening time. Flies over houses. Next door kids in pool, a couple of splashes, but basically quiet. Just jumped in cannonball style—big splash! Sidestroke, relaxed. Get out and lie in grass. Mom gets in on her float and reads. Water laps against it. Sunglasses fall in. Paddles after them. Bam! Jumps in. Swims around, then climbs back on. Kids get back in. Play tag in water. Rowdier, splashing, neighbors join in. Full of people. Yard gathering for barbecue. Watch fireworks. Oooh's and aaah's. Quiet except for water. Kids get distracted and start swimming again. Diving, no splashes though (good divers). Mom trying to teach toddler how to swim. Keeps sinking then coming back up for air, laughing. Good time had by all. Everyone good friends, lively music, food, games, everyone in. Getting late fast. Winds down. Resident family left. Cleaning up. Kids are very tired. Go to bed. Mom and Dad dance in moonlight, content summer night. Everyone is happy. Hold hands, walk to house.

DAY 6: Short breathy toot, then contrasts with distinct long note. Piano leads in for the trumpet and ties it together. Sometimes connects the two. Smoky bar. Dim lights. Quartet in the corner, just making music. One couple in the corner. Student trying to study. Bartender just listens, dusts around the bar area. Couple starts dancing. Four more people walk in. Bartender gets busy. Drops a glass, spills a lot, student gets frustrated and leaves. Two more couples take the floor. Slow dance. One couple gets more drinks. Watches band. Thinks they're pretty hot. Bartender makes his way over to the piano and they give him a solo—pretty good. Drummer gets riled up. Bass increases volume. Original pianist taps his foot, but wants his piano back. Gets it and tries to match bartender's solo. Pretty good. Dancers want slow. They get it, close, hardly moving. Bar is closing up. Everyone's out.

CONCERTS AND GUEST ARTISTS

Many musicians' musical journeys began with a memorable concert experience. Watching someone playing on stage, something stirred inside and a voice said "I want to do that."

I try to keep students and parents abreast of jazz events in San Francisco and offer extra credit for students who attend concerts and write a short pieces about them. At least once a year, I organize a field trip to a local jazz club and invite the parents as well (the school pays for the kids, the parents pay for themselves). After the concert, we often stay to meet the artists and I always invite them to come to school to see what the kids are up to. (Teachers take note! Perhaps because of years of being close to the audience in nightclubs, it is an unspoken general rule that anyone can often meet the artist backstage without a special pass. My kids have met Wynton Marsalis, Dave Brubeck, Jon Hendricks, Marian McPartland, Gary Burton and others in this way.) You may be surprised by the generosity of jazz artists—vibraphonists Milt Jackson and Stefon Harris both came and played with the kids, as did pianist Sonny Bravo from Tito Puente's band. We also have a budget for guest artists and have had many fine local musicians come play for—and in some case, with—the kids.

Stefon Harris working with 8th graders.

PERFORMANCE

The Oxford English Dictionary's first two definitions of the word "perform" are "to complete, to finish." Music is a performing art and it is indeed important to share the fruits of our creative process. Performance takes on many levels in the program—from running into the hall and grabbing whoever is available to come listen when a piece feels ready to preparing a full-fledged concert. Typically, our students perform for each other, for the grandparents on a special "Grandparent's Day," for the parents in a spring concert, and for our annual school CD.

THE CHILDREN'S VOICES

Here we come to the end of beginning jazz education. In the first chapter, we outlined some cornerstone principles, and this is a good time to look at them again.

- The whole of jazz must be taught to the whole class using the whole range of our intelligences.

- A study of jazz is a study of culture.

- A study of jazz is a study of history.

- A study of jazz is a study of the repertoire.

- A study of jazz is a study of theory.

- A study of jazz is a study of ourselves.

Now we know some of the details—homework, tests, theory work, listening, videos, field trips, performances and, of course, playing the music itself via the practice of Orff Schulwerk. How effective is this approach? Now's the time to hear from the children themselves and find out what this program means to them (groupings mine):

- ## JAZZ NEEDS SCHOOLS TO GUARANTEE EXPOSURE

> "I learned about many jazz musicians that I have never heard of before. I will always remember what the bridge is."
>
> —HAI CHI

> "I never would have listened to jazz without taking this course. I didn't know there were so many styles of jazz. I thought jazz was just some boring type of music, but you taught me otherwise."
>
> —JESSIE STAR HOWELL

> "I learned a lot about jazz history. And I feel lucky to be able to learn these things because many people aren't able to."
>
> —JOEONNA BELLORADO

> "I learned to play jazz which is really cool because I can't play anything. I've always thought that you couldn't learn music, but being in your class has really changed my mind."
>
> —CAROLINA DAMIAN

> "I am most happy in that I got to learn about a whole world of things I probably never would have heard, but now will enjoy forever."
>
> —ERIC MORRILL

• APPRECIATION GROWS THROUGH UNDERSTANDING

"In the beginning of our jazz study, I lumped all kinds of jazz together. The blues, swing, be-bop, they were all the same to me and I didn't really like any of it. But now I can identify different kinds of jazz and some of the different musicians and singers. I've come to appreciate jazz and truly enjoy many kinds of it."

—GILLIAN CLAYCOMB

"I really like being able to hear the beat, the bass line, the form and all the different aspects of a piece when I listen to jazz—it makes it a lot more meaningful."

—KERALA GOODKIN

"I really like to learn about the musicians and learn how to play their songs on the instruments. It lets me understand the pieces better than just listening to the piece or hearing about it."

—SIANNON GALL

"The most important thing I learned this year was how to play and hear the AABA structure of some pieces. Being able to recognize it makes it easier to understand the music and predict the next part that will be played."

—NICK ROLLINS

• HISTORY IS VITAL TO JAZZ STUDY

"After a class when we learned about Charlie Parker, I went home and tried to improvise like he did. I really think it is important to learn about the history of what you are playing, so you can incorporate things that are in the very beginning."

—SAM ARKIN

"I liked learning how all the musicians started their careers, whether they be in night-clubs or in the streets. It's very inspiring to learn about people like Duke Ellington when you play piano yourself."

—CHRISTINA ZANFAGNA

"I feel that jazz music has the most complex and interesting history of any other music style. Each jazz musician has interpreted jazz in his/her own way and put in something more to create his/her own personal style. This way, there are many variations in jazz. I like to play different styles because you get an even better perspective on how jazz is played and how many feelings can be portrayed through jazz."

—THEA HORNER

"I appreciated learning about such people as Billie Holiday, Dizzy Gillespie, Ella Fitzgerald and Charlie Parker. I learned more about blacks and my history in music."

—ANYA ROBINSON (AN AFRICAN-AMERICAN STUDENT)

"I really appreciated learning about jazz. This is because it made me realize how jazz is the "mother" of Soul and R&B. Every time I would listen to a song on the radio, it reminded me of Billie Holiday or another singer. We really got to learn about other people's cultures through the biographies. I got to learn the struggles of the black experience in the United States."

—NADIA GROSFOGUEL

"I think that knowing the history of the jazz musicians is really important. If you don't know about where jazz comes from, you won't be able to really appreciate what you are hearing or playing. When you know about the history of these people, you can understand what they went through and maybe have a better understanding of the meaning of the songs."

—Rachel Gelfond

"One of the highlights of the year was the feeling I got as I performed in the concert. Not only did I know how the play the songs, I knew the people, the history, the form, the stories behind them and the practice I went through to learn them. I was proud not only of my playing, but also how I learned to play it and what I knew about the music."

—Ella Christoph

• JAZZ EXPANDS THE RANGE OF OUR FEELING LIFE

"While I am listening to jazz I get a feeling that no other music can offer. I feel so many mixed emotions of sadness, happiness, passion and loneliness. All of the singers or players and their music add their own personal feeling to their pieces."

—Ashley Slater

"I like jazz a lot. I like the swing and the feel of it. I like to play it and dance to it. I also like to listen to it. There are so many different types of jazz, you can get so many different feelings from it. I think it's fascinating how it originated. It was like a cross of cultures and jazz was the result!"

—Sarah Davidson

"While listening to the Ragtime and Dixieland tape, I realized that any type of music can give you either a happy, cheerful feeling or a sad, blue feeling. This depends on the musicians and their techniques. I also noticed how there can be so many different versions of one song just from improvisation and style preference. It's almost as if the song were an heirloom being passed down through different musicians, each with their own way of looking at it and playing it."

—Sarah Davidson

"I actually like jazz very much. When I was listening to the different jazz players, I especially liked Scott Joplin's music. It really got me feeling a lot better and happier. Even though I like blues now I think I'll like it a lot more when I get older (I'm not sure why). I also think that I like playing jazz more than any other type of music. I really start feeling the music. On one of the days when we listened to jazz for music homework, I was really surprised how much I like it. It was really better than I thought."

—Max Corwin

"It's wonderful to have an appreciation for modern as well as historical jazz. In my opinion, good jazz is the best thing in life. I've listened to jazz since I was an infant and I've loved it the whole time. This jazz study has just furthered my interest in jazz."

—Zachary Shedd (now a high school senior performing around town!)

"It's all about soul and having fun."

—Emily Delaplaine

What does a jazz study mean to the *adult* students who get a formal introduction that includes the full range of playing, improvising, listening and learning history? Let's hear from some of the graduates of my annual jazz course—*Jazz in Elementary Music: An Orff Schulwerk Perspective.* Their words highlight other key points:

• JAZZ EDUCATION IS BEST BEGUN EARLY IN LIFE

"Before this class, I never thought that I could learn to appreciate and understand jazz. My only regret is that I wished I learned all this at an earlier age."

—(ANONYMOUS)

"As Tom Robbins wrote, 'It's never too late to have a happy childhood'. I wish I'd had this in my early teacher education."

—MOLLY SCHOLZ

• WE ALL HAVE AN INNATE "JAZZ SELF" AWAITING RELEASE

"This class was like a journey to a place I always wanted to visit—everywhere I looked and listened was something new."

—DIANE GLAZER

"This class opened up a door to a whole new world. Jazz is something that I have always enjoyed, but never in a participatory sense. Doing all aspects from instruments to movement to singing brought it alive and made it real for me. It gave me a chance to unleash the musical soul inside me."

—ALISON KENNY-GARDHOUSE

"I was a classically trained opera singer and jazz was a foreign element. I'm getting 'into it' now and feel like I'm in so far I can't back out...there's so much more to learn!"

—JOAN SWEET

"I learned about a genre of music I have always shied away from. Jazz intimidates me because of the improvisatory aspect of it but at least I have begun an appreciation of this music."

—BARBARA MARTIN

"I feel like I've been at a vast and delicious banquet, with a generous and knowledgeable host and very congenial and talented fellow diners. For the first time, I feel a significant connection to the music of my own country—jazz."

—KATE MUNGER

"I have always enjoyed listening to jazz, but have always felt like I can't play it myself. This week's active participation has made me realize that I can be part of a jazz group enjoying the freedom of expression and experiencing the joy of the rhythms."

—PEARL CHAN

WHERE TO FROM HERE?

"This book leaves off where others begin," I wrote in the Introduction, and so we arrive at the end of the beginning. For many, these foundation experiences will be the first and last time that they actively play jazz. Knowing their interests lie elsewhere, they can rest content having tried their hands at improvising a solo on the xylophone, sung the blues and danced the Lindy Hop. Having lived briefly as a player inside of this music, they are prepared to listen to it on their own. The many alumni who come back and say things like "I'm into Bill Evans right now" confirm my hope that this indeed is only the beginning of a lifetime of listening pleasure.

What awaits those encouraged to continue to play? Simply put—a lot of work. Having played our way into the basic feelings, forms and structures of jazz, the next step is the work of precision that will allow us to gain more control, mastery and complexity of expression. We'll need to choose *one* instrument instead of switching back and forth and practice long and hard to master techniques that allow for fuller expression. We'll need to continue the theory work, move into advanced harmonies, practice scales and tunes in twelve keys, and learn classic jazz riffs and solos. We'll need to enlarge our repertoire, in both listening and playing. We'll need to improve our reading skills as we sight read tunes or play from charts in bands. We'll come up against the wall of our limitations time and time again and decide at each point whether our passion for mastery is worth the time required. We'll eventually settle at our level of desire—some determined to play someday in the presitigious San Francisco Jazz Festival, some happy to play in the community band, some content to jam occasionally with a group of friends and some simply enjoying sitting down at the piano on a lazy Sunday afternoon.

Yet amidst all the serious discipline needed to advance, there's no reason not to keep in touch with the playful side of things. I've done workshops for award-winning high school jazz bands and the students have testified that it was not only fun to put their instrument down and play *Johnny Brown*, improvise with the sound of their name, beat rhythms on their body and dance to Dizzy Gillespie, but that they returned to their instrument with fresh inspiration. My belief is that the successful artist is one who has never lost touch with this playful self. The move from playful exploration (Romance) to the details of the craft (Precision) to mature self-expression (Synthesis) is a seamless one—all three stages are present in each step of the journey. The mature jazz artist is still playing around with musical ideas with the freshness of a three year old, still pressing against the wall of the technical demands of craft and daily striving for an aware and honest self-expression.

I once heard a panel discussion with Herbie Hancock, Terence Blanchard, Patrice Rushen and Marcus Miller and was impressed to hear these famous musicians affirm some of the ideas set down in this book. Some choice quotes:

> Marcus Miller: "On the surface, jazz is doing well. It has become institutionalized, which is both good and bad. If all we do is learn the repertoire, who will add to the lexicon? Jazz has become a language preserved rather than something alive. In the last 10 to 15 years, nothing new is happening. We have to be careful about creating an unhealthy reverence for the canon. I want to see the music live.

> "I say show the young people videos of people dancing to jazz. That's how my mother learned to love it—she went to the University of Count Basie, dancing to the music. Also, the kids should learn the words to the songs so they can understand better the jazz improvisation."

Herbie Hancock: "We should teach young people in a way that's not separate from the meaning of their lives."

Terrance Blanchard:"The problem with this business is that jazz has become business."

Patrice Rushen: "Young artists need the space to make mistakes. It's death to creativity to get signed too young to a label that is only interested in duplicating what sells well."

Dancing to jazz, learning the songs to better follow the improvisation, giving freedom to make lots of mistakes, teaching a repertoire while encouraging continual search for new forms, keeping the process away from business and connected to the meaning in the children's lives—such a joy to hear the approaches suggested in this book affirmed by these master musicians at the top of the food chain. I could imagine these musicians teaching my three year olds—and having a great time doing it!

And so the loop is complete—as it begins, so it ends. The three year old and the 63 year old are not so very far away after all. What works for one—letting the need to freely sing, shout, move, rise up without inhibition—works for the other. What works for the other—learning how to do things well and precisely—works for the one. There are different needs at different points on the journey, but we're all on the same trip.

Stefon Harris working with 8th graders.

JAZZ HISTORY RESOURCES FOR CHILDREN

The following are some materials geared toward children that my students have enjoyed.

- BLACK AMERICANS OF ACHIEVEMENT SERIES: Chelsea House; NY Philadelphia

  This excellent series is written for middle school age and beyond, with great photos and further resources. The books tend to be 100+ pages and the series includes biographies on Louis Armstrong, Duke Ellington, Ella Fitzgerald, Billie Holiday, Scott Joplin and more.

- *Giants of Jazz:* Studs Terkel; The New Press—This is the book that inspired the storytelling-style homework assignment, with 13 short biographies (around 10–15 pages each) ranging from King Oliver to John Coltrane at an upper-elementary and beyond level.

- *Duke Ellington:* Andrea Davis Pinkney and Brian Pinkney; Hyperion Books for Children—a picture book geared for ages 5 to 9.

- *New Orleans Stories:* Edited by John Miller; Chronicle Books—This anthology of short stories set in New Orleans includes Louis Armstrong's wonderful piece *Growing Up in New Orleans.* I read this aloud to the 8th graders every year and never get tired of it.

The author with Milt Jackson at The San Francisco School.

CHAPTER 11: CONCLUSION: THE LEGACY OF JAZZ

"It was last Monday mornin,' Lawd, Lawd, Lawd

It was last Monday mornin,' Lawd, Lawd, Lawd

My daddy went a huntin', Lawd, Lawd, Lawd

My daddy went a huntin', Lawd, Lawd, Lawd

He was huntin' for the grey goose, Lawd, Lawd, Lawd,

He was huntin' for the grey goose, Lawd, Lawd, Lawd,..."

—AFRICAN-AMERICAN FOLK SONG*

So opens a long song about the grey goose. He gets shot down by the hunter and takes six weeks to fall from the sky. He gets taken to the big house and it takes six weeks to pick his feathers, another six weeks to cook him. Once cooked, the fork can't stick him and the knife can't cut him. When the people realize they can't eat him, they throw him in the hog pen. The hog tries to eat him, but breaks his jawbone. They put the grey goose on the sawmill, but he breaks the saw's teeth out. At the end, he's back up flying in the sky and "the last time I seen him," there was a long string of goslings flying behind him.

And there we have the history of Africans in America. Our European forefathers went a-huntin' for cheap labor and after shooting the goose, they picked him, boiled him, stuck him, cut him, threw him to the hogs, threw him to the machines, but never could kill him.

The grey goose spirit proved so durable, so strong, so powerful, that nothing could touch it. If you take away everything that defines us as human beings—our native land, our community, our families, our names, our language, our music, our dance, our dignity, our freedom—and *still* something in us survives through centuries of denied humanity,

---

* See Appendix 3 for the full song.

not only survives, but gets up and soars through the sky (is that bird Charlie Parker?)—well, if anyone knows a story more inspiring than that, I'd like to hear it.

I believe it was the historian Arnold Toynbee who said that Africans contributed nothing of consequence to civilization. He was looking for the Taj Mahals and scientific breakthroughs and technological inventions and missed the essence of the African genius—an inner core with a direct line to the spirits that animate this world, a spiritual dimension that does not crystallize into dogma or theology or written texts, but emerges as a song and dance. A song and dance so potent, so robust, so vigorous, that the body language of an African-American child born in Chicago still has resonance with an African child born in Accra.

That we as an American people have not grieved sufficiently for the acts of our forefathers nor attended enough to our own current prejudices is self-evident. But perhaps what is worse is that we've neglected to pass on to the children one of the most uplifting stories in the whole of history. Jazz is the story of the triumph of the human spirit. We learn the story on one level when we dance to Count Basie, on another when we listen to Billie Holiday and yet deeper when we ourselves play and sing their music. But we also need to say out loud the story of their difficult lives, go down with them into the vale of tears before ascending to the mountain of glory. And here another game comes to our aid, a way to go into grief and arise jubilant in an African style—by playing, singing and dancing.

LITTLE SALLY WALKER

That's where the story starts. But jazz is more than the African spirit alone. As George Gershwin noted, "Jazz is the result of the energy stored up in America." It comes from a confluence of many spirits from many traditions creating something new from their meeting. My mentor Avon Gillespie once told me of the profound sense of belonging he felt when he first heard Bessie Jones sing, the deep feeling that he had found his people. As a second generation Russian Jew brought up Unitarian in New Jersey, I lamented that I never would have the same feeling. And then one day, playing some Gershwin songs, it struck me, "This is as close as I'll get." Gershwin, like my father, was a first generation Russian Jewish immigrant brought up in New York. Like me, he rubbed shoulders with African-American culture and something entered his bloodstream. He saw the same lights of the New York skyline that I saw from the Staten Island ferry. As much as I love the blues, the jazz standards that Gershwin and his fellow songwriters wrote touch something a bit deeper. This is *my* music as well.

Americans need jazz to help us understand who we are, who we've been and who we might be. Our story is the tale of a country struggling to match the inspired ideals of its founding documents with the actual practice of true democracy. The Declaration of Independence is the talk, but the practice of jazz is the walk. As Wynton Marsalis so eloquently sums it up, "Jazz is what America could be if it ever became itself."

Schools Need Jazz

If "America is to become itself," the process must begin young, and what institution has a better opportunity to create the America of the future than American schools?* But without a clear vision or intention, schools will continue to do what they mostly have done since their inception—reflect the status quo and train people to fit into it. Jazz offers a vision that can profoundly change us as individuals and as a people, but are schools prepared to receive it? Schools may have jazz programs, but do they welcome jazz's deeper ideals and ideas? Consider:

- Schools want brightly lit hallways. Jazz prefers the dim light of nightclubs or the natural light of sunny fields.

- Schools keep freedom outside at recess and discipline confined to the classroom. Jazz knows that they belong together.

- Schools are content to merely learn about information. Jazz insists on living it.

- Schools keep you seated in your private desk in your assigned row. Jazz brings you into the circle.

- Schools study subjects. Jazz tells stories.

- Schools separate head, hands and heart. Jazz knows they're a trio.

This book began with the premise that **jazz needs schools** to establish its rightful place in American culture. It ends with the idea that **schools need jazz** to fulfill *their* rightful place in the culture—to become a training ground for the expressive potential of the human spirit. Not jazz as a subject, as an entertainment, as notes on the page, but as an idea, an ideal, a metaphor, a way of thinking, a way of doing, a way of being, a way of living.

Having come through these pages with a look at how schools might teach jazz, I end with a look at how jazz might teach schools. The following is a graduation speech I gave at my school in 2002 that sums up my vision of what jazz can contribute to a democratic education that honors and actively builds community—and with this, I close this book.

---

* My own vision of what schools could be is set down in my book *The ABC's of Education: A Primer for Schools to Come.*

Jazz, Democracy and Community—A Graduation Speech

"This is my third graduation in three weeks—first my daughter from college, then my daughter from high school and now, these marvelous 8th graders. I've heard a lot of graduation speeches and they all said similar things—thanks to families, friends and teachers, encouragement to pursue your dreams, reminders to be true to yourself and all those lovely sentiments that have been spoken at countless graduations from time immemorial. But I had the nagging sense that one crucial thing was missing and I finally figured out what it was—a sense of a collective purpose, a common goal, a unified meaning.

"As a music teacher, this is easiest for me to describe in musical terms. For if music is anything, it is the joining of strong individual voices in a collective and coherent whole, a whole that is greater than the mere sum of its parts. And this is what makes music unique. When two or more people are speaking at a time, the words clash and we can't make sense of them. But in music, one rhythm is joined by a counter-rhythm, one pitch by another, and music is born from their union. That is the unique pleasure of musical conversation and musical thinking—not only can two or more people talk at the same time, they frequently must to create coherent music. Listen to a whole concert of just drums or just bass or just melody or just piano chords and you'll want your money back. But when the four are in conversation, each offering their point of view in service to the whole—well, that's music.

"I think we have done a good job recognizing the gifts and genius of each and every one of you graduates and you have done a good job working hard to learn all that we had to offer. Each of you is a finely tuned instrument with a special timbre, technique and even your own song. But that's just the beginning. Now we must ask, 'What orchestra or band will you play in? What kind of music will you play?'

"I'd like to suggest that the piece we should playing is called Democracy and all our practicing should lead towards fulfilling its promise. The right to "Life, Liberty and Pursuit of Happiness" is a brilliant idea, but it has yet to be played well—too many instruments are left out, too many are playing out-of-tune, too many people are just reading the notes without really hearing the music, too many are just listening to their part and not hearing how it fits in, too many are cranking up their expensive, powerful amps and drowning the rest out. Where we should be hearing a beautiful blend of contrasting parts, it's a formless cacophony out there. It's going to need you, the next generation, to figure out how to bring the music together and you're going to need some guidance.

"Since you have spent the year studying jazz with me, it should be easy for you to imagine democracy as a jazz ensemble. A good jazz ensemble—and by extension, democracy—requires eight things."

1. **Every instrument must contribute.** The rhythm of the drums, the harmonic outline of the bass, the piano chords and the saxophone melody are all needed for the music to be full. In the democracy yet to be, no voice can be left out.

2. **Every instrument must come prepared to the rehearsal.** To be a functioning jazz citizen, you have to do your homework before you have your say—learn your instrument, learn your parts, know your theory. In jazz parlance, you've got to pay your dues to earn the freedom to express yourself—and that means disciplined study.

3. **A contribution in the background is as important as one in the foreground.** Though each voice is equally important, some are more in the background in a supporting role and some in the lead. Both are equally honorable and necessary.

4. **Everyone gets a turn to solo.** The bass may not solo as much as the horn, but it will have its moment to speak alone. That means as democratic musicians, you can't simply read the notes or follow the conductor—you must develop a personal voice that says something that no one else can say in quite the same way.

5. **Everyone must support the soloist and listen and respond in every moment of the music.** When we went to the jazz concert, many of you commented on the interplay between the musicians. That's where the real pleasure and excitement lies— speaking for a common purpose that is unraveling as it goes along. Every moment in which the give and the take, the call and the response, click, the meaning is revealed.

6. **The group should stay alert to the times and continue creating new music.** 'Things Ain't What They Used to Be' says Ellington's tune and that means that every musician who plays it doesn't play it the way it used to be played, but makes it new, makes it now. We need new solutions to old problems and that means keeping your minds fresh and alert.

7. **No matter how wonderful the music, we need to share the stage with other groups.** Jazz musicians from the beginning didn't just listen to jazz—they opened their ears to every style of music that crossed their paths, enjoyed it for what it was and absorbed it into their own way of talking. Democracy shares the stage equally with all musics and keeps its ears open to what they might have to contribute.

8. **The purpose of musical teamwork is to bring beauty to the world.** I chose a musical metaphor rather than a sports, corporate or engineering one because the group is not working to merely win the game, make the most money or build the most useful bridge—it aims to bring harmony to the discord that surrounds us, to bring healing to our afflicted souls. Democracy's new song will need to be practical, but it also must be beautiful.

We live in an age when people can buy multi-track synthesizers to make music with themselves, where bands can hire drum machines, where kids can sit at parties each plugged into their own Walkman, where three year olds have their personal Website. On the last plane I rode, everyone had their own private screen with their personal choice of four movies. Our time is a time of excessive individualism when what we so desperately need is common purpose. Democracy cannot work with everyone pursuing his or her own personal dreams and fantasies in isolation. Democracy cannot work when we depend upon machines to entertain us. Democracy cannot work when we only talk to the people we put on our speed-dial cellphone.

It's time to get back to what is tried-and-true—solitude in the woodshed getting your chops together, group experimentation in the after-hours club and communion on the bandstand, sharing the beauty with a world that needs to hear what you have to say.

So keep singin,' keep swingin,' keep alert through the changes, keep calling *and* responding, keep playing the tune of democracy's promise, and go forth into the future *together*—like the song says, "Side by Side." And most important, remember that feeling you get when the band is swingin' and the trumpets are wailin' and every note is in its place. No matter how hard it gets, beauty makes it all bearable. So embrace the world, love the world and sing along with Pops at the end of each song...

"Oh yeeaahh!"

APPENDIXES

Appendix 1: ORFF SCHULWERK AND JAZZ: A PARALLEL HISTORY

While Louis Armstrong was making history in New York in 1924, an experiment of a different nature was taking place across the ocean in Munich, Germany. Carl Orff, an emerging young composer, collaborated with dancer Dorothy Gunther to create a daring experimental approach to dance training. Orff's and Gunther's improvisations were as radical in their challenge to established conventions in Germany as jazz was to American music. Breaking the mold of music *accompanying* dance, the seventeen young women in the Guntherschule were both musicians and dancers. They slapped their bodies and clapped their hands while they danced, recited rhythmic speech and played simple percussion instruments. Later, influenced by West African balaphones, Indonesian gamelan instruments and German glockenspiels, Orff had special xylophones, metallophones and glockenspiels built that later became known collectively as Orff instruments. These instruments inspired new compositions in an elemental style, some composed in response to a choreographed dance and some inspiring, in turn, new dances.

While the Guntherschule students were creating new music on metallophones, the Deagan Company in the United States had just invented a new instrument called the vibraharp (later to be called the vibraphone). In 1930, Lionel Hampton went into a recording studio with Louis Armstrong and played the first vibraphone jazz solo on record.

In the early 1930's, the Guntherschule's students performed throughout Germany, with several pieces created by a brilliant graduate of the school, Gunild Keetman. Lola Harding Irmer, a young student who later attended the Guntherschule, describes a performance in Berlin:

> "It was astounding because the girls came and some were sitting at the side playing the elementary music instruments under the direction of Gunild Keetman and for the girls who were moving and dancing, the leader was Maja Lex. In the midst of the show, the girls would interchange, so they had to be musicians as well as dancers and that, first of all, was unique. Secondly, their deportment was beautiful, they were very, very rhythmic and impressive with their dynamic change." [1]

Meanwhile, a different kind of marriage between music and dance was being joyfully celebrated in the Savoy Ballroom of Harlem, as big band musicians and Lindy Hop dancers spurred each other on to greater creative heights. These dancers were also "very, very rhythmic," with a unique stylistic deportment and an impressive dynamic in the subtlety of their movement.

The political climate in Germany and subsequent war interrupted the momentum of the Guntherschule's work. Orff turned his energies to composing stage works that included his famous composition, *Carmina Burana*, first performed in 1937. This epic work was based on medieval drinking songs, love songs, dance songs and laments transformed to an art music form of "scenic cantata." The composition likewise drew from medieval musical practices, emphasizing lively rhythms, modal scales and elemental harmonies. A few years later, Duke Ellington premiered his *Black, Brown and Beige Suite* (at Carnegie Hall) which he described as "a tone parallel to the history of the American Negro." Drawing from the love songs, dance songs and blues laments of his culture, he transformed the rhythms, scales and harmonies of earlier musical forms into a dramatic and evocative art music format.

Orff's teaching resumed in 1948 when a Bavarian radio station asked him to recreate the elemental music formulated in the Guntherschule, only this time for children. He re-united with Gunild Keetman and created a series of compositions for children to be broadcast. Their success led Orff to turn his attention towards forming the pedagogical approach that became known as the Schulwerk (German for schoolwork). That same year, another collaboration began as Miles Davis and Gil Evans joined forces in their first project together that led to the historic *Birth of the Cool* recording.

While Charlie Parker and Dizzy Gillespie were solidifying the language of be-bop in the early 1950's, Gunild Keetman began teaching children's classes at the Mozarteum in Salzburg, Austria. Interest in the Schulwerk grew, fueled by the publication of five volumes of compositions by Orff and Keetman, *Orff-Schulwerk: Music For Children*, between 1956 and 1961. In 1962, Orff travelled to Toronto, Canada to share his avant-garde vision and changed the face of American music education. The next year, Sonny Rollins returned the favor by performing avant-garde jazz with Don Cherry in Paris, France, offering new inspiration to the European jazz scene. In 1963, when John Coltrane's fiery quartet was making jazz history in the States, the establishment of the *Orff Institut* in Salzburg as a training ground for the Schulwerk made a profound impact on music education worldwide. In 1968, the connection between Salzburg and the United States (ironically, the year that Helen McInnes wrote an espionage thriller titled *The Salzburg Connection*!), was formalized by the founding of The American Orff Schulwerk Association. Meanwhile, jazz paused at the crossroads of distinctly different directions— fusion, free, hard bop, funk, bossa nova, revival, and more.

Over the next 35 years, jazz continued in many directions at once—back into its own history, forward into further development and sideways into increased influences from other musical cultures, with many foreign-born jazz innovators. Orff Schulwerk likewise worked the music of the original Volumes, developed new material and opened out internationally, with significant Orff associations in Canada, Australia, Taiwan, Greece, Finland, Spain, Belgium, Italy, England, and Japan, and with growing interest in Estonia, Russia, China, Iceland, New Zealand, Argentina, Brazil and other countries.

Orff and jazz grew up side-by-side in the same historical time period, but were separated by both geography and culture. Jazz musicians didn't stop at the Guntherschule in their European tours and Orff and Keetman never danced at the Savoy. (What marvelous material for a drama! Lionel Hampton sits in on a class in Munich, Orff jams with

Count Basie in New York!) But what is the quality of the Orff approach that accounts for its adaptability across this immense cultural gap? As described by Orff himself:

> "Elemental music is never music alone, but forms a unity with movement, dance and speech. It is music that one makes oneself, in which one takes part not as a listener, but as a participant. It is unsophisticated, employs no big forms and no big architectural structures and uses small sequence forms, ostinato and rondo. Elemental music is near the earth, natural, physical, within the range of everyone to learn it and experience it, and thus, suitable for the child." [2]

This quote describes African-American folk tradition and even much of jazz into the 30's. Orff's genius was to recognize traditional musical practices of various cultures and historical periods and recreate them in a contemporary western framework. While grounded in the western tradition, he challenged the prevailing assumptions of 20th century composition and teaching. The genius of jazz was to join traditional African musical practices and sensibilities with a contemporary western framework, also challenging assumptions about the European model. Now these parallel histories have finally intersected and a new chapter in American music education has begun.

Endnotes

1. Private interview in Sydney, Australia 1/94

2. Orff, Carl: *The Schulwerk* : V. III: Schott

ORFF—JAZZ Timeline: 1895–1995

ORFF	JAZZ
1895-Carl Orff born	
1898-Orff experiments at piano with meat pounder	
1899-	Maple Leaf Rag published/ Duke Ellington born
1902-Jelly Roll Morton experiments at piano with elbow	
1905-Orff gives his own puppet theater	
1917-Original Dixieland Band makes first jazz record	
1924-Guntherschule founded in Munich	Louis Armstrong joins Fletcher Henderson in N.Y. Harlem Renaissance in mid-stride
1925-Maja Lex comes to Guntherschule	Hot Five records—first scat vocal
1926-African balaphone/recorders arrive Keetman enrolls at Guntherschule	Jelly Roll's Red Hot Peppers record
1928-First Orff xylos built	Armstrong/Hines duet *Blackbirds* musical—Cab Calloway/Bill Robinson
1930-First public performances of dance group	Lionel Hampton records a vibraphone solo
1932-Discusses new music program for Berlin schools	Bennie Moten/Count Basie at Savoy
1936-Performance with 6,000 children at Berlin Olympic Games	Lindy Hop national dance craze with Benny Goodman/Teddy Wilson
1937-Premiere performance of *Carmina Burana*	Katherine Dunham performs concert dance
1938-	First Carnegie Hall jazz concert
1943-	Pearl Primus debuts traditional African dance
1944- Guntherschule closes	First bebop recordings—Bird & Diz
1945- Guntherschule destroyed in bombing	
1948-Bavarian radio Schulwerk programs	Dizzy's Afro-Cuban works
1953-Schulwerk demonstrated at an International Music Conference	Modern Jazz Quartet formed
1956-6-Music for children published, recordings made, TV series and workshops throughout Europe	Be-bop absorbed and extended: Monk, Miles, Mingus, Horace Silver, Bill Evans
1962-First North American Orff Conf. in Toronto	
1963-*Orff Institut* established in new building	Coltrane's *Love Supreme*
1968-American Orff Schulwerk Association founded	
1969-First American Conference	Miles Davis fusion group forms
1972-*Step It Down* published—Avon Gillespie introduces material to Orff world	Louis Armstrong dies
1982- Carl Orff dies	Thelonious Monk dies
1988-First Orff/jazz course taught by Doug Goodkin	
1990-Gunild Keetman dies	
1991-	Miles Davis dies
1995-Carl Orff Centenary celebrations held worldwide	U. S. Post office issues jazz musician stamps

Further Orff training and Institutions

American Orff Schulwerk Association: www. aosa.org

The Orff Institute, Salzburg, Austria: www.Orff.forum@nextra.at

The San Francisco School, 300 Gaven St., San Francisco, CA 94134, (415) 239-5065 www.sfschool.org

The San Francisco Orff Certification Course: www.douggoodkin.com

Jazz and Orff Schulwerk Course with Doug Goodkin: www.douggoodkin.com

Appendix 2: SOUL AND SPIRIT IN JAZZ

In his book, *Revisioning Psychology*, James Hillman makes some useful distinctions between Soul and Spirit. Describing the qualities of Spirit, he remarks:

> "Its direction is vertical and ascending; it is arrow-straight, knife-sharp, powder-dry and phallic. It is masculine, the active principle, making forms, order, and clear distinctions. Although there are many spirits, and many kinds of spirit, more and more the notion of 'spirit' has come to be carried by the Apollonic archetype, the sublimation of higher and abstract disciplines, the intellectual mind, refinements and purifications."

Following our chart (see Chapter 1), we might say that Europe, and its subsequent American incarnation, is more concerned with Spirit. Beginning in its Christian roots separating body and soul, good and evil, light and dark, European culture attempted to grow towards one in negation of the other. The cathedrals pointed ever upwards, the dancers tried to leap off the earth, the eyes gazed to the heavens. The Spirit of European culture consigned evil to the underground, preferred the clear light of day to the vague dark of night, centered itself in the city and feared the forest, deemed the clear logic of intellect superior to the murky realm of emotion, extolled male images of extroversion over female images of introversion. It was European Spirit that spawned phallic spaceships with dry, brightly lit interiors shooting into the heavens to gather data. It also gave birth to the music of Bach and the spiritual clarity of Meister Eckhart.

Soul gives us images of water, of night, of the moon, of the feminine, of salt, present in blood, sweat and tears. The West African cultures honor Soul with dancers embracing the earth, homes close to the ground, the intellect periodically subsumed in trance. Soul is at home in the forest, moves in the night, feels good and evil mixed. Soul fosters depression, unpredictable emotion, explosive passion. It also gives us the great polyrhythmic drum choirs and the wisdom of elders unknown to us by name in the western world.

Throughout their history, the African-Americans' association with Soul surfaces time and time again: stowed *underground* in the ship's holds when captured as slaves, held captive in the *South*, escaped in the *Underground* Railroad, played their music in the basement *underground* nightclubs, "got *down*" when dancing, played the blues with the *Devil's* interval (the tritone), spilled their *blood, sweated* in the cotton fields and shed *tears* under the barbaric tyranny of a racist culture. Years later, Motown was churning out "Soul music", barbecue joints were cooking "Soul food", teenagers were dancing on the TV show "Soul Train", Eldridge Cleaver published "Soul on Ice" and Sam Cooke was singing, *"He's got Soul and everybody knows, that it's all right."*

The story of the African-American experience is Soul meeting Spirit. African-Americans transformed everything they touched through the alchemy of Soul. Likewise, they themselves were transformed through their contact with European Spirit. This doesn't imply an evolutionary *advance*—West African culture has its own blend of Spirit and Soul, as does European. But it clearly created something *different* at each new meeting point. (A modern jazz musician may have more in common with a contemporary German intellectual than with a 17th century slave.)

The most eloquent statement of that changing story is the art form in which Soul and Spirit marry— jazz. The jazz musician practicing for hours on end to master technique, studying extensive theory, analyzing solos, searching for higher levels of musical clarity, is in the realm of Spirit. The same musician expressing herself in the moment of improvisation, telling her story, singing her grief, pain and joy, is working in the world of

Soul. The Soulwork grounds the Spirit and the Spirit gives wings to the Soul. Jazz needs both. And so do we.

European Building—masculine ascending spirit.

Painted house in Sirigue, Ghana—feminine earthy soul.

Jazz Resources:

International Association for Jazz Education: www.iaje.org

Jazz for Young People Curriculum: written and narrated by Wynton Marsalis www.jazzforyoungpeople.org

THE GREY GOOSE

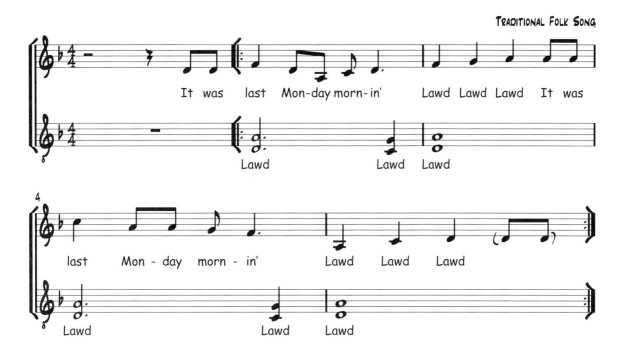

2. My daddy went a'huntin', Lawd, Lawd, Lawd (2x)
3. He was huntin' for the grey goose, Lawd... (2x)
4. The grey goose came a'flyin'...
5. My daddy pulled back the trigger...
6. And the gun went 'Boo-loo!'...
7. The grey goose came a'fallin'
8. He was six weeks a'fallin'
9. They put him on the wagon...
10. He was six weeks a'haulin'
11. They took him to the big house...
12. They brought him to the kitchen...
13. They gave a feather pickin'...
14. They was six weeks a'pickin'...
15. They put him in the oven...
16. He was six weeks a'cookin'...
17. They brought him to the table...
18. But the knife couldn't cut him...
19. And the fork couldn't stick him...
20. So they throwed him in the hogpen...
21. The hogs tried to eat him...
22. And he broke the sow's jawbone...
23. So they took him to the sawmill...
24. And he broke the saw's teeth out...
25. Well, the last time I seen him...
26. He was flyin' 'cross the big sky...
27. With a long string of goslings...
28. And they all singing "Quonk! Quonk!"

SUMMARY OF MATERIAL BY ORDER OF PRESENTATION

Chapter 2–Games

Chapter 3–Speech and Body Percussion

Chapter 4–Jazz Movement

Chapter 5–Beginning Ensemble Pieces

ALPHABETICAL INDEX OF MATERIAL

---

* These activities work best with chromatic Orff instruments

ABOUT THE AUTHOR

Doug Goodkin is an internationally recognized music teacher in the field of Orff Schulwerk, training teachers in over 25 countries worldwide. He teaches music and movement to children between three and fourteen years old at The San Francisco School. where he has taught since 1975. He also directs the San Francisco Orff Certification Course, teaches frequently at the Orff Institut in Salzburg, Austria, and has taught his own course on jazz and Orff-Schulwerk since 1988 in North America (San Francisco, Minneapolis, Vancouver, Toronto, Montreal, Calgary), Europe (Reykjavik, Madrid, Tenerife, Rome, Salzburg), Australia (Sydney, Melbourne) and Asia (Taipei, Bangkok).

Doug has written numerous articles for international music journals, is an author of the McGraw-Hill textbook series *Share the Music* and his written five other books. He has performed as a jazz pianist in the San Francisco Bay Area and is a founding member of the Orff performance group, Xephyr. He is also the recipient of the prestigious Pro Merito Award given by the Orff Foundation in Munich in recognition of his contributions to the development of Orff Schulwerk.

With studies ranging from jazz piano to African xylophone to Balinese gamelan to Bulgarian bagpipe, Doug's work reflects an international perspective on music, culture and education. As described by one student: "His work conveys a long, earnest and continuing struggle to present music of integrity in a way that affirms our collective humanity."

To contact Doug, go to: www.douggoodkin.com or e-mail: goodkindg@aol.com